Popular Performance

Popular Performance

Edited by
Adam Ainsworth,
Oliver Double and Louise Peacock

methuen | drama
LONDON • NEW YORK • OXFORD • NEW DELHI • SYDNEY

METHUEN DRAMA
Bloomsbury Publishing Plc
50 Bedford Square, London, WC1B 3DP, UK
1385 Broadway, New York, NY 10018, USA

BLOOMSBURY, METHUEN DRAMA and the Methuen Drama logo are trademarks of Bloomsbury Publishing Plc

First published in Great Britain 2017
Paperback edition first published 2018

Cover design: Louise Dugdale
Cover photography by Idil Sukan www.idilsukan.com

A catalogue record for this book is available from the British Library.

ISBN: HB: 978-1-474-24734-4
PB: 978-1-350-08968-6
ePDF: 978-1-474-24733-7
eBook: 978-1-474-24735-1

A catalog record for this book is available from the Library of Congress.

Typeset by Newgen Knowledge Works Pvt Ltd., Chennai, India.

To find out more about our authors and books visit www.bloomsbury.com and sign up for our newsletters.

Contents

List of Illustrations vii
Notes on Contributors viii

Introduction: What is Popular Performance? *Oliver Double* 1

1 From Domestic Song to Drawing Room Recitation: Dan Leno's Music Hall Repertoire *Caroline Radcliffe* 31

2 American Vaudeville *Leigh Woods* 55

3 It's 1922 and at the Munich Kammerspiele Karl Valentin and Liesl Karlstadt Perform *Das Christbaumbrettl* at *Die rote Zibebe* *Michael Wilson* 75

4 Packed From Pit to Ceiling: The Kingston Empire (1910–1955) and British Variety *Adam Ainsworth* 97

5 Grock: 'Genius Among Clowns' *Louise Peacock* 119

6 Something Wicked: The Theatre of Derren Brown *Michael Mangan* 137

7 Performing the Burlesque Body: The Explicit Female Body as Palimpsest *Lynn Sally* 161

8 'Hiya Fans!': Celebrity Performance and Reception in Modern British Pantomime *Simon Sladen* 179

9 With Them, Not at Them *Bim Mason* 203

10 What's Special about Stand-Up Comedy? Josie Long's Lost Treasures of the Black Heart *Sophie Quirk* 223

11 'It Feels Like a Group of Friends Messing Around Onstage': Pappy's and Live Sketch Comedy *Oliver Double* 247

Conclusion *Louise Peacock* 269

Index 283

Illustrations

1.1 Dan Leno in 'Clever Mr. Green' 39

2.1 Olga Petrova in the year of her entry into vaudeville, *Green Book Magazine*, August 1912 56

4.1 Programme from the Kingston Empire, Monday, 1 February–Saturday, 6 February 1943 105

7.1 MsTickle performing at the Burlesque Hall of Fame, Las Vegas, NV in 2011 170

8.1 Pamela Anderson as the Genie of the Lamp in First Family Entertainment's pantomime *Aladdin*, New Wimbledon Theatre, 2009 187

9.1 Bighead at *Juste Pour Rire* Festival, Montreal 2005 204

10.1 Illustration by Josie Long, part of her series Another Planet for the *Guardian* newspaper 240

11.1 Pappy's perform Last Show Ever at the 2012 Edinburgh Fringe 256

Notes on Contributors

Adam Ainsworth is a senior lecturer and the current head of Drama at Kingston University. His research interests include pantomime, music hall, variety theatre and the live performance culture of Kingston upon Thames. He is the co-founder of the Theatre and Performance Research Association's Popular Performance Working Group.

Oliver Double is reader in Drama at the University of Kent. He is author of *Stand-Up! On Being a Comedian* (1997), *Britain had Talent: A History of Variety Theatre* (2012) and *Getting the Joke: The Inner Workings of Stand-Up Comedy* (2nd edition, 2014). Before becoming an academic he was a professional comedian, and he continues to explore the creative possibilities of stand-up, performing both locally and sometimes as far afield as Orlando, Florida.

Michael Mangan is professor of Drama at Loughborough University, UK. He has published books and articles on theatre and society, Shakespeare and Elizabethan theatre, theatre and social justice, theatre and gender, contemporary British drama and popular performance. He has also worked professionally as a director, dramaturg, literary manager, musician and playwright. His books include *Performing [Dark] Arts* (2007), *Staging Ageing* (2013) and *The Palgrave Companion to Drama, Theatre and Performance* (2013).

Bim Mason is co-founder and Artistic and Education Director of Circomedia. He has been a professional performer since 1978 and is also a triple award-winning director of circus and physical theatre productions. He has worked with numerous pioneering circus-theatre groups as well as his own companies including Mummer&dada, Dark Horse and Bigheads. Bim's writing work includes *Street Theatre and Other Outdoor Performance* (1992), *Popular Theatre: A Contradiction in Terms* (1994), 'The Well of Possibilities' in *Jacques Lecoq and the British Theatre* (2002), *Towards a Healthy Circus Ecology* (2007), *Provocation* *in Popular Culture* (2015) and 'Bouffons and the Grotesque' in *The Routledge Companion to Jacques Lecoq* (2016).

Louise Peacock is an associate professor in Theatre Practice (Comedic Acting) at the University of Southern California. Prior to that she was senior lecturer in Theatre at the University of Hull. She teaches in the areas of Commedia dell'Arte, Clowning and Stage Comedy. She is the author of two books, *Serious Play: Modern Clown Performance* (2009) and *Slapstick and Comic Performance* (2014). She has written numerous peer-reviewed papers and chapters on Commedia dell'arte, stand-up comedy and clowning. She is currently editing the Modern Age volume of Bloomsbury's *A Cultural History of Comedy*.

Sophie Quirk is a lecturer in Drama and Theatre at the University of Kent where she teaches popular and comic performance. She is the author of *Why Stand-up Matters: How Comedians Manipulate and Influence* (2015). The book explores the social and political influence of contemporary British stand-up comedy.

Caroline Radcliffe is a lecturer in the Department of Drama and Theatre Arts, University of Birmingham. Caroline publishes on popular performance and Victorian drama. Her PhD thesis was entitled *Dan Leno: Cultural Hegemony in the Victorian Popular Theatre*. Caroline has edited and published (with Andrew Gasson) two original plays by Wilkie Collins, *The Lighthouse* (2013) and *The Red Vial* (2016) and she is currently working towards a monograph on Collins's dramas.

Simon Sladen is senior curator of Modern and Contemporary Performance at the Victoria and Albert Museum, London. Recent publications include *The Globality of Pantomime: A Brief Excursion* (2012) and *The Death of the Dame? Tales from the National Database of Pantomime Performance* (2015). Simon is the founder of Panto Day and has been reviewing pantomime for the British Theatre Guide since 2009.

Lynn Sally is an associate dean and associate professor in the Visual and Performing Arts Department at Fairfield University. Her research interests include American popular culture, gender and performance. Her publications include *Fighting the Flames: The Spectacular Performance of Fire at Coney Island as Elemental Performativity*, and articles in *The Journal of American Drama and Theatre*, *Journal of Popular Culture*, *Senses & Society Journal*, and *New York History* among others. She received her PhD in Performance Studies from New York University.

Michael Wilson is professor of Drama at Loughborough University. His research focuses on popular and vernacular performance and he is author of *Storytelling and Theatre* (2005) and co-author (with Richard Hand) of *Grand-Guignol: The French Theatre of Horror* (2002); *London's Grand Guignol and the Theatre of Horror* (2007); *Performing Grand-Guignol: Playing the Theatre of Horror* (2016). He has also translated and published (with Oliver Double) work on Karl Valentin.

Leigh Woods has taught at the University of Michigan since 1987. He has written about performance and the history of acting in *Garrick Claims the Stage* (1984), *On Playing Shakespeare* (1991), *Public Selves/ Political Stages*, with Agusta Gunnarsdottir (1997), and *Transatlantic Stage Stars in Vaudeville and Variety* (2006), and has co-edited *Playing to the Camera* (1998). A member of Actors' Equity Association, he has performed over 100 roles onstage.

Introduction: What is Popular Performance?

Oliver Double

Little Tich is not a stage play

In April 1912, the actor, playwright and theatre manager Granville Barker brought a test case against the Tivoli music hall, claiming that it was illegally presenting 'stage plays that had not been allowed by the Lord Chamberlain' (*The Stage* 1912a). Music halls were licensed differently from theatres and had been getting into trouble with the authorities for decades for staging sketches, which technically counted as stage plays. This case took things a step further. Granville Barker had attended the Tivoli on 1 March and picked out two solo acts as examples of supposed stage plays – those of the great comedian Little Tich and the ventriloquist Johnson Clark. The case was eventually dismissed on 8 May after Henry Tozer, the chairman and managing director of the New Tivoli Ltd., argued that 'the generally accepted definition of a stage play was a story in action developed by dialogue between two or more persons' and commented, 'You cannot make a play out of one person any more than you can make matrimony out of one person' (*Daily Mail* 1912).

What was it that made a theatre manager want to prove that Little Tich's comical songs, dance and patter and Johnson Clark's ventriloquism should legally be defined as *plays*? After all, most people, then and now, would think of these more as *acts* than plays, more entertainment than theatre.

The immediate motivation for the case was commercial interest. Theatre managers clearly felt that music halls had the commercial advantage, and wanted to reduce this by suggesting that the licensing laws should restrict and regulate them. Twenty years earlier, the actor-manager Henry Irving had argued against changes in licensing to allow music halls to present sketches, particularly objecting to the fact that music hall audiences were allowed to smoke and drink in the auditorium. He asked why music hall managers were unprepared to apply for licences to become theatres – which would deny audiences the pleasures of alcohol and tobacco while watching the show – and concluded: 'It can only be that the drink and smoke profits where drink and smoke are allowed in the auditorium are advantages too valuable to forego' (*Era* 1892).

However, the dispute went much deeper than money, being a symptom of a long-established division between the artistic and respectable *theatre* on the one hand, and the disreputable entertainment of *music hall* on the other. In fact, this is just one example of a Great Divide between different types of performances – high versus low, legitimate versus illegitimate, formal versus informal, literary versus improvised, publicly subsidised versus purely commercial, aesthetic versus entertaining, improving versus frivolous.

This is a book about one half of this Great Divide, a tradition which we call *popular performance*. Historically, popular performance has been seen as being entirely separate from what is often called legitimate theatre. In *The Empty Space*, Peter Brook argued that since Ancient Greece, 'the "legitimate" theatre has been considered the important one' and popular performance – which he labels 'Rough Theatre' – 'has been thought less serious' (1972: 76). In 1660, this divide was enshrined in law, when King Charles II granted the two Royal Patents, giving us the term 'legitimate theatre' and granting it an 'immediate hegemonic advantage' over illegitimate theatre (Radcliffe 2016: 93).

As Brook suggests, popular performance has often been thought of as being not just separate from legitimate theatre, but also distinctly inferior. Henry Irving objected to drinking and smoking in the music halls because 'we hold that play-acting is an Art, and requires to be treated as such, and to have its necessary and suitable environment. It is to the conditions of the music halls that we object' (*Era* 1892). The implication is clear. The Art of theatre requires sober and smoke-free conditions, and the smoky, boozy environment of the music hall is only suitable for an inferior type of performance. Two years later, the *Era* reported the views of the temperance and purity campaigner Ormiston Chant, who was more explicit about the inferiority of music hall: 'The music hall catered for people who had a small proportion of brains' and thus its audiences 'could hardly appreciate a play' (in Radcliffe 2016: 86).

Such attitudes survived well into the twentieth century, long after music hall had evolved into variety theatre. Peter Prentice, of the unicycling and lassoing speciality act El Granadas & Peter, recalled the landlady of a theatrical lodging house introducing him to a legitimate actor. She asked the actor if he knew Prentice, to which he replied, 'I don't know anyone on the bastard side of the profession' (Double 2012: 199). The wording gives a hint of the animosity between theatre and popular performance, as 'illegitimate' is replaced by the more pejorative synonym 'bastard'.

This might sound quaintly old-fashioned today, but the Great Divide continues to separate popular performance from legitimate theatre. For example, live comedy – stand-up, sketch and improv – is normally listed separately from theatre in events listings in newspapers and magazines. This reflects the fact that comedy and theatre are seen as completely separate forms. So do the perennial news stories about comedy taking over the Edinburgh Fringe at theatre's expense. As early as 1991, Joanna Coles reported in the *Guardian* that 'Comedians … are frequently accused of squeezing new theatre out.' The same kind of complaint has rumbled on, year after year. In 2005, the *New Statesman* asked comedian Stewart Lee to refute the idea that 'the proliferation of comedy has … wrecked the Fringe as a hotbed for alternative theatre', which he did by arguing that, 'There is much that comedy can learn from theatre; but there is probably more, about pacing, accessibility, simplicity of staging and the way to sell strange ideas to suspicious crowds, that theatre can learn from comedy' (Lee 2005: 29). Two years later, another comic, Shazia Mirza, was defending comedy again after Fringe director Jon Morgan accused it of getting out of control at theatre's expense. 'The complaint has surfaced again,' she noted, wryly (Mirza 2007).

Moreover, the comedy versus theatre debate goes much wider than the Edinburgh Fringe. In 1992, *Guardian* theatre critic Michael Billington wrote an article called 'Noises Off: How Alternative Comics Took Over the World', in which he noted that 'comedy has absorbed much of the talent that a generation ago would have gone into straight theatre.' Although broadly praising live comedy, he worried that it 'offers a short, intense, hour-long experience that makes few of the emotion-stretching demands of narrative drama' and confessed: 'it unnerves me a little that the comedy industry is increasingly siphoning off the writers, the performers and even the audiences that were once drawn to drama.' Again, there is the implicit idea that theatre is superior to comedy. Theatre is more demanding of its audiences – and therefore more virtuous – and we should be worried if comedy draws talented people away from it.

Over 20 years later, in 2015, *Guardian* comedy critic Brian Logan wrote a piece which was essentially a variation on the same theme. He uses a discussion between stand-up and sketch comic Tom Parry (of Pappy's) and theatre-maker Hester Chillingworth (of Getinthebackofthevan) to ask, 'What can contemporary theatre learn from comedy?' and concludes that 'it opens up [the possibility] of dialogue between comedy and theatre. There is often mutual suspicion between the two worlds: snobbery flowing one way, inverted snobbery flowing the other.' The use of the snobbery/inverted snobbery binary suggests a clear cultural hierarchy, leaving us to infer that theatre is the snob (i.e. in the superior position, looking down), and comedy the inverted snob (looking up from below).

Being seen as culturally inferior is not just abstract – it can have material consequences. In 2009, Lisa Keddie applied for Arts Council England (ACE) funding for a comedy project. She was refused on the grounds that ACE only funds 'art', under the categories combined arts, dance, literature, music, theatre and visual arts (Davis 2009). The implication is that comedy cannot be publicly funded because it qualifies as neither art nor theatre.

Step back from the current partition between theatre and comedy, or indeed the historical Great Divide, and it becomes difficult to find a rational basis for it. Peter Brook's seminal text takes its name from its opening sentence, which offers a crystal clear definition of what theatre is: 'I can take any empty space and call it a bare stage. A man walks across this empty space whilst someone else is watching him, and this is all that is needed for an act of theatre to be engaged' (1972: 11). Little Tich's music hall songs and Johnson Clark's ventriloquism act may have been legally defined as not stage plays, but by Brook's definition, they are certainly forms of theatre. After all, both of these performers did much more than simply walking across a space, and they were watched and enjoyed by hundreds or even thousands of people every night. By the same token, the live comedy of today – or indeed any of the examples of popular performance discussed in this book – pass the Peter Brook test with flying colours.

Definitions

So what is it that makes popular performance so very different from legitimate theatre that the two have been divided from each other for a period of centuries? In order to answer this, we must arrive at some kind of convincing definition of popular performance. Earlier definitions of popular *theatre* – as it has often been called – tend to take a broadly sociological approach, by focusing on audience. Popular theatre is defined as being 'of the people' (Mayer 1977: 263; Bradby et al. 1980: 276; Prentki & Selman 2003: 9). The implication of this is that its audience is either specifically working class, or drawn from sections of society which David Mayer describes as having 'lower per capita income, lower level of education and literacy, lower interest in or knowledge of aesthetic criteria, lower level of political influence' (263). For Bernard Sharratt, 'the people' implies 'a dominated class struggling to identify itself against an imposed and degrading definition by a ruling class' (in Bradby et al. 1980: 276).

Sometimes, popular theatre has been separated into different categories, like folk drama, popular theatre and mass entertainment, each with its own nuance and meaning (see Price 2016, chapter 1 for a detailed discussion of this). The word 'mass' implies a political analysis which takes a dim view of the popular. Louis James notes that, 'Scholars of mass entertainment in the capitalist era have tended to focus on popular theatre in terms of the exploitation of the working classes' (in Bradby et al. 1980: 1–2).

On the other hand, popular theatre is sometimes seen as a weapon in the fight to liberate the poor and downtrodden. Joel Schechter sees it as 'democratic, proletarian, and politically progressive' (2003: 3). In Tim Prentki and Jan Selman's particularly specialized definition, popular theatre is seen as what might otherwise be referred to as community theatre or applied performance. For them, it means 'theatre created with, by and for communities most involved in the issues it seeks to address', which 'seeks radical change … question[ing] the social and political structure, and presum[ing] that there is a more egalitarian social make-up possible' (2003: 8–9).

When its artistic properties, rather than its sociological importance, are discussed, this is sometimes in relation to its influence on legitimate theatre. Peter Brook rather grandly declares that, 'It is always the popular theatre that saves the day' (1972: 73). He goes on to spend 28 pages of his 37-page chapter on Rough Theatre discussing its influence on Brecht and its relevance for the work of Shakespeare. While both may have real connections to the popular, both Brecht and Shakespeare are inarguably recognized as key figures of the legitimate theatre. Brook spends little time discussing actual concrete examples of truly illegitimate popular theatre.

Another approach is to identify a series of key attributes which popular theatre possesses. John McGrath drew up a list of nine qualities which, he argued, appeal to working-class audiences: directness, comedy, music, emotion, variety, effect, immediacy, localism (in the sense of 'characters and events with a local feel'), and localism (in the sense of 'a *sense of identity* with the performer') (McGrath 1981: 54–59). There are a number of similarities between this and a list Bim Mason came up with 15 years later: direct contact, participation, spectacle, craft, emotions, comedy, sex and horror (in Merkin 1996: 3–4).

The definition we are proposing in this book focuses very much on performance technique, more than idea of theatre 'of the people' – or even that which simply puts the most bums on seats. For us, popular performance is theatre from the wrong side of the Great Divide, seen as being low, disreputable and unworthy of serious attention because of particular artistic qualities it possesses. These make it instantly recognizable and distinct from what is normally thought of as actual theatre, in spite of the fact that – on closer inspection – it clearly is just a specialized form of it.

Popular performance is what Peter Brook describes as 'the theatre that's not in a theatre' (1972: 73), often taking place outside of conventional theatre buildings. This is certainly true of many of the twelve examples discussed in this book. *Cabaret* and early *music hall* usually took place in drinking establishments, and although *vaudeville* and *variety* happened in theatres, both grew out of earlier tavern-based entertainment. The ground level of today's *stand-up*, *live sketch* and *burlesque* tends to be staged in licensed premises, for a drinking audience. *Clowns* often appear in circus tents, even if they sometimes work in theatres. *Magic* has been performed in various contexts, including variety theatres, comedy clubs and even – like *street theatre* – in the open air, outside of any building. *Pantomime* has probably made the most significant inroads into legitimate theatre buildings, but even so it has been seen as a seasonal interloper, a commercial cash cow that helps to subsidize the less profitable shows. As music hall mogul HE Moss wrote in a letter to the *Era* in 1894: 'Many of the "theatres" in this country would not survive but for the Christmas pantomime' (in Radcliffe 2016: 92).

As for its artistic qualities, we propose that the particular strand of popular performance that we are concerned with shares *four key features*:

1. It involves *direct connection between performer and audience*, eschewing any notion of a fourth wall.
2. It embraces *skill* and *novelty*.
3. It is *rooted in the present moment*, directly acknowledging the performance situation and engaging with topical events.
4. It involves an *interlacing of performer and role*, which might, for example, involve the performer playing him- or herself.

It is crucial to our argument that this is not just a list of discrete individual attributes, but instead a set of interrelated performance strategies that work together to create a particular kind of show, based on an immediate, intense relationship between performer and audience, which makes it quite different from legitimate theatre. These strategies have evolved partly because of the ramshackle array of venues within which popular performance tends to happen, which often create greater demands of the performer than the rather more orderly surroundings of a conventional theatre auditorium.

Direct connection between performer and audience

In popular performance the audience are addressed directly, and their presence is never forgotten. They sit – or stand – at the very heart of the performance, and the lines of communication between them and the performers always remain open. According to Stuart Hall and Paddy Whannel, for music hall singers, 'the making of rapid connections with the audience was … *a condition of the kind of art* in which they were engaged' (1964: 58). Marinetti wrote in 1913 that, 'The Variety Theatre is alone in seeking the audience's collaboration. It doesn't remain static like a stupid voyeur, but joins noisily in the action, in the singing, accompanying the orchestra, communicating with the actors in surprising actions and bizarre dialogues' (in Double 2012: 140). The celebrated variety singer Vera Lynn made a similar point: 'The variety stage involved direct contact with the audience, then and there. Everything had to be right, you couldn't stop and start again, and reaction was immediate' (in Double 2012: 130). Clowns are just as direct: 'The clown does not simply perform in front of the audience, he or she plays with the audience, connects with them' (Peacock 2009: 34). For the veteran alternative comedian Tony Allen, it is this directness of communication that separates comedy from theatre: 'A stand-up comedy performance involves direct communication with an audience. Performing rather than acting' (2002: 28).

For the popular performer, the fourth wall has not been removed so much as it never really existed. There is sometimes an assumption that the fourth wall is a given in theatre, that it is the default setting, and to work without it requires it to be actively got rid of. Brecht, for example, probably inspired by his experience of watching and even performing in cabaret, boldly stated: 'We want to demolish the fourth wall' (2002: 44–45). Similarly, Dario Fo – whose work arguably straddles the Great Divide – claimed that: 'The intention of doing away with the fourth wall was already an obsession with the commedia players' (1991: 73).

For all his brilliance, Fo is making the common mistake of assuming that the roots of the fourth wall go deeper into history than they actually do. It has been claimed that Molière used the term in his 1663 play *L'Impromptu de Versailles*, in which the great comic actor and playwright is supposed to have asked 'whether this invisible fourth wall does not conceal a crowd observing us' (Pavis 1998: 154). In fact, the quote has been wrongly attributed. It actually comes from a similarly titled play called *L'Impromptu du Palais-Royal*, written by Jean Cocteau almost 300 years later in 1961–62, which imagines an encounter between Molière and Louis XIV. The king angrily dismisses some marquises and declares, 'This time we are alone.' Molière responds by smiling and indicating the audience, which leads the king to deliver the line in question: 'Sait-on si les trois murs de notre vie n'en sont point quatre et si ce quatrième mur invisible ne dissimule pas une foule qui nous observe?' (Do we know if the three walls of our life aren't in fact four and if the invisible fourth wall doesn't hide a crowd watching us?) (Cocteau 2003: 1275–76, my translation).

The concept of the fourth wall probably dates back to Diderot's 1758 work *On Dramatic Poetry*, in which he advises: 'Whether you write or act, think no more of the audience than if it had never existed. Imagine a huge wall across the front of the stage, separating you from the audience, and behave exactly as if the curtain had never risen' (1918: 299). However, this reflected Diderot's ideals for the theatre rather than the actual theatrical culture he experienced. For example, in his later work *Paradox of the Actor*, he describes common conventions of direct communication across the footlights, with actors 'casting an eye around the boxes' and 'as almost all of them do, speaking straight to the pit' (2013: 31–32). He recalls a specific incident in which an actor called Quinault-Dufresne was heckled with, 'Speak louder!' to which he replied, 'And do you, Sirs, speak less loud!' (2013: 47). Diderot's ideals of theatrical realism only really started to be strictly implemented in the late nineteenth century, when Antoine's radical staging innovations at the Théâtre Libre 'moved the focus of the action from the auditorium to the stage' so that

> The actors, no longer playing directly to the audience, are, by implication, no longer playing for it. No longer the acknowledged core of the action, the audience experiences the illusion of looking in on another real, self-centred world, of being the unseen witness of a moment of actual existence. (Chothia 1991: 24–25)

It was in relation to Antoine's work that Jean Jullien coined the phrase the 'fourth wall', and the concept was developed by Stanislavski, who devised precise acting techniques to allow his actors to ignore the audience and thus preserve their sense of the reality of the fictional world they were evoking. These included focusing the eyes, 'Almost at the same angle as if you were looking at the tip of your nose' to simulate looking at an object on the fourth wall itself, rather than making the 'physiological error' of focusing on somebody in the orchestra (Stanislavski 1980: 90).

Such careful use of the eyes to avoid any possibility of direct connection with the audience would be absurd in the context of popular performance. Rather than focusing on an imaginary fourth wall, popular performers look directly at the audience and share their gaze around the auditorium so that every section feels included. There is no need to demolish the fourth wall, because it was never built in the first place. The concept of the fourth wall assumes a proscenium arch, and in many cases popular performance is not performed in conventional theatre spaces. In cabarets or comedy clubs, with the audience seated around tables and chairs, the stage is just a platform without a literal second and third wall, never mind a notional fourth one. In street theatre, there are no walls at all.

For popular performers, the trick is to break down any barrier between them and the audience, rather than develop techniques to establish an artificial one. Popular performers play straight to the crowd, establishing a direct, intense relationship and continually working to avoid the noisy consequences of losing them. Direct address is fundamental to the art of the music hall comedian, the cabaret conférencier and the stand-up comedian. Magicians talk directly to their audience, and interact freely with the volunteers they bring onto the stage to help with their tricks. Pantomime performers break out of their fairy tale narrative to talk to the audience – in or out of character – and lead the audience in ritualized participation. As Louise Peacock points out, 'In the circus, the audience expects the clowns to invade the audience space. This is, in effect, part of the contract you enter into as a member of a circus audience' (2009: 66). In street theatre, the performers have to conjure an audience into existence in the first place, using a range of skills to persuade passers-by to stop, arrange them into a suitable shape and keep them entertained enough to stop them drifting away (Mason 1992: 90–100). Direct communication with individuals or the crowd as a whole is an important part of each of these stages.

Of course, playing directly to the audience is not a single technique with a single aim in mind. Direct address and audience interaction are as subtle and varied as any other facet of performance, and they encompass a range of different approaches and seek to create a range of different effects. For example, magicians seek to amaze where burlesque performers seek to arouse. Contact between stage and auditorium can build the collusion which makes laughter more plentiful, heighten the audience's appreciation of the skills on show, or join them together in collective celebration when they clap along with the rhythm of a song or join in the chorus. A skilled popular performer can cue the audience to laugh or applaud without making them aware that they are being manipulated.

This is not to say that the fourth wall is entirely ubiquitous in legitimate theatre. When Antoine built the imaginary fourth wall at the Théâtre Libre, he was reacting against the traditional French acting style in which everything was played straight out to the audience (Chothia 1991: 23). Nor has legitimate theatre always enjoyed audiences as well behaved as they are today. Richard Butsch's book *The Making of American Audiences* documents the long history of audience rowdiness in America, tracing it back to its European origins in, for example, the noisy, lively Elizabethan playhouse (3–4). More recently though, theatre audiences tend to be quieter and more formal. As Susan Bennett put it, 'by the exchange of money for a ticket which promises a seat in which to watch and action unfold, the spectator accepts a passive role and awaits the action which is to be interpreted' (1990: 177).

For some, the comparatively recent innovation of the fourth wall is a historical aberration. Brecht argued that demolishing the fourth wall was, 'The hardest advance of all: backwards to common sense' (2002: 45). Artaud saw fourth wall Naturalism restricting the theatre to 'probing the intimacy of a few puppets, thereby transforming the audience into Peeping Toms' and suggested that it was this that had encouraged the masses to turn away from it in favour of the cinema, circus and music hall (1977: 64).

Immersive theatre companies like Punchdrunk have now started to challenge the dominance of the fourth wall, involving the audience much more directly in the fictional worlds they create. Theatre critic Lyn Gardner argues that the 'contract with the audience' has 'changed a lot over the past 20 years': 'That's true of the proliferation of Punchdrunk-inspired shows, but even quite traditional work can involve an element of audience participation' (2015). Some critics have proven resistant to this trend. In a review of Belt Up's adaptation of Kafka's *The Trial* at Southwark Playhouse, Charlotte Higgins declared: '[I]f you've seen one too many "immersive" pieces of theatre, the shock and excitement of sharing a space with the actors can just simply wear off ... As we left the theatre, I found myself saying to my friend: "For god's sake, bring back the fourth wall. And seats"' (2009).

This tends to suggest as well as being a dominant feature of legitimate theatre in the twentieth century, the fourth wall largely continues to be so today. Importantly, Gardner sees legitimate theatre's challenges to the fourth wall as comparatively recent – within the last 20 years – and the fact that they are worthy of note suggests that they are still the exception and not the rule. Even among radical theatre-makers, the convention of ignoring the audience has often gone unchallenged. Grotowski, for example, tried various ways of configuring the auditorium to create new relationships between performers and audience, but in each case the people watching the show were given a 'passive role'. Even when the performers were playing among the spectators, they ignored them, 'looking through them' (1975: 20).

Although comedy is a genre defined by creating a tangible response in the audience – making them laugh – in legitimate theatre, the jokes often remain within the fictional frame of character and situation. There is a reluctance to break the illusion by addressing the audience directly. Athene Seyler was a much-admired comic actor throughout much of the twentieth century, and in *The Craft of Comedy* (written with Stephen Haggard and first published in 1944) she wrote interestingly about the performer-audience relationship. She argued that Stanislavskian identification with character was inappropriate for comedy, which involves 'standing outside a character or situation and pointing out one's delight in certain aspects of it'. This creates a particular kind of relationship with the audience:

> [I]t demands the co-operation of another mind on which this observation is to be made – the audience, and is in essence the same as recounting a good story over the dining table. It must have direct contact with the person to whom it is addressed, be it one's friend over the port or one's friends in the stalls and pit.

However, this 'direct contact' did not mean direct address as such:

> I hope this does not give you the impression that I would take a low view of comedy as something to raise the 'laughter of the injudicious', nor that you will confuse it with the vulgar wink across the footlight to establish good fellowship, or any of the perfectly legitimate tricks employed in the music-halls or revues to 'get a joke across' as the saying is. This branch of comedy acting is a very great one, but I'm afraid I haven't any knowledge of it or its technique. (2013: 25)

This subtle psychological reaching out to the audience is a far cry from the full frontal direct address of the music hall comic or the stand-up.

Here, then, is the dividing line between legitimate theatre and popular performance. Actors in theatre are not just less likely to work straight to the audience, when they do it tends to be in a much subtler, less direct way. For the popular performer, on the other hand, working the crowd is a core skill and is elemental to what they do. The American stand-up Shelley Berman had trained as an actor, and a key lesson when becoming a comedian was how to talk to audiences:

> I didn't even *address* the audience, because I was used to the Fourth Wall. I was really trained to ignore that, you do not penetrate that Fourth Wall unless you are doing a soliloquy … And one night I tried it, and I got much more laughter … I somehow realised that it's dealing with an audience that a comedian does, and, you know, I'd better stop being such a snob. (in Double 2014: 190–91)

What is slightly remarkable here is that a nightclub audience would have put up with a comedian who did not talk to them directly. Audiences for popular performance are prone to unruliness, which means they require careful handling, and there are often specific reasons for this. In objecting to smoking and drinking in music halls, Henry Irving was picking up on something significant. When an audience smokes, drinks or eats, it changes the nature of their night out, making it as much about socializing as watching the show. It has often been noted how alcohol and tobacco make for a more active, rowdy audience (Brook 1972: 73; Bennett 1990: 129; Butsch 2000: 50). As Bim Mason has argued, for such a crowd, '[t]he barrier of the invisible fourth wall will either feel like a protective barrier that a fearful actor has erected, or a snobbish superior ignoring of all the other people in the same space' (in Merkin 1996: 3).

Direct communication is demanded by the kind of loud, rumbustious, even drunken audiences that popular performance tends to attract. Tom Parry advises Hester Chillingworth that if Getinthebackofthevan wanted to appear in comedy clubs, they would have to adapt by 'signal[ling] clearly from the get-go that you're going to make them laugh', because audiences in such venues know that 'if they're not enjoying something, they have the right to communicate that to the act' (Logan 2015).

The implication of this is that the popular audience is in a powerful active position which allows them to sit in judgement over the performance playing out on the stage and make their feelings known. They can show approval by laughing, cheering and applauding, or their disapproval in the form of heckling, booing or ugly silence. The direct relationship with an active audience means that popular performers have to actively seek approval, in a way that has often been seen as suspicious in legitimate theatre. Diderot suggested a fourth wall, because he believed it is 'necessary that both author and actor forget the spectator, and that all the interest should be centered [*sic*] in the characters' (1918: 298). Similarly, Grotowski advised, 'One must not think of the spectator while acting', warning that playing to the audience would lead to '[a] sort of prostitution, bad taste', and 'a kind of flirtation that means he is playing for himself, for the satisfaction of being accepted, loved, affirmed' (1975: 181, 202).

Skill and novelty

Popular performers have no such qualms and are perfectly prepared to present things to the audience in order to entertain and delight them. A good example is novelty. As Richard Butsch points out, 'As a general rule, audiences attend to, even are absorbed by an entertainment when curious about some novelty' (2000: 11). Novelty often has negative associations, the *Oxford English Dictionary* using adjectives like 'useless', 'trivial', 'frivolous' and 'nonsensical' in its various definitions of the word.

Grotowski would probably see it as 'bad taste', but popular performance is happy to embrace novelty in the form of something new, fresh, unusual, quirky or idiotic, possibly a new twist on an old idea or an unexpected juxtaposition. Novelty is often presented to the audience in such a way as to make whatever is novel about it as conspicuous as possible. For example, in variety theatre, Valantyne Napier would finish her human spider contortionism act with a twist ending which made the audience realize just how unusual the act had been: 'I came through the tabs to take my "call" and as I removed the hood of my costume there was always an exclamation from the audience as my long blonde hair fell down and they realized that the "spider" was a girl' (in Double 2012: 187).

Another strategy for winning the audience's approval was to present them with a display of skill. Bim Mason argues that, 'Quite rightly, a popular audience won't have much time for a performer until he or she shows themselves to be capable of doing something out of the ordinary – merely acting is not enough. So skills whether they are musical, acrobatic, comic or whatever are essential' (in Merkin 1996: 4). The two acts which Granville Baker argued were stage plays might each have involved the display of skill – the remarkable leaning and balancing stunts in Little Tich's famous Big Boot Dance and the ventriloquism skills of Johnson Clark.

Indeed, popular performers dazzle audiences with a dizzying array of skills, as they sing, dance, juggle, tumble, throw, catch, imitate, pratfall, ride unicycles, walk on stilts, swing on trapezes, escape from chains or handcuffs or barrels, practice sleight of hand, do motorbike stunts, display the animals they have trained and demonstrate feats of extraordinary strength. As Louise Peacock points out, 'Stunts and acrobatics serve, among other things, to remind the audience of the level of physical skill possessed by slapstick performers' who show 'an ability to do things with their bodies that the watching audience could never conceive of doing with their own' (2014: 33).

As with novelty, skill has to be correctly framed for maximum impact, because there is no direct correlation between the difficulty of a stunt and the amount of applause it will receive. One way of framing skill is to challenge audience volunteers to try the stunts out for themselves, so that their failure makes it all the more impressive when the performer subsequently pulls it off. The strongwoman Joan Rhodes, who worked in variety, would challenge men in the audience to feats of strength, asking them to try bending six inch nails in their hands, or taking four of them on in a tug-of-war. She observed that 'the harder it looked the louder the applause' (Rhodes 2007: 83).

By contrast, there are other skills which are deliberately kept hidden, passed off as natural and spontaneous, without revealing the effort and experience that have gone into developing them. Ernest Short recalled how the actor Louis Calvert praised music hall comic Harry Lauder for 'the consummate skill with which he used his voice. He gave the impression of perfect spontaneity, and, though he always appeared to be "just talking," he, in fact, used an astonishing range of voice'. As Calvert explained:

> The delectable, winning inflections, which somehow cajole and stroke an audience into just the warm mood he wishes, are not, I venture to say, so unstudied as they seem. Night after night he deftly touches the identical notes so expertly and easily that it all seems the naïve and almost accidental charm of a delightful personality. (in Short 1946: 21–22)

Lauder is supposed to have taken a year to perfect the laugh he used in his song 'Tobermory' (Short 1946: 22). Similarly, Short wrote of the variety double act Flanagan & Allen: 'If they have a fault, it is that their methods tend to be so casual that one can never be certain that success is not a happy chance rather than the product of craft skill, but then this comment applies to so much of current art' (1946: 245).

Some popular performers – particularly those who play for laughs – may not have any obvious, dazzling skill to frame for maximum effect, but instead use this type of invisible skill in order to win the desired responses from the audience. In addition to vocal rhythms and inflections, they learn how to keep the rapport they enjoy with their audience warm and immediate, constantly reading their reactions and adjusting the act accordingly, and making sure that all sections of the audience feel included. Frankie Howerd recalled how he acquired the skills he needed to perform in variety theatres:

> One music hall technique I had to learn was to perform to three layers of people at once: stalls, circle and gallery. I had to please them all – especially the gallery, which was where the whistling and cheering (or boos and catcalls) came from ... So [my sister] Betty would move around the theatre to make certain people could see and hear me; make sure I was projecting my voice and facial expressions – especially those made by my eyes. (Howerd 1976: 67)

Rooted in the present moment

Another effect of direct communication between a performer and an active, vocal audience is to firmly root the performance in the present moment. The performers can not only engage with topical events but also directly acknowledge the reality of the performance situation. The venue, the audience and even the performance itself can be commented on by the performers and incorporated into the show. All live theatre exists in the moment, but popular performance places immediacy and spontaneity at its core. As Tony Allen puts it, 'The "Now" agenda defines stand-up comedy' (2002: 28). Mark Thomas makes a similar point, speaking at the Linda Smith Lecture in Canterbury in 2015:

> The thing is, though, that actually it's about addressing the situation and being honest, and that's a really key, key fact in performing and comedy, to address the reality of what is happening ... This is an encounter not a recital. What is happening here – is I am talking to you. We are meeting each other. We are meeting each other and actually this moment in time – none of us know what's going to come out of my mouth next, including me. [audience laughter] ... it's a one-off, it's an encounter.

This means that improvisation has to be much more central to popular performance than most legitimate theatre. Joseph Wilson, the manager of the Tivoli music hall, spoke for the defence in the Granville Barker case, arguing that 'in the course of a long experience he had never before heard it suggested that a performance like that of Little Tich was a stage play. His "patter" varied nightly, and dealt with current events of the day' (*The Stage* 1912a). Topical gags and references are liberally strewn across cabaret, pantomime and stand-up, being changed and updated night after night as events in the outside world develop.

Meanwhile, events within the venue itself constantly offer themselves up for comment. The audience's own noisy contribution to the show, its laughter, its applause and crucially its heckling, remind it of the nowness of the event – as do the performers' spontaneous responses to its interjections. The performers can also comment on the process and mechanics of the performance, drawing the audience's attention to how it is all being done. Peter Davison points out how variety comics Max Miller and Frankie Howerd would talk to the conductor of the orchestra so that, '[i]n effect, a "hidden" part of the theatrical event ... was made apparent, something which would not be done in a "straight" play in the days when a small orchestra would "accompany" the performance' (1982: 22).

This commentary on the reality of the performance situation can even occur in forms of popular performance which are structured around a narrative. In pantomime and sketch comedy, for example, the performers can step out of the narrative frame to answer a heckle or comment on how a particular joke has gone down and then get straight back to the story. Davison argues that this forces the audience to respond 'multiconsciously', so that, 'At one moment disbelief could be suspended; at another, the audience could be made conscious it was in a theatre; and then it could again suspend disbelief' (1982: 12). This implies that the noisy popular audience is more sophisticated than its reputation would suggest.

Shows must be structured to allow for improvisation to sit alongside planned material. Louise Peacock writes of:

> the mutability of any clown performance in which, whilst an overall structure may exist for a performance, a clown will still respond to his audience. The nature of the interaction between the clown and the audience is spontaneous and here, genuine play occurs, creating an energy which also affects the planned sequences of the performance. (2009: 9)

Successful improvisations can be brought back and recreated in subsequent shows. This not only means that the material of the show changes and evolves over time, but also that what is apparently spontaneous and improvised might actually be performed in the same way night after night. Tony Allen confesses:

> Stand-up comedy . . . can give the appearance of being wholly improvised. In reality, of course, very little is spontaneous and it is only the potential for spontaneity that exists. An honest stand-up comedian will admit that the moments of pure improvisation account for less than five per cent of their act . . . What eventually made me such an inconsistent stand-up was that I couldn't hack the fundamental deceit involved in presenting only a semblance of spontaneity. (2004: 93)

Interlacing of performer and role

Granville Barker testified that in the third song he saw Little Tich perform at the Tivoli, 'he might be said to have appeared as Little Tich himself, wearing a more or less conventional music hall costume' (*The Stage* 1912a). The idea of the performer appearing as him- or herself is another defining element of popular performance, and it partly relates to the idea of being rooted in the present moment. If performers have to acknowledge the reality of the immediate performance situation, then part of this reality is their own identity.

Even though Little Tich performed many of his songs in character, he could also appear as 'himself'. More than this, there was a kind of consistent persona underlying all of his characters. The voice he used was fairly similar whether singing as a gamekeeper or a gas inspector, and he drew on running comic themes, particularly playing on his own short stature. The implication of this is that whatever character he was presenting, the audience would still essentially have thought of him as the stage personality Little Tich.

Similarly, many of the performers examined in this book present consistent stage identities which underlie all of their performances, providing a context for the act, and giving it its own particular tone. Grock, for example, had established his stage persona by 1911 and enacted his childlike struggle to understand the world from then on. Josie Long's personality – earnest and idealistic as well as playful and childlike – has been a constant throughout the stages of her evolving stand-up act. Meanwhile, Derren Brown's magic is uniquely flavoured by his intelligent showman persona, promoting scepticism while apparently accomplishing impossible feats, using pop psychology to dismiss any mystical explanations.

Performing in the first person means that the performer's inherent physical properties become an important part of the act. For example, Little Tich made frequent jokes about his diminutive size, while the cabaret comedian Karl Valentin exploited his lanky physique for all it was worth. Revue star Maisie Gay offered the following career advice to Jessie Matthews: 'Develop your own personality, and don't mimic. Think of your own face. Never forget your round face, straight hair, and fringe. Visualise it all the time, while you are working, and exploit it for all you are worth' (Short 1946: 237).

The idea of *stage personality* or *persona* involves a certain amount of ambiguity. On the face of it, when Little Tich appears as 'himself' he might seem more authentic than when he presents characters. He seems to be acknowledging the reality of his own personality so that what the audience see is what they get. However, even Granville Barker's words suggest it is not quite as simple as that. By using the phrase 'might be said to have appeared', he allows for a certain amount of artifice.

Clive Barker argued that, 'The image or persona is a fabrication. It is a part played as consciously as the actor assumes his role.' However, he also acknowledged that the persona is 'a very personal creation' and that there are 'cases where the inevitable feed-back from continual performance of the role and the interlacing of personal and fictional qualities bring the personal character close to the stage persona'. He also suggested that, 'In certain cases the private life of the performer forms an important part of the performer's persona' (Barker 1978: 8). Little Tich would probably have agreed that his persona was a fabrication. He saw his stage identity as being quite separate from his private personality, one symptom of this being that he disliked being called Little Tich offstage, preferring to be addressed by his birth name, Harry Relph.

On the other hand, Tony Allen argues that, 'A raconteur comedian walks on stage relatively naked. He speaks directly to the audience in the first person. There is no contract, only a nebulous agreement that the performance is spontaneous and authentic' (2002: 28). Many of today's stand-ups agree that they do perform in the first person, appearing pretty much as themselves. Jo Brand says her onstage and offstage selves differ 'hardly at all, to be honest', Sarah Millican believes that her persona 'is exactly as I am', and Josie Long argues that when she is performing, 'It *is* me and I try to be, like, as earnest as possible with it' (Double 2014: 128). Similarly, Teddie Beverley – of variety singing trio the Beverley Sisters – is adamant that onstage identity is an authentic expression of self: 'It's not an act really, it was *us*, you see. It wasn't assumed. It was us. It was us in the absolute raw … It doesn't succeed with the public over time if you put on an act' (Double 2012: 106).

However, Maisie Gay's words suggest that there is a process of selection and exaggeration in the creation of a stage self. The personality must be 'developed', the performer's physical properties – her face and hair – must be 'exploited'. The particular way that personalities are developed, the blending of truth and artifice, differs between different historical forms of popular performance.

Bernard Sharratt wrote of the 'complex interplay between the player and the role' in pantomime, arguing that 'the panto dame, or villain, makes no sense unless we simultaneously see through the character to the actor, and react "exaggeratedly" to the personality of both character and performer' (in Bradby et al. 1980: 282). Here, there is a layering of identity, with performer and role both visible to the audience. We might add that the performer's own personality becomes particularly conspicuous when breaking from the action to comment on how a gag has gone down.

In clowning, it is not so much a case of layering character and performer, but rather the building of a persona out of the raw material of the performer's personality. Louise Peacock explains that:

> When a clown performs, the audience sees the ideas and attitude of that individual conveyed by an adopted persona that has developed out of the individual's personality and which could never be adopted and lived in the same way by anyone else. The clown is not an interpreter. In his or her performance the view of and reaction to the world is the same for the creation (the clown persona) as for the performer. (2009: 14)

Even when the stage personality is an invented character – bearing little or no resemblance to the performer who inhabits it – the boundaries of truth and fiction can remain blurred. Madame Olga Petrova, for example, was born and began her career as the English actor Muriel Harding, but once she had adopted her Russian persona, she maintained it consistently, both onstage and off. This must have created a sense of an authentic personality, in spite of her shaky accent.

Regardless of the particular way that the performer's personality is manifested in the stage act, the fact that it is used at all tends to separate popular performance from legitimate theatre in general and fourth-wall Naturalism in particular. For Antoine, 'The fundamental battle was for characterization by the actor and against display of stage personality … The traditional seductiveness of the actor, the titillation of the audience by self-display, what Antoine even described as, "solicit[ing] at any price the approval of the public", was sternly rejected' (Chothia 1991: 29).

This suggests a strong link between addressing the audience directly and first person performance. The fourth wall creates a separation between the fictional world of the stage and the reality of the auditorium and allows the actors to immerse themselves deep into their characters. On the other hand, once a performer starts talking to the audience, it is likely that his or her personality will peep out from behind any fictional role he or she is adopting. For Tony Allen, any kind of characterization at all involves some kind of separation from the audience. He suggests that when stand-up comedians act out 'a character, short scene or conversation', they have chosen to 'erect a temporary fourth wall' (2002: 28).

A distinct mode of performance

The four key features discussed above interact with each other to create a distinct mode of performance, which is vibrant, exciting and intensely commercial. Performers play straight to an active audience, displaying skill and novelty to delight and surprise them, responding spontaneously to the immediate performance situation, and appearing in a role built out of elements of their own personality.

Some or all of these features may be found in legitimate theatre, and some or all were once common before fourth wall Naturalism recalibrated it and became 'the dominant twentieth-century mode' (Chothia 1991: 29). However, while they might occur in theatre, they are not the defining features. In the Little Tich case, Granville Barker defined acting as 'The assumption of character and the general development

of character', and Henry Tozer defined a stage play as 'a story in action developed by dialogue by two or more persons and with a connected plot' (*The Stage* 1912b).

By contrast, direct address, skill and novelty, the sense of immediacy, and stage personality are the beating heart of popular performance, as vital to it as character, plot and dialogue are to legitimate theatre. It is these four qualities that give popular performance its intense vitality and mark it out as being in a separate category of its own – hence the legal verdict that Little Tich's act was not a stage play.

Of course, our four key features work differently in different contexts. Each chapter focuses on a detailed case study – of a performer or act, a venue, or even a particular performance – and by doing so draws out how the key features are manifested in a particular form of popular performance.

Chapters are organized in two sections, starting with *historical* examples, before moving onto more *contemporary* ones. The historical section examines some different forms associated with the variety tradition, as well as examining contrasting comic performers (Caroline Radcliffe on the changing repertoire of the hugely successful music hall comic Dan Leno; Leigh Woods on the celebrated vaudeville act Madame Olga Petrova; Michael Wilson on Karl Valentin and Liesl Karlstadt's appearance in Brecht's cabaret *Die rote Zibebe*; Adam Ainsworth on the Kingston Empire, a typical suburban variety theatre; and Louise Peacock on the iconic Swiss clown Grock's appearances in circus and onstage)

The contemporary section starts with chapters which focus on issues relating to the identity of the performer (Michael Mangan on the reconfigured mentalism act of magician Derren Brown; Lynn Sally on burlesque artist MsTickle's subversive take on her own art form; and Simon Sladen on Pamela Anderson's appearance in the New Wimbledon Theatre's pantomime in 2009). These are followed by chapters which focus on the kind of relationships which performers build with their audiences in the popular performance of today (Bim Mason on his own experiences of performing street theatre with the Bigheads and Mummer&Dada; Sophie Quirk on cult comedian Josie Long's monthly club, Lost Treasures of the Black Heart; and my chapter on the influential live sketch trio Pappy's).

Our aim in this collection is to take these various forms of popular performance seriously as legitimate artistic endeavour. We are particularly interested in how popular performance is made, and we aim to analyse and evaluate the complexities of production and presentation techniques. Traditionally, it has been seen as the disreputable bastard relative of legitimate theatre, but we hope to show that for all its noise and apparent roughness, popular performance is as complex and sophisticated as anything else presented on stage for the amusement of an audience.

Bibliography

Allen, Tony (2002), *Attitude: Wanna Make Something of It? The Secret of Stand-Up Comedy*. Glastonbury: Gothic Image Publications.

Allen, Tony (2004), *A Summer in the Park: A Journal of Speakers' Corner*. London: Freedom Press.

Artaud, Antonin (1977), *The Theatre and its Double* (trans. Victor Corti). London: John Calder.

Barker, Clive (1978), 'The "Image" in Show Business', *Theatre Quarterly*, 8 (29) Spring: 7–11.

Bennett, Susan (1990), *Theatre Audiences: A Theory of Production and Reception*. London and New York: Routledge.

Billington, Michael (1992), 'Noises Off: How Alternative Comics Took Over the World', *The Guardian*, 14 May, 22.

Bradby, David, Louis James and Bernard Sharratt (1980), *Performance and Politics in Popular Drama*. London, New York and Melbourne: Cambridge University Press.

Brecht, Bertolt (2002), *The Messingkauf Dialogues* (trans. John Willett). London and New York: Bloomsbury Methuen Drama.

Brook, Peter (1972), *The Empty Space*. Harmondsworth: Penguin Books.

Butsch, Richard (2000), *The Making of American Audiences: From Stage to Television 1750–1990*. Cambridge: Cambridge University Press.

'Cases in Court' (1912a), *The Stage*. 18 April, 25.

'Cases in Court' (1912b), *The Stage*. 9 May, 28.

Chothia, Jean (1991), *André Antoine*. Cambridge and New York: Cambridge University Press.

Cocteau, Jean (2003), *Théâtre complet*. Paris: Gallimard.

Coles, Joanna (1991), 'Arts: Edinburgh Festival – A Tale of Empty Houses, Emptier Pockets', *The Guardian*, 29 August, 26.

Davis, Hazel (2009), 'Why Isn't Comedy Funded by the Arts Council?' *The Guardian*, 3 November.

Davison, Peter (1982), *Contemporary Drama and the Popular Dramatic Tradition in England*. Totowa, NJ: Barnes & Noble.

Diderot, Denis (1918), 'On Dramatic Poetry' [1758] in Barrett H. Clark (ed.), *European Theories of the Drama*. Cincinnati: Stewart & Kidd.

Diderot, Denis (2013), *The Paradox of Acting*. Miami, Florida: Hardpress Publishing.

Double, Oliver (2012), *Britain Had Talent: A History of Variety Theatre*. Houndmills, Basingstoke and New York: Palgrave Macmillan.

Double, Oliver (2014), *Getting the Joke: The Inner Workings of Stand-Up Comedy* (2nd edn). London and New York: Bloomsbury.

Fo, Dario (1991), *The Tricks of the Trade* (trans. Joe Farrell). London: Methuen Drama.

Gardner, Lyn (2015), 'When Does Poking Fun at Your Audience Turn into Bullying?' *The Guardian*, 25 August.

Grotowski, Jerzy (1975), *Towards a Poor Theatre* (ed. Eugenio Barba). London: Methuen.

Hall, Stuart, and Paddy Whannel (1964), *The Popular Arts*. London: Hutchinson Educational.

Higgins, Charlotte (2009), 'Immersive Theatre – Tired and Hackneyed Already?' *The Guardian*, http://www.theguardian.com/culture/charlottehigginsblog/2009/dec/07/theatre-punchdrunk [accessed 19 April 2016].

Howerd, Frankie (1976), *On the Way I Lost It*, London: Star Books/WH Allen.

Lee, Stewart (2005), 'When a Knob Joke Is Better than Brecht', *New Statesman*, 22 August, 28–29.

Logan, Brian (2015), 'What Can "Chin-Strokey" Theatre Learn from Raw Standup?' *The Guardian*, 12 March, http://www.theguardian.com/stage/2015/mar/12/can-theatre-learn-from-raw-standup-comedy.

Mason, Bim (1992), *Street Theatre and Other Outdoor Performance*. London and New York: Routledge.

Mayer, David (1977), 'Towards a Definition of Popular Theatre' in David Mayer and Kenneth Richards (eds), *Western Popular Theatre*. London: Methuen, 257–77.

McGrath, John (1981), *A Good Night Out. Popular Theatre: Audience, Class and Form*. London and New York: Methuen.

Merkin, Ros (ed.) (1996), *Popular Theatres?* Liverpool: Liverpool John Moores University.

Mirza, Shazia (2007), 'Don't Make Me Laugh: Comedy Isn't Out of Control at the Fringe, It's Popular for Being Fresh and Aventurous', *The Guardian*, 10 August, 36.

'Mr. Granville Barker's Test Licence Case Dismissed' (1912), *Daily Mail*. 9 May, 5.

Pavis, Patrice (1998), *Dictionary of the Theatre: Terms, Concepts, and Analysis*, Toronto and Buffalo: University of Toronto Press.

Peacock, Louise (2009), *Serious Play: Modern Clown Performance*. Bristol and Chicago: Intellect.

Peacock, Louise (2014), *Slapstick and Comic Performance: Comedy and Pain*. Houndmills and New York: Palgrave Macmillan.

Prentki, Tim, and Jan Selman (2003), *Popular Theatre in Political Culture: Britain and Canada in Focus*. Bristol and Portland: Intellect.

Price, Jason (2016), *Modern Popular Theatre*. Houndmills, Basingstoke and New York: Palgrave Macmillan.

Radcliffe, Caroline (2016), 'Theatrical Hierarchy, Cultural Capital and the Legitimate/Illegitimate Divide' in Peter Yeandle, Katherine Newey and Jeffrey Richards (eds), *Politics, Performance and Popular Culture*. Manchester: Manchester University Press, 75–95.

Rhodes, Joan (2007), *Coming on Strong*. Darlington: Serendipity.

Schechter, Joel (2003), *Popular Theatre: A Sourcebook*. London and New York: Routledge.

Seyler, Athene with Stephen Haggard (2013), *The Craft of Comedy* (ed. Robert Barton). Abingdon and New York: Routledge.

Short, Ernest (1946), *Fifty Years of Vaudeville*. London: Eyre & Spottiswoode.

Stanislavski, Constantin (1980), *An Actor Prepares* (trans. Elizabeth Reynolds Hapgood). London: Methuen.
'The Drama at the Music Halls' (1892), *The Era*. 23 April, 15.
Thomas, Mark (2015), [live performance] *The Linda Smith Lecture*. Gulbenkian Theatre, Canterbury, 12 May.

1

From Domestic Song to Drawing Room Recitation: Dan Leno's Music Hall Repertoire

Caroline Radcliffe

Dan Leno was the most popular male performer of the Victorian music hall, yet few people of the present generation are aware of his centrality to the British comic tradition. His fame was eclipsed by one of his most renowned imitators, Charlie Chaplin, who overshadowed Leno soon after his death as the medium of film took hold of the popular imagination. Like Leno, Chaplin worked his way up through the British music halls and popular theatres, performing clog-dances, slapstick and character acting; Stan Laurel followed the same route. Both Chaplin and Laurel acknowledged their debt to Leno, and traces of his act frequently appeared in their work, but from the age of twenty-six until his death in 1904, Leno had remained at the pinnacle of his profession, elected as the professional representative of music hall artistes and adored by his public.

Despite Leno's seminal position as a popular performer, he has received no scholarly attention other than through my own work (Kershaw 1994; Radcliffe 2006, 2010, 2015). Prior to an intensive and fruitful period of academic analysis during the 1980s and 1990s, music hall performance in general, has, historically, been celebrated and remembered through the lens of ideologically mediated theatrical mythology and a conservative nostalgia for 'the good old times'. Leno has been documented by a narrative that frames him as an archetypal comic genius who ironically but inevitably succumbs to overwhelming depression and madness, hence parallels with Spike Milligan, Peter Sellers and Tony Hancock are frequently, and, from a stylistic point of view, inappropriately, made.

Contrary to the common narrative that presents music hall as a romanticized, working-class art form, I argue that it was Leno's ability to adapt and keep up with the managerial ambitions and changing environment of the music hall as 'big business' that ensured his long-lasting popularity and success as a performer. It was this 'professional acumen' that served him most successfully and which, in turn, reveals an alternative narrative to the interpretation of the music hall stage.

In this chapter I explore Leno's mid- to late- career when he was at the peak of his success, focusing on his repertoire of music hall songs. I will demonstrate how his professional judgment led him to adapt his performances to conform with and survive within the dominant cultural hegemony. Leno's 'genius' was in choosing songs that complied with the changing policies and aims of the London music halls, appealing to the corresponding social composition of a newly emergent middle-class audience and management sector. I thus disprove the myth of Leno as a champion of a working-class audience by demonstrating that he consciously moved away from his early material (undoubtedly rooted in the personal hardships of his youth), complying instead to an ethos of 'improvement', endemic to the late-nineteenth-century music hall. A survey of Leno's songs from 1885 to 1903 demonstrates a clearly defined repertoire. Leno's early, bleakly ironic depiction of lower-class domestic violence transforms into a musical and textual satire of middle-class drawing room music and dance repertoire.[1] As Leno rose to stardom through his roles in the Drury Lane pantomimes, he relinquished his preferred performance style, successfully formulating a new style that complied with the increasing aggrandisement of both pantomime and music hall.

Born in 1860, Leno's life and career coincided with the music hall's most prolific and successful period. Leno's immense skill as a performer was grounded in disciplined family performance training, encompassing forms of dance, sketch performance, satirical ballads, burlesque and pantomime. These traditional, theatrical skills demarcated him from many other music hall performers, enabling him to bring otherwise standard songs to life through his accomplished character acting. His early immersion in popular theatre forms, contemporary drama and popular literature and his determination, adaptability and self-reliance as a performer secured his initial success as a music hall performer.

Leno's first performance was over one hundred and fifty years ago. But a few seconds of Kinetoscope reels and a number of gramophone recordings survive, unable to convey his particularly spontaneous, and by all accounts, hilariously funny acts. It would be misleading to attempt to offer a reconstruction of *how* he performed on the music hall stage. Music hall song sheets and photographs provide visual means with which to interpret his act, but the texts, with their absences and omissions, cannot be regarded as representative. What can be ascertained for sure is that Leno's performance style was an amalgamation of diverse elements of Victorian popular performance, creating a highly physicalized, slapstick style, including the gestural and choreographed comic vocabularies of the Harlequinade, traditional and contemporary dance and music, and popular drama – from melodrama and burlesque to Shakespeare; an unbroken clog dancing tradition acknowledges and still displays his influence.

Musical form, performance and patter

At the time of his London 'debut' (cited as 1885 by his biographer, Hickory Wood [Wood 1905]), although billed equally as 'Vocal Comedian and Champion Dancer', Leno stated that he was already earning £10 a week in the provinces as a comic singer long before he got his 'London chances' (*The Era* 1901). At this time, Leno's songs employ a strictly formulaic and limited musical structure, reliant on standard musical genres and subject matter common to the majority of music hall songs from the 1870s through to the early 1900s. As with the popular repertoire of hymns or folk music, the melodic range of the music hall song is extremely limited, accommodating the typically untrained voice of a music hall performer such as Leno, and easily manageable by audience members in their communal rendition of a chorus. Each music hall song contains a number of musical pointers, identifiable by the audience as signals to listen, join in, laugh or applaud. Characteristic musical motifs were integral to Leno's act, for example, an introductory eight bars of song melody followed by eight bars of music with diminishing note values (giving the impression of acceleration into the verse, not dissimilar to the 'hurry' music of early pantomimes and accompanying later silent film chase scenes) served to bring Leno onto the stage – he would make a fast entry, running down to the footlights, slamming his foot on stage to gain the audience's attention. Four bars of similar 'hurry' music are frequently repeated at the end of each chorus, as a transitional passage into the next verse, during which Leno performed comic 'business'. These four bars also served as a 'walk-off' at the end of the song; in Leno's songs, this concluding section often extended into an eight bar section in which he performed an eccentric dance break. Further musical clichés serve to reinforce stereotypical characterization; for instance, Leno's song 'Dear Old Mike', which concluded with a fast Irish reel.

But Leno's individuality as a performer did not rely on the song itself. His 'genius' is frequently attributed to his development of 'patter' – spoken interjections between the verses and choruses of a song. Leno included patter in all of his songs. In the earlier songs the patter consisted of a few lines but soon expanded to become the main body of the act.

Patter provided Leno with a particularly direct form of audience address, creating an intimacy between the performer and the spectator. It also strengthened the song's narrative; the patter was key in illustrating the songs. Undoubtedly, Leno's skill at the form singled him out from other performers but he was certainly not unique in using patter. Patter is reproduced in much earlier songs such as 'Villikins and his Dinah' (published 1853), and there are numerous theatrical precedents from Charles Matthews to Albert Smith. Leno's published patter is unusually substantial compared to other published music hall songs, considerably outweighing the musical content. He was clearly a leader in the field of spoken comedy. Although sometimes cited as the precursor to today's 'stand-up' comedian, his act still remained within a framework of character and parody, not situational nor political nor overtly topical comedy.

It is evident that Leno planned a clear structure to his patter, maintaining links to the song it was based on and building a framework on which he could then improvise.[2] A comparison of the published song sheet texts with Leno's phonograph recordings of the same material illustrates this. The recordings contain small differences (generally an improvement on the published texts), demonstrating that there was a certain amount of development and improvisation. It is possible that the published texts were already a polished rendition of versions that he had tried out and improved over months of repetition as he took the song from hall to hall. Considering that he would often perform the same song for well over a year, it is not surprising that he eventually established a set patter. Leno was emphatic, however, that he invented his own patter, improvising at each performance:

> Do I have my own patter written for me? No; not a single word of it. What's more, I've tried to write it down myself, and failed. I could no more sit down and write you the patter of a single song now than I could fly. But when I'm on stage it comes natural. You hear me sing the same song at three halls, and you will not find the patter the same at two. (*The Era* 1893)

Jimmy Glover, the musical director of the Drury Lane pantomimes, maintained that Leno was a bad study, never knowing his part or his songs on the first night; reviews were often optimistic that he would 'work up' a song, making a success of one that was not an immediate hit (Glover 1911: 75). Contrary to Leno's description of his own methods, Glover insisted that Leno had no powers of initiation, claiming that the song writer, Herbert Darnley (who wrote many of Leno's later songs), provided him with material which Leno would then build on: 'Once provided with the material he had the best contributory and constructive power' (153). Glover's account perhaps explains why the few songs that Leno wrote himself were parodies.

Leno, as with most other music hall performers, bought his songs from professional composers and writers. Once paid for, he changed them as he pleased.

> I get hundreds of songs and buy lots of them for a good chorus or a funny line, then work them out myself again. Lots of my songs are absolutely rewritten by me, except the refrain or a catchy bit like that (*The Era* 1893: 11).

In the same interview, he explained how he would sometimes be the one to formulate the idea for a line or phrase sending it to the writer to develop into a full song. Leno commissioned songs to suit his own imagination, allowing for spontaneous improvisation onstage. Few of his songs were failures, for each was meticulously adapted to his particular set of performance skills and the audiences he was playing to.

'The Shopwalker': Naturalism and a shifting class appeal

In 1939, Herbert Darnley, one of Leno's most prolific writers during his late career, defined Leno's style as a character singer as opposed to a comic one:

> Leno was not in any shape or form a comic singer – that is to say, he was not a singer of comic songs. Neither was Albert Chevalier. They were both delineators of character comedy, quite a different line of business. It may be asked how do I differentiate between a comic song and a comedy number? Well, the former is a humorous ditty that, from the first word almost, starts off with, as Clarkson Rose calls it, a wise-crack, and then, romping through an eight or sixteen-line stanza containing as many jokes as is possible to squeeze in, runs on to a chorus in which there may be a twist or a slogan, but invariably a strong

> last line. As an example, take R. G. Knowles' old song *The Benches in the Park.* This was Knowles telling the audience what funny people he had seen sitting on the park benches. Or Herbert Campbell asking the folk to *See Me Dance the Polka.* Or Harry Champion likening a gold chain to *Any Old Iron.* These were comic songs (and jolly good ones) in which the singer, without disguise, was putting himself, as it were, over the footlights. But no characterisation, to be somebody ... Leno was not merely a great comic, he was a great actor. Whatever the number he was the character true to life. Never for a moment stepping out of the picture, never burlesquing or exaggerating the little worries of existence, nor belittling its joys, Leno gave to his songs a realism by which they came to life. (Darnley 1939)

Darnley was clearly looking back to Leno's high career – forgetting, or perhaps never having witnessed his early, aggressive style of domestic humour which grossly parodied the 'little worries of existence', cynically 'belittling the joys' of lower-class marriage and courtship. By the time Darnley was writing for Leno in the 1890s, there had been a distinct move towards dramatic naturalism in the legitimate theatre influencing theatre criticism in general; thus it was Leno's 'truthfulness to life' that was consistently admired by commentators. While the legitimate theatre was rapidly modernizing, the music hall was also seeking a move away from the precedents of the last thirty or forty years. Song writers such as Darnley moved towards the acting styles of the legitimate theatre, the seeds of which appeared in Leno's later work. As his career progressed, comparisons were made between Leno and legitimate actors such as Henry Irving. The following anecdote demonstrates the moment of change, as the music halls transformed from the older-style hall, designed and geographically situated to attract a 'popular' audience, to the new 'Empires' of London's West End, attended by the new, middle-class, upper-class and bohemian spectator. The anecdote demonstrates Leno's awareness of this changing audience, signaling the moment for him to develop a new style in order to maintain his popularity.

J. B. Booth refers to Leno's song 'Dear Old Mike', by Harry King, performed in 1889 and sung in the character of an Irish labourer's wife:

> I can do what I like with dear old Mike,
> All the days of the week but one day,
> He's as happy as you please with a bit of bread and cheese,
> But he likes his bit of meat on Sunday.

> … Leno sang it first one night at the Empire, and Lennard (Horace) went round to see him in his dressing room. The new song had not gone particularly well.
>
> 'Come round with me, and hear me sing it at the "Mo"', said Dan; 'This audience doesn't know the type, but they'll see it alright at the "Mo"'.
>
> He drove Lennard in his brougham to the Old Mogul, where on his appearance he had the usual tremendous reception. He let himself go, as only Leno could, and when as a frowsy yet loveable old harridan, he produced from his marketing basket Mike's 'little bit of meat', in the shape of a belly-piece of pork, which he referred to as the 'waist-coat piece with the buttons', the house became hysterical with delight. (Booth 1943: 52–53)

When Leno produced the actual 'bit of meat' – representative of every-day life and perhaps laced with sexual innuendo – the audience at the Empire could not relate to it but when taken to the Middlesex Music Hall (the 'Old Mo'), a hall renowned for a lower class of patron, the 'bit of meat' got the biggest laugh. The picture on the sheet music cover illustrates Leno dressed as a middle-aged woman in a plain, drab dress, with an old-fashioned bonnet adorned by a flower and a red shawl, holding a shopping basket. With meekly clasped hands and a benevolent look, Leno seemingly portrays a passive, humble woman but her red nose undermines any pretense at moderation. The red nose was worn by Leno as a signifier of the carnivalesque, representing a state of intemperance embodied through drunkenness or sexual impropriety. The red nose subverts the image into a figure of derision, reflecting the content of the song. By emphasizing his small stature and distinctive facial features with ill-fitting, overly large costume and makeup, Leno conformed to the 'low' comic convention of exaggerated physicality.

Figure 1.1 Dan Leno in 'Clever Mr. Green' (author's collection)

The song-sheet cover also contains a small, inset picture in which a rowing couple is depicted as lower-class domestic stereotypes – the brutish husband, throwing his supper out of the window and the woman, who, far from being passive, is portrayed as a screaming harridan. Onstage, as he performed an eccentric dance to an eight-bar Irish reel, Leno concluded by pulling a particularly grotesque and ugly face in the limelight, signalling the audience to laugh at his exaggerated and misogynistic rendition of the wife.

Darnley cannot be referring to Leno's early songs such as 'Dear Old Mike'. He is describing a more refined characterization, a less obviously stereotyped realism, the criteria of which could only be met with a different style of song, a style which Darnley himself would shape for Leno.

Accordingly, in 1891, Leno's songs took a new direction, cementing the transition from the old style to the new. Walter De Frece's song, 'The Shopwalker', achieved phenomenal success and is, without doubt, the Leno song that was most popular with contemporary critics. The oft-quoted chorus is hardly indicative of a ground-breaking success, but 'The Shopwalker' became Leno's most popular song, the refrain recalled by many for years to come:

Walk this way! Walk this way!
The sale's now on; we've a grand display.
Upon my word, we're giving them away!
Walk this way, madam! Walk this way!

The chorus contains no apparent narrative or humour; it was Leno's characterization that captured the imagination of the new music hall public. The title on the music sheet cover implied that this was something new – *Dan Leno's Celebrated Pantomime, Patter Song* (sic). The song had not featured in any pantomime, the reference was to Leno's extended use of his physical pantomimic and verbal patter skills that defined 'The Shopwalker' as something new and different. The music hall performer Charles Coborn fondly remembered it:

> It is a joyful memory to have seen Dan Leno, and the procession of his 'characters' often rises before my mental vision. It was a sublime treat to see him as the shopwalker, when he placed a ladder, which did not exist, against a set of steps and drawers which were not there, run up and down it, and then spread upon an imaginary counter the articles which had never been. Your own imagination provided readily the boxes, drawers, ladder, and counter as he expatiated upon the excellence of the goods he had to sell. And the screamingly funny comments and recommendations he made concerning all of them! Verily, he was a supreme artist. (Coburn 1928: 151)

Contemporary commentators consistently focused on Leno's ability to 'truthfully' characterize real types. George Smith, in the *Dictionary of National Biography* of 1912, wrote:

> Although essentially a caricaturist, with a broad and rollicking sense of fun which added myriad touches of extravagance beyond experience, the groundwork of his creations was true, and truth continually broke through the exuberance of the artist ... 'The Shopwalker' perhaps convinced the great public of his genius. (Smith 1912)

Texts such as these contribute to the Leno mythology, isolating him from his music hall act and the larger part of his audiences while exposing the negotiations occurring between popular and high culture. 'The Shopwalker' became a signifier in the cultural mythology surrounding Leno. The *National Biography* notes it as the pivotal song that 'convinced the *great public* of his genius' (emphasis added). Leno was already well established, at the head of his profession by 1891 when the song was sung, with many published songs and a full working diary as testimony to his success. Leno was a top performer with a dedicated lower-class audience in both the halls and the Surrey Theatre pantomimes; from 1888 he was also starring at Drury Lane, but perhaps by 1891 his success had not convinced the middle classes – the great public. 'The Shopwalker' was the song that secured a wider following. It was the first of a new genre of Leno songs. Unlike the exclusively lower-class domestic songs hitherto performed by him, 'The Shopwalker' was the first of many songs representing the 'petit-bourgeoisie' or lower middle classes of Victorian society. Jane Traies in her article, 'Jones and the Working Girl', bases her evidence on the increasing marginal working-class/lower-middle-class audience. Traies is seminal in locating 'the voice of the clerks and the shop-assistants' as 'one of the voices of music-hall culture' (Traies 1986: 25). From around 1870 there was a demographic rise in clerks and administrators coming from working-class families. There was also an increase in the small businessman. Together they created a new lower middle class, coinciding with a rise in consumerism and bureaucracy. Leno turned to these subjects as he witnessed a rise in their numbers among music hall audiences and in the respectable suburbs of London where he himself now lived. As his own standard of living rose, parallel with his career rise through the more 'respectable' halls, his observations turned away from the lower class, to the characters around him, as he began to take an active interest in the middle-class world of mortgages, local councils, shop assistants and holidays reflecting not only a change in society but also in the rising economic status of the music hall performer.

Leno's new songs expose a contemporary perception of the Victorian lower-middle-classes as small-minded and hypocritical, satirizing the newly emerging relationship between the dishonest businessman and the put-upon employee. The subtexts of songs such as 'Our Stores' or 'The Doctor' indicate the rise of the individualistic, small-time capitalist – the small businessman exemplified by Leno's shopkeeper in 'Our Stores'. Each of Leno's new, economically driven characters deceives his customers in one way or another to increase his own profit. Each is prepared to sacrifice morals and quality service in his own interests. The doctor whose 'medicine's weak' but his 'fees are strong' announces at the end of his patter, 'But there you are, I'm making such a fortune!' and the proprietor of 'our nineteenth-century stores' serves rotten old food, passing it off for fresh new goods. A host of downtrodden employees followed 'The Shopwalker' in similar songs, such as 'The Waiter' and 'The Bootman'. Leno played the overworked shop assistant, spending long hours on his feet: 'And no-one knows but my poor corns, how I've walked up and down.' These songs represent the social-climbing, commercial employee, obsequious to and suspicious of his superiors in equal measure. Like Leno's other members of the lower-middle-class capitalist system, the shopwalker's subservience is a front for his tricks and dishonesty as he tries to earn more, raising his social status. The figure of the shopwalker as he attempts to sell off last year's stock must have appealed to the clerks and administrators, the new class of consumer, viewing the insistent salesman with suspicion, while the higher-class audiences of the Empire perhaps looked down on the grasping little shop assistant from a position of satisfying superiority. The man or woman who seeks to rise above his or her station has ever been a comic target. Other songs, such as 'Buying a House' by Herbert Darnley and Dan Leno, reveal the agonizing dichotomy of the character who, by taking on a mortgage, seeks to make an investment, but in fact gains nothing, becoming a slave to the capitalist system.

> Verse:
> Once I bought a house thro' a Building Society,
> Thinking when I paid for it it would belong to me;
> But oh! I was wrong, for the more I spent on it,
> The further off from being mine the dwelling seem'd to be . . .
>
> Chorus:
>
> Am I the Landlord, or am I not?
> Sometimes I think I am, and then I think I'm not,
> The Building Society wants to claim the spot,
> And my Landlord he wants to have the lot;
> Now what I want to know, before I'm off my dot,
> Is who does the house belong to?

Leno had often performed his earlier, domestic songs cross-dressed as a woman; although only a handful of his pantomime roles were female, it is for these that he is chiefly celebrated. The new genre of song reversed the gender of Leno's earlier songs and the sexual targets. Sexually aware wives had previously played on comic innuendo ('he likes his bit of meat on Sunday') with male characters played as naive innocents, emasculated by their ferocious or predatory female counterparts. Male characters now became the norm, their 'knowing' comments directed at the female:

> The obsequious and bewhiskered counter-jumper, with his automatic politeness and everlasting 'walk this way,' lending an attentive ear to the wants of his female customers and telling them that the gloves he sells will 'stretch like a woman's conscience,' is a sight to make the proverbial cat laugh, as is also the alacrity with which he takes the place of the female attendant and smoothes over the bashfulness of his female patrons by assuring them that he is a married man, and fully aquainted with the mysteries of feminine attire – immediately proving it by recommending an article that is better than the old-fashioned kind that buttoned at the back. (*The Era* 1897)

Leno realized that his characterizations, based on familiar types, should have a general class appeal; in an interview from 1899, he references his conscious use of mimesis:

> Songs must suit all classes of the audience and without that there is no success. 'The Shopwalker' and *Our Nineteenth Century Stores* are my favourites so far, because they are real studies of human character. You know the amount of humour there is in a shopwalker. His politeness to the buyers, and his courtesy to non-purchasers are proverbial. I knew a real genius in that line – a marvel indeed. He is my prototype for the song. Then the storeman, he is great. He usually sells something and you too. I know 'em. (*The Era* 1899)

By 1899, the year of the interview cited above, Leno's performances had fully conceded to the hegemonic demands of the 'great public'.

The ballroom: Music hall song and social dance.

The very existence and numerousness of Dan Leno song sheets is further evidence of his middle-class appeal. The music hall song sheet was costly and out of economic reach for the working-class earner. Leno's most popular songs were arranged as polkas, one of the most popular ballroom dances of the time, catering to middle-class pastime of social dance. This is an important indicator, not only of Leno's wide popularity across the classes, but also of the interdependence between late-nineteenth-century music hall repertoire and middle-class social dance repertoire. The first example of a polka arrangement appeared in 1892, 'The Dan Leno Polka', by Fred Eplett. It included music from 'The Moving Job', 'The Grass Widower' and 'The Railway Guard'. Its publishers, taking advantage of 'The Shopwalker's' phenomenal popularity, included a picture of Dan Leno as 'The Shopwalker' on the cover, even though the song was not included in the musical arrangement. In 1892 'The Shopwalker Polka on the Melody of Dan Leno's Great Song' by Josef Meissler was published as part of a series of 'new and fashionable dance music'. Only a handful of music hall songs appeared in the series, which was mainly composed of fashionable dances based on Victorian light repertoire suitable for the ballroom. Meissler's polka incorporated both the words and the tune of the chorus – an acknowledgement of the song's popularity. Both polkas also appeared in arrangements for full orchestra and 'octuor' (octet), intended for balls and public gatherings.

As Leno's style progressed, the songs became increasingly less defined in terms of class as he sought to encompass the whole music hall audience demographic. 'No More Fancy Balls for Me' references the upper-class aristocracy, the middle-class clergy and the lower-class pawn shop within the four-line chorus, reflecting a simplistic, triadic view of society often depicted in Leno's later songs.

> No more fancy balls for me!
> They suit the aristocracy and parsons;
> But if I have to go to any more balls,
> It'll be to the old three brass 'uns.

The references to costume hire situate the song in a higher class bracket:

> SPOKEN: Oh there's no doubt I've made a blithering idiot of myself. I had no business to go like this, I ought to have gone as a Roman Gladiator, but they wanted £4 10s. for that, and I'd only got 15s. to do the whole evening on

The hire of a costume was a considerable expense; at the time of 'No More Fancy Balls for Me' an evening's entertainment at a music hall could be purchased for as little as 2d. or 6d. Although the song jokes about having only 15 shillings, it would be a prohibitive expense for a working- or even lower-middle-class person.

The musical introduction breaks away from the usual formula by incorporating a waltz motif – another popular ballroom dance. It sets the scene of the fancy dress ball by presenting sixteen bars of genteel waltz music, comically switching to a four bar verse introduction followed by four bars of 'hurry' music bringing Leno on for the song. Herbert Darnley's style of introduction served to reinforce the setting and characterization of the song, creating a musically descriptive picture. The song also references another social dance – 'the Lancers', popular at middle-class gatherings:

> I soon forgot my sorrows as I mingled with the dancers,
> And begged of 'Joan of Arc' to be my partner in the Lancers.

Leno juxtaposes contrasting class material within his patter, bringing the affluent world of the country house down to the lower-class world of the pawn shop – the 'three brass 'uns':

> I was invited down to her father's house to a shooting party – I got there just in time to help them out with the piano … Oh, what a head I've got this morning! When I woke up, the servant – I mean the policeman – gave me a cup of coffee, and I said, 'What have I been doing?'

Leno performed songs such as 'No More Fancy Balls for Me' not only to satirize but also to encourage audiences to identify with the subject matter within their own experiences. In a previous article (Kershaw 1994: 42) I cited Leno's interview for *The New Penny Magazine* in which, when asked how he viewed the future of music hall, he replied:

> I think that in a very few short years that title will have vanished. We shall have no music halls, only variety theatres, and I also think that in a few years we shall be on a level with the legitimate theatres. Whether this remark will bring down the house around my ears, I hardly dare to think, but as an instance of what can be done with the business, look at Mr Charles Morton, and the Palace Theatre. A few years ago, no lady would be seen at a music hall, and especially no lady in evening dress. Now it is the lady who goes in her very best and prettiest evening dress, and after a smart restaurant dinner party, a visit to the Palace is 'de rigeur' … The Alhambra under Mr Slater's direction, has established a favourable reputation, and even the once much discussed Empire is becoming the fashion … I have also noticed a change at the Tivoli and the Oxford, two of the halls with which I have been identified for

> some years ... The Pavilion in its present condition is far more likely to attract than before, but I always got on well with the audience. (*New Penny Magazine* 1900: 112)

It is worth citing again to emphasize Leno's awareness of the changing social structure of the music halls and the need to adapt his repertoire. He predicts the impending transformation from music hall to variety theatre, recognizing a move towards a morality set by the legitimate theatre. His statement that the music hall would soon be on par with the legitimate theatre forecasts a challenge to the legitimate theatre's leading hegemonic status, a change sought by the music hall but never achieved. When asked, in the same interview, whether the public taste in songs moved with the times, Leno replied:

> Most decidedly. Some five years ago, I sung a song about a 'fried fish' man. It was encored nightly, but I am sure if I were to revive it it would not do. The standard of music halls is rapidly rising, and though some people pretend they are unnecessary and not to be taken seriously, the idea is absurd. Night after night these places are crowded, and what turns get the most applause? Good knock-about business, and the ultra-melodramatic ballad, especially when the refrain is sung by some tiny boy or girl from the upper circle.

Far from remaining true to an 'authentic working-class culture', suggested by writers Bailey and Stedman-Jones as being the prevalent music hall class culture, performers such as Leno consented to the hegemonically driven, moral and class elevation taking place in the music hall during the 1890s, choosing material that was unchallenging, with universal appeal.[3] Commentators who failed to recognize the new, class-encompassing music hall chose to read Leno's material as class-specific, attaching a sentimental nostalgia to it, unable to view it as an element of the new entertainment for the petit-bourgeoisie.

> Leno ... stood for the understructure of life from which it emerged, by means of a comic transmutation of its dark privations and necessities of suffering. Dan Leno is the supremely comic figure emerging from

> a tragic conflict ... His material was the sum of all the small things in the life of his class. It was full of babies' bottles, Sunday clothes, pawnshops, lodgings, cheap holidays and the like. *There was no change in his material after he had ceased to be affected by all these problems.* He remained, as Grimaldi remained, a member of his class, and was *innocent* of basing any behaviour on the assumption that he had left it. (Scott 1946, emphasis added)

Despite this claim, as Leno gained popularity in the London West End halls, most critics were viewing his work exclusively in the light of character songs such as 'The Recruiting Sergeant', 'The Waiter' or 'The Jap'. It is these, along with later songs such as 'The Beefeater' or 'The Huntsman', that are most frequently cited, eclipsing his prolific output of earlier, mainly domestic songs of specifically lower and frequently harsher content.

Recitations: Parodies and the national-popular

Towards the end of the 1890s and the beginning of the new century, Leno's songs became increasingly neutral, influenced by a national-popular hegemony. Songs such as 'The Swimming Master' or 'The Lecturer' avoided specific class reference, the subject matter was sufficiently universal to appeal to a general, mixed-class audience. Leno also started to introduce more of his own parodies and monologues. He recorded many of these spoken items. The parodies 'Where Are You Going to My Pretty Maid' and 'The Mockingbird' are based on well-known ballads; 'Poppies' is a burlesque 'coon' song and 'McGlockell's Men' a burlesque Scottish ballad. Other spoken recitations included 'My Wife's Relations' and 'The Robin'. Leno performed these at the beginning of the twentieth century by which time he was an established 'celebrity' or 'star' of the music hall, acknowledged even by royalty. It is unclear whether he performed these recitations in costume or not, but given his widespread fame and established status as a 'national treasure', it is likely that he was able to abandon all characterization and finally perform as 'himself'. The only other occasion for which he appeared onstage as an un-costumed, 'non-actor' had been the clog dances he had regularly performed as part of his music hall act until the mid-1880s.

In 'Where Are You Going to My Pretty Maid', and 'The Mockingbird', Leno subverts the ballads by taking each line literally, reducing the poetry to humorous banality, transporting essentially poetic characters to a world of pleasantries and social conventions:

> Do you believe in old songs? Well – I do to a certain extent, but I picked up one the other day and I think the man must have been silly who wrote it – it was called 'Where are you going to my pretty maid'. Now that's how it commenced, but there's no explanation whatever. But from what I could see it was a gentleman walking across a field and there was a lady – or a working girl – coming in the opposite direction with a bucket on her arm. Well this gentleman, well he was no gentleman or he wouldn't have spoken to her first without an introduction of course – that's very plain – but however, he turned round and he said, without any introduction 'Where are you going to my pretty maid?' And then he repeated it – he said, 'Where are you going to my pretty maid?' You see now – what was it to do with him where she was going – but an entire stranger – but she turned round – now this is very wrong – she oughn't to have taken any notice of him – she turned round and she said, 'I'm going a-milking sir' she said, 'sir' she said, 'sir' she said. Now why three times – what for! Once would have been enough and she should've gone on about her business.

Leno's monologues parodied the recitation, a prevalent late-nineteenth-century drawing-room entertainment published in collections suitable for the amateur reader for respectable home entertainments. Leno's biographer Hickory Wood, for example, published many volumes of humorous recitations, and an extract from Leno's ghosted pseudo-autobiography, *Hys Booke*, went through at least eight editions in *Routledge's XXth Century Humorous Reciter.*

Leno's monologues or recitations could be viewed as part of an inevitable progression of his style. As his patter increasingly dominated his songs, Leno began to sing just an introductory song verse and an end verse, or even to end with just a chorus; as the subject matter became oriented to a wider class spectrum, it was an easy transition from song to recitation. Leno's later humour conforms to Gramsci's definition of a 'national-popular-cultural-character' – a cultural identity which could be understood, experienced and felt by a whole nation (Forgacs and Nowell-Smith 1985: 122–23). 'The Robin', for example, satirized the pervasive Victorian sentiment for Christmas, reflecting a shared religion, shared traditions and the shared values of the Victorian family. Leno parodied the Dickensian image of the warmth and friendship of the Christmas dinner, punctuated by instances of 'good-will'. His style of recitation becomes a pompous monotone in which he eventually loses the thread:

> There you sit and you think of Christmas, and just then the little Robin comes hopping outside the window, hopping on his little hop, and you throw the windows open – (weather permitting of course, and you're not sitting there with your neck against it) – and there the Robin hops along and hops and – I often think it's a pity he hasn't got two more feet to hop on, give his hopping legs a rest – and you say 'Oh Merry Christmas!' and you throw him a loaf of bread and he picks it up and flies away with it and you say 'This is Christmas!'. Just then in comes the Christmas pudding, all hot and smoking with a little bit of holly sticking on the top and made of currant and lemons and bits of string and all the brandy burning all round it, all the beautiful brandy burning, and you say 'Oh, ooh, oh! What a pity the brandy's burning!' and there you sit on the pudding and you eat the robin with the pudding – you put the rob – er – well that is the reason I want to give you this impersonation of the bird and his song.

Leno had perfected a style that appealed to a wider national identity thus guaranteeing his popularity. Unlike his early domestic songs, which included slang and specifically lower-class references, Christmas was a nationally understood ritual. The symbolism of the robin, the holly and the Christmas pudding was engrained in the Victorian consciousness. As a hegemonic drive to improve popular entertainment gathered momentum, music hall managements sought to appeal to higher-class audiences. Leno recognized and readily consented to the hegemonic change, consciously adapting his material accordingly. Far from remaining the youthful, clog-dancing champion of the lower classes, the mature and successful Leno entertained all classes of audience, turning to performance material that enshrined the national-cultural experience.

Notes

1 See my article (Kershaw 1994) and my PhD thesis (Radcliffe 2006) for a full discussion of Leno's early repertoire.
2 See, for example, Johns's *Theatre World* interview with Dan Leno Junior (n.d.); Herbert Dan Leno's (1978) letter to the *Sunday Telegraph* and Wood (1905: 110).
3 See Stedman-Jones (1974) and Bailey (1998).

Bibliography

'A Chat with Dan Leno' (1901), *The Era*. 26 October, 21.

Bailey, Peter (1998), *Popular Culture and Performance in the Victorian City*. Cambridge: Cambridge University Press.

Booth, J. B. (1943), *The Days We Knew*. London: T. Werner Laurie, 52–53.

Brandreth, Giles (1977), *The Funniest Man on Earth, the Story of Dan Leno*. London: Hamish Hamilton.

Coburn, Charles (1928), *The Man Who Broke the Bank – Memories of the Stage and Music Hall*. London: Hutchinson, 151.

'Dan Leno at Home' (1893), *The Era*. 7 January, 11.

'Dan Leno in America' (1897), *The Era*. 24 April, 19.

Darnley, Herbert (1939), letter to the *Stage*. 2 February (page number unknown).

Forgacs, David, and Geoffrey Nowell-Smith (eds) (1985), *Antonio Gramsci. Selections from Cultural Writings*. London: Lawrence and Wishart, 121–23.

Johns, Eric (n.d.), 'Idols of the Past', *Theatre World*, 226.

Kershaw, Caroline (1994), 'Dan Leno: New Evidence on Early Influences and Style', *Nineteenth Century Theatre*, 22 (1): 30–36.

Leno, Herbert Dan, (1978), letter to *Sunday Telegraph*. 8 January, 13.

'Music Hall Gossip' (1899), *The Era*. 11 November, 20.

New Penny Magazine (1900), 9 (112) (December): 309–314.

Pertwee, Ernest (ed.) (1904), *Routledge's Humorous Reciter*. London: Routledge.

Radcliffe, Caroline (2006), 'Dan Leno: Cultural Hegemony in the Victorian Popular Theatre', PhD thesis. Royal Holloway, University of London.

Radcliffe, Caroline (2010), 'Dan Leno: Dame of Drury Lane', in Jim Davis (ed.), *Victorian Pantomime*. London: Palgrave, 118–35.

Radcliffe, Caroline (2015), 'Henry Irving and the Music Halls: Theatrical Hierarchy, Cultural Capital and the Legitimate/Illegitimate Divide', in Katherine Newey, Peter Yeandle and Jeffrey Richards (eds), *Politics, Performance and Popular Culture: Theatre and Society in Nineteenth-Century Britain*. Manchester: Manchester University Press, 75–95.

Scott, Harold (1946), *The Early Doors: Origins of the Music Hall*. London: Nicholson and Watson.

Smith, George (1912), *The Dictionary of National Biography* (ed. Sir Sidney Lee). Oxford: Oxford University Press.

Stedman-Jones, Gareth (1974), 'Working-Class Culture and Working-Class Politics in London, 1870–1900: Notes on the Remaking of the Working Class', *Journal of Social History*, 7 (4) (Summer): 460–508.

Traies, Jane (1986), 'Jones and the Working Girl: Class Marginality in Music-Hall Song 1860–1900', in J. S. Bratton (ed.), *Music Hall; Performance and Style*. Milton Keynes: Open University Press, 23–48.

Wood, Hickory J. (1905), *Dan Leno*. London: Methuen.

Songsheets, instrumental music and song collections

Bowerman's 1st Monster Comic Song Annual (n.d.). London: Bowerman.

Bowerman's 2nd Monster Comic Song Album (1905). London: Bowerman.

The Dan Leno Album (n.d.). London: Herman Darewski Music Publishing.

Darnley, Herbert and Norbert Atkins (1895), 'No More Fancy Balls for Me!' London: Francis, Day & Hunter.

Darnley, Herbert (1897), 'Clever Mr Green'. London: Charles Sheard.

Darnley, Herbert (1898), 'The Beefeater'. London: Francis Day & Hunter.

Darnley, Herbert (performed 1899), 'The Swimming Master', reproduced in *Bowerman's 2nd Monster Comic Song Album* (1905). London: Bowerman.

Darnley, Herbert, and Dan Leno (performed 1901), 'Buying a House', reprinted in *Bowerman's 1st Monster Comic Song Annual* (n.d.). London: Bowerman.

de Frece, Walter, and George Le Brunn (1892), 'The Shopwalker' *or Walk This Way Step This Way! Dan Leno's Celebrated Pantomime, Patter Song*. London: Charles Sheard.

Eplett, Fred (1892), *The Dan Leno Polka, Arranged on Dan Leno's Popular Songs*. London: Charles Sheard.

Eplett, Fred (n.d.) 'Our Stores' *Ltd*. London: Charles Sheard.

Jones A. Boy, W. Bernott and George Le Brunn (1892), 'The Waiter'. London: Charles Sheard; reprinted in *McGlennon's Star Song Book* (1900), October.

King, Harry (performed 1888) 'Has Anyone Seen a Moving Job'? in *The Dan Leno Album* (n.d.). London: Herman Darewski Music Publishing.

Le Brunn, George, and Richard Morton (1893), 'The Jap'. London: Charles Sheard.

Leno, Dan, and Albert Hall (n.d.), 'The Bootman'. London: Orlando Powell, *News of the World*, reprinted in *McGlennon's Star Song Book* (1900), October.

McGlennon's Star Song Book (1900) October (no publishing information given).

Meissler, Josef (1892), *The Shopwalker Polka on the Melody of Dan Leno's Great Song' Composed by George Le Brunn*. London: Charles Sheard.

Morris, A. J., and George Le Brunn (1893), 'The Doctor', words by A. J. Morris. London: Charles Sheard.

Sedgwick, T. B., Dan Leno and Denham Harrison (performed 1900), 'The Lecturer' reproduced in *Bowerman's 1st Monster Comic Song Annual* (n.d.). London: Bowerman.

St. Clair, F. V., and George Le Brunn (performed 1890), 'The Railway Guard', in *The Dan Leno Album* (n.d.). London: Herman Darewski Music Publishing.

Stevens, George A., Albert Perry and Fred Eplett (performed 1900), 'The Huntsman', reproduced in *Bowerman's 2nd Monster Comic Song Album* (1905). London: Bowerman.

Woodhouse, J. H., and Fred Eplett (performed 1891), 'The Grass Widower or She's Going out of Town', in *The Dan Leno Album* (n.d.). London: Herman Darewski Music Publishing.

Wright, Harry, and Fred Eplett (performed 1893), 'The Recruiting Sergeant', reproduced in *The Dan Leno Album* (n.d.). London: Herman Darewski Music Publishing.

2

American Vaudeville

Leigh Woods

Vaudeville was a variety entertainment that flourished between the 1880s and the early 1920s in parallel with industrialization and the headlong urbanization it brought the United States and Canada. In festive response to large-scale mechanization, vaudeville inspired the catch-phrase 'lunch-counter art' to encapsulate its fast-paced, highly varied bills of turns numbered and ordered strictly by convention and cultural standing (Royle 1899: 495). Vaudevillians at each of its tiers called 'small-time', 'medium-time' and 'big-time', personified speed, mobility and honest labour. They moved across the continent by rail to be grouped into aggregates that were shuffled and changed by the week.

Lunch-counter art applied most literally to daily matinees attended by many who had caught a bite on the quick or would do so after the show. Women were well-represented, especially at the matinees when some of them would arrive with children in tow. Most adults were out for a good time in the middle of, or for the nighttime shows after, a full day's work. Many kids would have been too young for school and so in women's custody, while a few older ones were playing hookey. At evening performances, New York's and many other cities' bright lights drew crowds that craved the night in ways mostly wholesome. The phrase 'big-time vaudeville' called to mind a giant clockface embossed on a map. Time was rendered a commodity that ran in synchrony with the industrial workday.

Vaudeville's most characteristic response to heavy industry's numbing sameness was to valourize individualism on both sides of the curtain. Even as lunch-counter art epitomized the entertainment's

Figure 2.1 Olga Petrova in the year of her entry into vaudeville, *Green Book Magazine*, August 1912 (courtesy of the University of Michigan Library)

assembly-line paradigm, its bills were attracting viewerships wide and diverse enough to lift it above the legitimate theatre in profitability and above every other diversion that defined itself by its exclusivity. Vaudeville offered more compelling evidence than the theatre or any other set of live venues could, that entertainment could be generated plentifully in the form of modular and interchangeable acts. In sheer quantity, these lent themselves to distribution on a massive scale. By 1900, vaudeville was being overseen by syndicates much as the theatre had been commandeered in lockstep with trusts' growing stranglehold on American commerce in general.

Big-time vaudeville's marquees were fed by electricity that featured leading performers' names in high wattage wired over generous footage. Beyond the overlit overhangs and the crack orchestras purring away inside lay surprisingly handsome and comfortable backstage quarters for performers who had made it that far. Even a labour economist hostile to vaudeville moguls' plutocratic airs had to admit that

> The big-time theatres which are being built today are equipped with every convenience and comfort for the artists. Beautifully appointed and comfortable rest and smoking rooms where the actors can await their call; dressing rooms that leave nothing to be desired; showers and baths where the actors can refresh themselves after their hard day's work; these, and many other luxuries and conveniences, minister to the well-being of the vaudeville actor in the big-time house of modern design. (Bernheim March 1924: 18)

Producers who sprang for such lavishness could 'point with pride', the technocrat conceded, to 'raising vaudeville to its present dignified position'. The enterprise maintained commercial advantage and promoted its dignity by drafting performers from higher-culture venues and other lands onto its otherwise polyglot bills.

Simon Nelson Patten held out the prospect of a veritable utopia of entertainment in his book *Product and Climax* (1909):

> The old world of pain is gone, except as it is perpetuated in the overwork of our factories and workshops. If this grim, sordid depression were removed, would men sink into vice and disorder, or would they rise to new levels of sobriety, morality and religion? We all know that pain can create a morality: Is there also a moral tendency in the growth of pleasure? (Patten 1909: 54–5).

Visions like these called out to new-world vaudeville goers and vaudevillians who wanted to feel as though they, and things, were looking up. Seamus Deane, with tongue in cheek, has invoked an American imperium that promulgates 'moral and material improvement' in even its most freely attended and escapist diversions (Deane 1995: 359).

Big-time vaudeville's auditoriums, like their backstages, fairly radiated Patten's 'growth of pleasure' principle in mercantile splendour. When Edward F. Albee took charge of designing his partner B. F. Keith's New Theatre vaudeville emporium in Boston in the early 1890s, news of its 'beauty of decoration and adornment traveled far and wide' (Grau 1912: 151). In 1906, Albee (adoptive grandfather and namesake of the American playwright) undertook major renovations at the Fifth Avenue to trumpet Lillie Langtry's vaudeville debut there in an abbreviated version of one of her perversely sacrificial stage roles. The Jersey Lily basked in the 'Parisian gray, chartreuse green and old ivory' Albee had chosen for refurbishing the auditorium. 'The draperies … are of a deep Chambertin red and the carpeting a Burgundy red', the reporter went on in rapt detail, while the new lobby had 'a cheerful aspect in its gilt-framed panels of red and absinthe green'. There lay 'spacious reception rooms … attractively treated in lavender and cream', and finally, 'In the dome of the theatre are eight panels painted with figures of heroic size, the work of the late [painter Domenico] Tojetti when he was at his best' (Locke Collection [LC], Langtry, vol. 310, 1906).

These were pleasure palaces, shrines to abundance in a land of dreams. With Mrs. Langtry to anchor the bill at the Fifth Avenue, Europhilia prevailed in the spot where her fellow Englishwoman, Madame Olga Petrova, would introduce herself to vaudeville five years later. Actress, entertainer, entrepreneur, producer, journalist, playwright, fantasist, film-studio star and executive, and vaudeville 'headliner' supreme, she far surpassed Langtry's fewer, slenderer, more perishable skills. Petrova, as a lesser Langtry, was better able to exploit vaudeville's institutional passion for colourful if oftentimes artificially enhanced personalities and the performances seen to derive from them.

The performing self

Olga Petrova established herself quickly at vaudeville's big-time halls known also as 'refined' or 'high class'. Her most striking talent lay in the symbiotic relationship she struck with her audiences. She saw them as an expression of who she was, whoever that may have been.

She quickly grasped the totemic importance of vaudeville's marquees as when, for her vaudeville debut in 1911, she remembered a functionary removing 'a name from an electric sign outside a theatre [the Fifth Avenue] ... and the name that took the place of the one removed was ... mine', which is to say, the one into which she sank her identity even away from the stage (Petrova 1942: 242). She offered a classic instance of personality reconfigured as performance, and the composite made her a headliner in vaudeville. It also made her a key instigator of films – some of which she helped produce – and in the several stage plays she saw through to production.

It was as a run-of-the-mill supporting player that English-born Muriel Harding struggled as a singing actress in London and provincial and Commonwealth playhouses. On finding herself chronically unemployed in her homeland, she was persuaded, she claimed, to change her name to Olga Petrova (Petrova 1942: 212). So redubbed, she showed a fresh and startling versatility first at British music halls' analogue to big-time vaudeville, known as 'variety' (Woods 2006: 1, 7). Her change of name, sound and image made her a natural in vaudeville with its own name bastardized from a French word that itself was of sketchy origin.

In America, where self-fashioning was easily and commonly done, she promoted her assumed identity more fervently than she had in the UK. She radiated foreignness by adopting a heavy if sometimes wandering Russian accent. In vaudeville she called on her exotic enunciation to deliver songs, stories, poetry, excerpts from bodice-ripping plays, ripe autobiographical accounts, and in her later turns, social tracts of her own devising. Her warm if regal presence graced the stage at the New York Palace especially well and often. It was there that she enjoyed some of her greatest triumphs at what quickly became, after its opening in the year she entered vaudeville, its leading showcase.

Petrova had taken that surname, she said, from a first husband not sufficiently present (or real) to contest her version of events. It was as Olga Petrova that she crossed the Atlantic where an American entrepreneur named Jesse Lasky had recruited her earnest Slavicism for his *Folies Bergère* cabaret in Manhattan. She drew critical praise there, but the American *Folies* did not meet with success despite its claim to be 'more Parisian than Paris' (Petrova 1942: 225), sans the topless dancing.

Sime Silverman, the trade publication *Variety*'s founder, lead critic and most indefatigable advocate for vaudeville, saw Petrova perform her variety act in the *Folies* and suggested she 'go in for the dramatic matter' in the heavier parts of her act and 'employ other numbers' for the musical portions. She should also, he wrote, 'change her name back to where it was' (Slide 1994: 397). Another performer might have been shamed. Never the former Miss Harding.

Under Lasky's management, she took a singing role in a revue called *The Quaker Girl*, whose producer would shortly go down with the *Titanic*. Lasky then introduced her into vaudeville with an act that used, for its dramatic component, *pace* Sime Silverman, a torrid cutting from *Sappho*, the full-length version of which had precipitated an obscenity trial in New York several years earlier. Petrova insisted, with a doggedness that baffled many, that she take no money or billing during her first week at the tony Fifth Avenue (Petrova 1942: 242). When Petrova's act went over big there, she demanded to be headliner of record for her second week and to earn a headliner's salary. These conditions were met for the rest of her time in vaudeville extending over the next fifteen years, with the occasional hiatus for filmmaking and stage plays. Through it all, her accent must have been her most constant companion. One wonders whether she used it to create a richer ambience at locations where she shot her silents.

She insisted on being called 'Madame Petrova', and in her early renown told an interviewer that she wanted a husband for six months only to rescue her from a contractual obligation to play a less lucrative engagement in Europe. She said that she preferred to stay in vaudeville where she was expecting to earn \$750 a week (~ US\$15,000 now) for her turn along thirty-week tours in each of the next three years (*Washington Post*, 10 November 1912: M8). The *Post* added her objection to such measly terms as she had agreed to before vaudeville dangled the prospect of what now would be about \$1.35 million in front of her. 'W'at s'all I say?', she said. 'The European contract *il est fait accompli* [French for 'It's a done deal'] – I am, w'at you call, stuck. Where is ze hole in ze European contract where I crawl out of eet?'

She made the most of her vaudeville earnings by taking the stage as a solo act, always. In her memoir she remembered vaudeville as an arena where 'an entertainer stands or falls alone', and that before 'an audience … drawn from all sorts and conditions of people, his job is to hold them, entertain them, whether he be a red-nosed comedian or an operatic star' (Petrova 1942: 321).

Her authenticity, strange as it may seem to call it that, derived from her ability to cast a spell. She created an hermetic world on stages which artful lighting turned into Shangri-Las that framed her chic wardrobe and camera-ready face. She evoked a world of make-believe to which her accent made one of several filigrees. She made it a point to gauge her crowds and accordingly adjust what she would offer them. Other venues would not have allowed her the same liberty she took on arriving at a vaudeville hall. She would walk 'past the box office and go down the side aisle through the auditorium to the door leading to the stage … to feel out the temper of the gathering and … size up the house' (Petrova 1942: 334). She could take patrons out of their quotidian reality and do it with an ease that lengthened her time as a headliner.

Vaudeville was known for the assurance it fostered in its veteran performers, and Petrova showed this in spades. By her own account, she 'usually worked forty minutes … instead of [the] thirty' that were standard for headlined acts (Petrova 1942: 321). Her suffrage-era call for 'self-motherhood' championed the premise that women did not need men's help in raising a child (*Washington Post*, 12 December 1914: 1). It made for an odd pronouncement, but it conveyed her independent spirit away from the stage and the mesmerizing and largely solitary presence she showed while on it.

The truth of disguise

Petrova's colourful English lent her cover from journalists who, impressed as they were, struggled to capture just exactly what she did. As one critic noted after her triumphant re-entry into vaudeville in 1919, 'Few actresses have caused editorial pens so much perplexity as to the proper classifying of her particular style of work.' 'Some of the scribes have got real mad about the difficulty' she posed, the reporter added before concluding that 'Such a state of editorial indecision makes her a distinct novelty' (Slide 1994: 398). This made high praise in a form where novelty was worshipped and celebrities like Petrova from other venues and foreign lands stood as novelties unto themselves.

Petrova seems never to have left a vaudeville crowd feeling perplexed. 'She owned the audience', *Variety* reported from the Chicago Majestic where she opened her 1919 tour, speaking in her own voice, or person at least, before singing 'a gentle ballad of her own' (Locke Collection [LC] Petrova, *Variety*, 20 October 1919). One reviewer who caught her bill in Boston noted that 'Her curtain speech was a classic and she got a whale of a hand' (LC Petrova, in a clipping dated only '1919'). *Variety*, reviewing her again in New Orleans, reported her provoking 'a tumultuous outburst that compelled a speech, another and then another' (LC Petrova, *Variety*, 19 November 1919). Six years later, she was still working her magic in vaudeville as 'a gloriously talented artiste' with whom 'one really doesn't feel acquainted until [she] steps to the front and begins her little talk' (*Washington Post*, 25 January 1926: 5). What she offered as a chaste and uplifting exercise in public intimacy was rehashed in journalists' accounts of vaudeville goers' delight with her and their less worshipful responses to other acts. In critics' eyes, vaudeville goers coloured any performance by forming an interactive loop between themselves and the stage. Vaudevillians like Petrova trained themselves to read these audiences closely enough to know what they wanted and liked.

Petrova rearranged the elements of her act at will and sometimes on the spur of the moment. Her dialect would waver at times, and this had one *Variety* reviewer report her dropping 'the foreign accent other than a Continental rolling of the r's' (LC Petrova, *Variety*, 7 May 1919). Her oversight of other details suggests her adjusting her accent to the ears of the group she had determined would hear it.

Her lightning adjustments were complemented by a more calculating temperament. Years after she had stopped performing in public, someone who knew her wrote that 'Her entire life was stage-managed and never under-rehearsed' (Slide 1994: 396). Her passion for control grew as she gained trust in her writing. She campaigned for women's rights at the height of the suffrage movement, and she raised money for war efforts during both the Great War and, years after her last vaudeville engagement, the Second World War when she solicited donations for Russia as well as the land of her birth (*New York Times*, 16 March 1941: D3). Her calls for birth control, for addressing 'social [i.e. venereal] disease' frankly, and for the necessity of sex education for girls and women were made more palatable by the charm she showed in voicing them. Her progressive views never found quite the same welcome in the theatre where her plays were deemed too polemical and her calls for action too lengthy and strident.

She championed one of her pet causes along her 1919 vaudeville tour when she recited a poem she had written, a birds-and-bees parable called 'To a Child That Enquires'. Its content bothered Albee enough that he threatened to prohibit her from delivering it at the Palace, though he might also have done it to drum up interest in her latest tour (Gilbert 1940: 346). At any rate, reviews have her reciting the poem away from Albee's stronghold in New York City, and wherever she spoke it, the verses would have sounded as limpid and teasing as they seem saccharine now. The final stanza is illustrative of the other five:

I carried you under my heart, my sweet,
  And sheltered you, safe from alarms –
  Till one wonderful day the dear God looked down,
  And my darling lay in my arms. (LC Petrova, *Houston Post*, 20 December 1919)

Schmaltz served as virtual currency for vaudeville. Petrova used it to test the limits of what was permissible at a time when disseminating information about contraception was routinely suppressed and its advocates were tirelessly harassed.

In vaudeville, continually in 1919 and for some of the year after, she used for her dramatic element *The Shulamite*, which made, as *Sappho* had, a tale of unstayed passion, this one's Biblical source notwithstanding. Her latest excerpt ended with her character choked to death by a jealous husband, and Petrova embodied the murderer with her own hand. Her death-fall was praised for 'exhibiting a process of physical perfectness that any acrobat' would envy, and her dancerly grace made a qualification less heavily worked than her accent was (LC Petrova, *Variety*, 7 November 1919). After rising, she would move directly into her gracious curtain speech which she began, customarily, by mentioning her silent-film career offhandedly. She would have known that women looking on had seen her play other endangered characters on the screen.

To follow her latest ill-fated heroine, she would call up a youngster from the auditorium whom she used as an object of address for her recitation of 'To a Child That Enquires', and this reportage suggests that she relied on children being present regularly to see her. Childless herself, she wanted the crowd to see each child she chose as the progeny of her heart. Courtesy of acts like Petrova's, the Francophonic 'vaudeville' exoticized – at the same time it pasteurized – an entertainment which, in North America, traced its roots to houses of strong drink and easy women. When it came to moralizing, vaudeville producers wanted to have it both ways, and so, collectively, did their patrons and performers like Petrova who purveyed righteousness with barely a smidgen of the racy.

Bills and climaxes

Different registers of culture were sounded when headliners like Petrova appeared with, for instance, classical singers, ballet dancers, animal acts, sword-swallowers, fire-eaters, sand-dancers and masters of the soft-shoe. In the absence of a considerable star like Petrova, any dramatic offering had to be tight and almost invariably light. If a turn was comical, the hijinks tended towards a slapstick Petrova studiously avoided. The apparent randomness of the bills bespoke chance even as their formulaic order made them predictable, and, in their incremental way, dramatic in leading up to a big-time headliner like Madame who provided a classic Aristotelian finish.

One bill she joined at the Chicago Majestic had a critic write of her 'acting even when she is not supposed to be acting' to praise her rather than deride her (LC Petrova, labeled only '*Variety* 1919'). Her performing self may have been manufactured in part, but her commitment to it was unremitting enough to persuade and inspire. 'Her bow is a combination of the devotional obeisance of a nun and the salute of a [First World War] doughboy.' It made a gesture that caught up viewers' topical preoccupation with a war only one year done. In her usual way, she sang four songs, recited a poem, gave a curtain speech and winced 'at the sound of an elephant trumpeting' from offstage in the middle of her torrid *Shulamite*. After she finished her speech, she accepted 'her bouquet with a smile more radiant than the footlights, bestowing the largest rose upon the gallant [house] orchestra leader' in a gesture of *noblesse oblige*.

The elephant was part of the 'chaser' or last turn on the bill that followed hers directly, and it had 'Capt. M. Gruber and Mlle. Adelina' putting their *ménage* of pachyderm, horse, pony and dog through their paces. Performers charged with opening a bill were called 'doormats', and at the Majestic the job fell to an interpretive dancer in 'The Beginning of the World' with 'scenic novelty … [in] living colors'. This was followed by a jazzy dance pair in Lloyd and Wells, who set time to their act by using 'four rhythmic pedals'. O'Donnell and Blair showed a sketch called 'The Piano Tuner' and were reported to have been 'hilarious' before finishing 'with a ladder balanced' on the house piano Petrova would shortly be playing to accompany some of her songs. Ben K. Benney, *né* Benjamin Kubelsky, who came to fame later as Jack Benny – deadpan tightwad and hapless violinist – seemed 'not to care whether' the crowd liked him in a way that contrasted with the more frenetic offerings before his. Charley and Henry Rigoletto and the Swanson Sisters undertook as large a 'variety of entertainment [as] it is possible for four people to give', including magic, yodeling, juggling, 'statue posing', songs and dances and 'an Italian musician street scene' in a way that primed the audience for Petrova's higher-toned if equally randomized offering (LC Petrova, '*Variety* 1919'). Stuart Barnes followed the foursome with a 'mild' exhibition of talking and singing intended to set Petrova's electrifying presence in higher contrast when she followed him on the stage.

The seven, eight or nine acts on big-time bills were sequenced into two builds, the first one longer and the second one shorter and steeper. Each act had its own climax, with the most striking one saved, ideally, for last. An intermission followed the lengthier if lesser build that took up the first four, five or six acts. The second build began with a turn which, however captivating in its way, led to a headliner followed briefly by the chaser who held stage while the hall emptied. When two chasers succeeded the most ballyhooed act, one would be live and precede short films or newsreels.

Immersed in routine as vaudevillians needed to be, they learned to think of themselves as numbers drawn from their places on the bills, the minutes their act lasted, the counts of laughter and applause they ran up and the weekly salaries they received for performing twice a day with no days off in the big-time and as many as six times daily in small-time halls that paid less for more work. Where the clock was ticking and everything was tallied, performers comported themselves as walking tabulations. House orchestras marked time as if they had been metronomes, while backstage functionaries timed acts down to the second. Even the most renowned entertainers from loftier venues could find themselves enmeshed in numerology when their towering salaries became matters of public record. There was plain truth in the jest that when it came to vaudevillians, 'By their numbers ye shall know them' (Pollock 1911: 339). The word 'headliner' trumped vaudeville's fixation on numbers, but headlining remained an honour never offered to the vast majority of vaudevillians.

Headliners like Petrova would have had plenty of vaudevillians for company along the circuits. One study set the number of acts at between

5,000 and 8,000 and estimated that something like 30,000 vaudevillians were touring the United States and Canada at any given time (Bernheim, February 1924: 42). The survey fixed yearly profits for vaudeville's chief managerial entity, the Albee-ruled United Booking Office, conservatively at $7.5 million, which would approach $100 million in twenty-first-century dollars (Bernheim, January 1924: 43). Big-time vaudeville flourished enough that it needed thousands of performers to keep its circuits running at full tilt and its bills changing by the week. Vaudeville circuits were strung out along railroad lines that reached from one ocean to the other, and the halls harnessed the electric power dispensed along wider electrical circuits by public utilities. Served by newer technologies, civic pride and familiar modes of transport, vaudeville had Spanish-language cousins that proved popular in Mexico. Measured by the number of its halls at its height, the enterprise left the largest commercial footprint yet seen from a live entertainment in North America.

When vaudeville was withering against the onslaught from films and radio in the mid-1920s, Petrova called more than ever on her life to regale her crowds. In a 1926 article titled 'Vaudeville Holding Its Own', the writer praised her as 'one of the hopeful signs of vaudeville' for discoursing 'on her struggle toward the top of the tree', as seemed more substantial and worthy to the critic than her singing and reciting had been. Paraphrasing the autobiographical account the reviewer heard her deliver, he wondered 'Who can remain unmoved in the presence of a girl [then in her forties] who recalls the night she sat in the gallery of a London theater, after paying her hard-earned sixpence, watching the figures on the stage below and hoping that the "star" would tell how he or she rose, and pledging secretly to herself never to deny an audience a speech in response to a call for it' (*Christian Science Monitor*, 3 February 1926: 14). Through every chameleonic change she executed, she understood her bond with audiences to be sacred. It moved her to share parts of her experience which, fabricated or not, would strike the richest chord among her listeners.

This mooted the occasional exaggeration or outright lie on her part, leaving aside her zany dialect with its implicit myth of her origin. She primed a 1914 vaudeville appearance at Keith's in Washington, DC, by claiming statesmanship for having the turn she had titled, with typical scope, 'Comedy and Tragedy', to the Czar and Czarina of Russia and to the King and Queen of England (*Washington Post*, 29 January 1914: 10). She maintained the fiction that she was born in Warsaw (LC Petrova, *Toledo Times*, 11 August 1918) and educated in Brussels and Paris as well as in London (LC Petrova, *Chicago Tribune*, 1 June 1919). Her voice embodied her constructed self while enticing her crowds to believe her flights of fancy.

Her fabrications lent texture to her more commonplace skills. She was a miniaturist first and foremost, and the single elements she showed included snippets that were each in its way familiar. It was her way of putting them together and keeping them coming that made her riveting to watch. In essence, her turns offered a microcosm of an entire vaudeville bill. The conviction she brought to her performance of her fabricated self gave her audiences to believe that she was giving them something extra and exotic for their money. Her common touch while wearing enviable couture made more than a few identify with her closely.

She excelled as a copyist and mimic. Her most natural voice seems to have been the fine-grained soprano she would alternate with the baritone and high falsetto she applied, the three of them in sequence, to an aria from an operetta called *The Chocolate Soldier* (Gilbert 1940: 342) and to the American folk-classic 'Carry Me Back to Old Virginny' (Slide 1994: 399). Her sounding like a man showed another sort of transformation, as did her bird calls, including parrots', and her impressions of cats. Her cuttings from *Sappho* and *The Shulamite* re-created performances by the English drama queens Olga Nethersole and Lena Ashwell, respectively, whom Petrova would have idolized during her neophyte years in London. Lightsome as many of her bits were, she strung them together and added a finish of high drama and disarming chat about her life, career and unshakeable convictions.

Her diction would have been far less routine than vaudeville's lingo that filtered into common usage. 'Headliner' paid tribute to the newspapers that covered vaudeville and advertised it. 'Playing the Palace' came to signify the pinnacle of success in any endeavour, while the word 'vaudeville' itself was tempered in the crucible of American exceptionalism. Its name lent it a French twist that sounded classier than the humbler variety and minstrel shows from which it had sprung.

Vaudeville theatres were named in ways that wreathed some of them in old-country royalty, and performers like Petrova added weight to the institutional project. The New York Palace joined a Palace in Chicago, which had been preceded there by an Olympic and the aforementioned Majestic. The Hammersteins' Victoria, with its nod to the British Empire, stood closer than the Palace did to the heart of what came to be called Times Square in 1904 with the move of the *New York Times*' offices there. The flashy Percy Williams's Colonial and Alhambra featured theatrical stars as headliners for more than a decade at Manhattan houses that charted a thriving transatlantic commerce. Petrova's doctored internationality served and celebrated vaudeville's mission to declare itself as worldly as it was up to date.

Not quite disappearing

Into the early 1920s, big-time vaudeville remained robust in the East, with the Keith-Albee Exchange of thirty-four halls around New York City and along the eastern seaboard joined by northerly halls extending westward through upstate New York as far as but not including Chicago. About twenty-eight more big-time houses made up the Orpheum Circuit of major Chicago auditoriums as well as the leading ones in western states extending to the Pacific (Bernheim, September 1923: 34). The two chains, taken together for purposes of bookings, comprised about sixty showplaces. Noted vaudevillians could stay on the road for a year or longer if they wanted to, and Petrova must have wanted the marathon that took her from coast to coast in 1919, directly after her brief if blazing vogue as a film star. Fewer headliners like her welcomed heavy travel once films and radio could offer them more money for less time riding the rails.

As early as the 1880s, Tony Pastor, progenitor of big-time vaudeville in New York City, had called the crowds he drew 'double' ones of women and men together (Gilbert 1940: 10). Novel and thrilling as this was at the time, a few pundits would deplore what they saw as the coarsening vaudeville's commercial vigour inflicted on the body populace. In 1908, William Winter, dean of American theatre critics, denounced what he insisted on calling 'the Music Hall', in his Anglophilic way, for being 'the deadly foe of the theatre' (Winter 1908: 328). 'Throughout the length and breadth of the land', he opined, 'speculators have captured the industry that they call "the Amusement Business" and have made "a corner in Theatricals"' (307–8). Petrova might have disputed such anti-mercantilism, but if so, she did it while reaping the rewards of vaudeville's prosperity. Acts as cosmopolitan as hers defused some of the quibbling about vaudeville's origins and legitimacy.

Before the First World War, its impresarios were planning to link their domestic monopolies to an international circuit they hoped would extend to Europe and beyond (Woods 1999: 82). Classic postcolonial priorities held Europeans more precious to be recruited, cultivated and impressed than more benighted demographics on other continents. Vaudeville would never be exported in any literal way, but many vaudevillians, more than a few of them among its elite, shopped their talents abroad, especially where foreign analogues to vaudeville existed as they did in the United Kingdom and its colonial outposts and protectorates. So were films exported, many of them made for screening first in vaudeville. They relayed American culture in greater bulk after the trauma the Great War inflicted on performers and the performing arts across Europe.

Edward F. Albee never stopped courting noteworthy attractions. He offered the native hero Charles Lindbergh $100,000 a month to show himself in vaudeville (~ US$1.15 million now). This came in 1927, shortly after Lucky Lindy's pioneering flight across the Atlantic. Lindbergh did not take the bait (Green and Laurie 1951: 216), saving himself for situations better suited to his photogenic taciturnity and retrograde political views. But even Lindbergh could not have saved vaudeville nor drummed up enough business to cover such an astronomical fee so near the end of its most vital phase.

By 1926, when Petrova was appearing in vaudeville for the last time, the small-time had outstripped the big-time in receipts and the number of film projectors it commanded. In 1929, when the stock market crashed, Joseph P. Kennedy, progenitor of the political clan and later US ambassador to the court of St James, already owned the Radio-Keith-Orpheum vaudeville circuit when he acquired another producer's smaller chain before assigning all the halls to other uses (Marston and Feller 1943: 154). Petrova must not have wanted to reboard what must have looked like a sinking ship. When she had to carry the show, however, on a legitimate stage or celluloid, she never gained the fanfare she had won as main attraction among a collection of lesser ones chosen and arranged to feature hers. She reached the apex of her career in vaudeville, and it made her viable in the other entertainments she tried.

Vaudeville never vanished entirely. By settling on fifteen- or twenty-minute increments for its standard acts, it was partly responsible for the intervals that have governed US commercial television since the late 1940s. Every ten minutes or so, advertising fills out the standard half-hour situation comedies or hour-long dramatic series produced under sponsorship. Music videos have crammed quick rhythms into shorter spans of time, staking their appeal on continual restless sequences of images set to music. Television ads, ever more digitized, have joined documentaries and videos in offering mediated glimpses of the wider world in vaudeville's spirit of adventure.

YouTube offers a later and more far-flung example of the variety that exists now, literally, at our fingertips. Live performances mixing men and women onstage and among viewers are so widespread that we barely notice them. Performers rule the internet who owe their content and style to ethnic and national groups across the globe. These days, vicarious travel needs to evoke even farther away places, or to simulate travel more alluringly, to claim the novelty vaudeville held for Americans of nearly every kind – so long as the two-a-day was headlining Madame Olga Petrova and stars of her magnitude. If vaudeville served up vicarious travel, so did Petrova during her elaborate, idiosyncratic, inimitable time as a vaudevillian.

Bibliography

Bernheim, Alfred L. (1923–4), 'The Facts of Vaudeville', *Equity* [magazine].
September 1923 (8:9), 9–13, 32–35, 37;
January 1924 (9:1), 15–16, 40–43, 45, 47;
February 1924 (9:2), 19–20, 39–43, 45;
March 1924 (9:3) 17–20, 37–39, 43–44.

Deane, Seamus (1995), 'Imperialism/Nationalism', in Frank Lentricchia and Thomas McLaughlin (eds), *Critical Terms for Literary Study*, 2nd ed. Chicago: University of Chicago Press.

Gilbert, Douglas (1940; rpt. 1963), *American Vaudeville: Its Life and Times.* New York: Dover Publications.

Grau, Robert (1912; rpt. 1969), *The Stage in the Twentieth Century.* New York: Benjamin Blom.

Green, Abel, and Joe Laurie, Jr. (1951), *Show Biz from Vaude to Video.* New York: Henry Holt and Company.

[Robinson] Locke Collection [LC], at the Billy Rose Theatre Collection, Public Library of New York at Lincoln Center.
LC, Langtry, Lillie, vol. 310.
LC, Petrova, Olga, envelope 1749.

Marston, William Moulton, and John Henry Feller (1943), *F. F. Proctor, Vaudeville Pioneer.* New York: Richard R. Smith.

Patten, Simon Nelson (1909), *Product and Climax.* New York: B. W. Huebsch.

Petrova, Olga (aka Muriel Harding; 1942), *Butter With My Bread.* Indianapolis, IN: Bobbs-Merrill.

Pollock, Channing (1911), *The Footlights Fore and Aft.* Boston: Richard G. Badger.

Royle, Edwin Milton (1899), 'The Vaudeville Theatre', *Scribner's* 26 (October), 485–95

Slide, Anthony (1994), *The Encyclopedia of Vaudeville.* Westport: Greenwood Press.

Winter, William (1908), *Other Days, Being Chronicles and Memories of the Stage*. New York: Moffat, Yard.

Woods, Leigh (2006), *Transatlantic Stage Stars in Vaudeville and Variety: Celebrity Turns*. New York: Palgrave Macmillan.

Woods, Leigh (1999), 'American Vaudeville, American Empire', in Jeffrey D. Mason and J. Ellen Gainor (eds), *Performing America: Cultural Nationalism in American Theater*. Ann Arbor: University of Michigan Press, 73–90.

3

It's 1922 and at the Munich Kammerspiele Karl Valentin and Liesl Karlstadt Perform *Das Christbaumbrettl* at *Die rote Zibebe*

Michael Wilson

'Meine Damen und Herren, introducing Karl Valentin and Liesl Karlstadt . . .'

Valentin Ludwig Fey was born on 4 June 1882 into a Protestant middle-class family in the Munich suburb of Au, where his father owned a furniture removals business. Following an apprenticeship as a cabinetmaker and a three-month stint under the tutelage of the comedian Hermann Strebel, the young Valentin briefly took over the family firm when his father died in 1902. Finding himself particularly ill-suited to a life in business, the firm was sold and the young Valentin invested the proceeds in building his own multi-instrumental music machine, with which he toured Germany under the name Charles Fey. The venture proved to be an unmitigated disaster, and after a few months he returned to Munich penniless. In 1908, however, his fortunes changed when, performing as Karl Valentin, the name he would carry through his professional career, he achieved a huge success with his monologue 'Das Aquarium' (The Aquarium).[1]

By the time he met the young actress Elisabeth Wellano (1892–1960) in 1911 and persuaded her to become his onstage partner, changing her name to Liesl Karlstadt in the process, Valentin had already established himself as a firm favourite on the Munich cabaret scene. Over the following three decades, as the senior partner in the enterprise, but with Karlstadt nearly always by his side, Valentin became the most successful and highly paid comedian in Germany. With a self-written repertoire that made the most of their contrasting physicalities and delivery styles, the pair conquered first their native Munich and then later Berlin itself.

Today Valentin is remembered in Germany as (perhaps unfairly) the main creative force in the partnership and for his innovative use of physicality and language, with parallels to the Dadaist tradition, whilst Karlstadt remains very much in his shadow. Outside Germany, Karlstadt remains largely unknown, whilst Valentin's legacy is inextricably tied to the fortunes of a young poet and playwright from Augsburg, whom he met in Munich in the chaotic years immediately after the end of the First World War. The name of the Augsburger was Bertolt Brecht and the story goes that it was the comedian Karl Valentin who helped him formulate the principles of epic theatre.

Exactly when the young playwright befriended Valentin is unclear, but Michael Schulte suggests that it was as early as 1918, when they planned to write a play together entitled *Herr Meier und sein Sohn* (Herr Meier and his Son) (1982: 167). Although the plan came to nothing, Brecht continued enthusiastically to attend Valentin's performances, and in 1919, after Brecht returned from completing his military service as an orderly in a VD clinic, they performed together at the Oktoberfest and Brecht wrote a series of five short Valentinesque plays.[2]

It was, however, not until the autumn of 1922 that the pair embarked on their first serious collaboration, *Die rote Zibebe*, an after-show cabaret at the prestigious Kammerspiele theatre in Munich.

1922: Bert's big break

The year 1922 had not started particularly well for the young, ambitious (one might even say, precocious) Brecht. Attempting to install some momentum to a theatrical career that was struggling to get out of the starting blocks, Brecht was travelling between Munich, where he had been living since 1917, and Berlin. His financial circumstances were precarious and he spent a period of time in hospital early in 1922 with malnutrition and suspected tuberculosis. He nevertheless made his directorial debut that same year, directing Arnolt Bronnen's new play *Vatermord* (Patricide) for the Junge Bühne,[3] and he was also given a paid engagement in January, performing at Trude Hesterberg's *Wilde Bühne* cabaret.

Vatermord turned out to be a disaster when the lead actor (the far from malnourished Heinrich George) walked out on the project, so that Brecht's own 'participation ended in fiasco when George refused to continue working with him' (Thomson 2006: 26). His cabaret performance at the Wilde Bühne turned out no better. As Klaus Budzinski states:

> In January 1922 Brecht appeared at the Wilde Bühne in Berlin – his one and only appearance at a genuine cabaret – where he performed his 'Legend of the Dead Soldier' and with it unleashed a scandal amongst the audience. (Budzinski 1985: 32)

Brecht, apparently pleased with having provoked a response from his audience, seems to have been the only person who considered his performance a resounding success. He was not included on the bill for the following evening.

According to Ronald Hayman, 'the change in Brecht's fortunes came abruptly' (1983: 90). As summer approached, it was announced that Otto Falckenberg, the director at the Munich Kammerspiele, upon the advice of the theatre's dramaturg and friend of Brecht's, Lion Feuchtwanger, had scheduled Brecht's *Trommeln in der Nacht* (*Drums in the Night*) for September. It was Brecht's first premiere and it was to take place on Friday, 29 September 1922.

Opening night at the Kammerspiele

According to Hans Otto Münsterer, one of Brecht's friends from Augsburg, who attended the premiere, there was great excitement about the event, with Brecht's family all in attendance (1998: 104). Valentin and Karlstadt were also there. Valentin's indifference towards the theatre, and particularly the contemporary theatre, was well-known: he usually only went to the theatre once a year and that was to see the same play, Ernst Raupach's *Der Müller und sein Kind* (The Miller and his Child), which Michael Schulte describes as an unbearable blend of sentimentality, bigotry and melodrama[4] (1982: 43). Although Valentin 'did his faithful disciple the honour of going' (Völker 1979: 61), it seems that he remained unimpressed by what the modern theatre had to offer:

> Brecht, Horwitz[5], Liesl Karlstadt and Valentin met afterwards in the 'Malkasten', a pub in Augustenstraße. Nobody dared ask Valentin what he thought of the play. Liesl Karlstadt smiled to herself, embarrassed, Valentin kept silent, Brecht and Horwitz were too polite, or shy, or both, to ask Valentin for his opinion. After some time Valentin broke the silence and said, 'You know, when it comes to these modern plays, you need to have someone to come along at the end of the performance and tap people on the arm and say, "Hey you – it's all over!"' (Schulte 1982: 105)

According to Münsterer, the opening night of *Trommeln in der Nacht* was a catastrophe as 'everything that had been meticulously worked out during the rehearsals and had been perfect only that afternoon at the dress rehearsal went horribly awry' (1998: 104). Nevertheless, the press reviews were broadly positive, with the Berlin critic Herbert Ihering famously declaring: 'The twenty-four year old poet Bert Brecht has changed the literary face of Germany overnight' (quoted in Völker 1979: 61). With the tensions and anxieties of the opening night out of the way, it was now time to shift attention to the next performance on Saturday, 30 September, which would be followed by a piece of *Mitternachtstheater* (Midnight Theatre), a cabaret entitled *Die rote Zibebe* (The Red Raisin), named after the tavern in *Trommeln in der Nacht*.

The idea of an additional performance after the main show was not in itself innovative. As Michael Schulte says, 'Such *Mitternachtstheater* shows after the premiere were no rare occurrence' (1982: 104). There was an existing tradition whereby the actors involved in the main production would stage a short piece after the opening night, parodying the very play they had just performed. In doing so, they were effectively drawing attention to the production's theatricality and commenting upon it, which is most probably exactly what attracted Brecht to the idea of using the convention to attempt to bring the Munich popular theatre tradition of cabaret into the respectable theatre tradition of the Kammerspiele. For Brecht *Die rote Zibebe* was an experiment and, moreover, an early experiment, into the principles of the emerging aesthetic of epic theatre.

Unusually *Die rote Zibebe* ran for two nights (on the Saturday and the Sunday) and may have run for more had its licence been renewed. It would appear from the various accounts that the programme varied slightly between the first and second nights, in accordance with the immediate and improvised nature of the show that Brecht had devised, but it is clear that in addition to the usual satirical contributions from the play's cast, Brecht himself also made an appearance, as did Joachim Ringelnatz and the poet Klabund, both regulars on the literary cabaret scene in Munich at the time. Most innovative, though, was the inclusion of Valentin and Karlstadt, who were from a different theatrical mould altogether.

The Munich cabaret scene

In the period leading up to and immediately following the First World War, the cabaret, or *Kleinkunst* (small art) scene in Munich was as vibrant as anywhere else in Europe, and possibly more so. Moreover it had developed its own distinct, arguably even local, identity. Principally it can be divided into three distinct strands: the *Volksänger* tradition, the literary cabaret and the *Salonhumoristen*. The *Volksänger* occupied the larger drinking venues and *Singspielhallen* and drew their audience principally from Munich's growing working class and petit-bourgeoisie[6] and largely exploited their nostalgia for a Bavarian rural past with a blend of self-composed music and comedy that drew on familiar, traditional forms, delivered in a Bavarian accent that would have been 'incomprehensible to anyone from outside the province' (Sackett 1982: 11). According to Robert Eben Sackett, there were almost four hundred *Volksänger* working in Munich at the turn of the century (11). The literary cabarets, the most renowned of which were *Die Elf Schafrichter*[7] and Simplicisssimus,[8] took place in the smaller *Künstlerkneipen* (Artists' pubs) and were the favourite haunts of the left-leaning, radical intelligentsia and artistic communities, for whom Munich, a city notorious for its political and cultural polarities, had become something of a magnet. The *Salonhumoristen* (exemplified by Karl Maxstadt [1853–1930]) were considered more exclusive, dressing formally and playing the better class of hotels.

Although these three strands were distinct, there was also a degree of blurring at the points where they met, particularly where audiences were concerned. Brecht, who saw Wedekind perform a number of times at the *Künstlerkneipen*, also frequently saw Valentin perform in the *Singspielhallen*. Valentin, though, was arguably unique as a performer who was able to span all three strands, in that, while emerging from the *Volksänger* tradition,[9] he was influenced heavily by Maxstadt and, as the photographic record in the 'Alter Simpl' testifies, he was also a favourite among the literary cabarets (Double and Wilson 2004: 204).

In his biography of Liesl Karlstadt, Theo Riegler describes how Valentin became involved in *Die rote Zibebe*:

> One evening at the Germania Hotel, a stranger announced himself, whose outward appearance did nothing to particularly inspire confidence. 'There's someone outside who wants to speak with you,' Liesl Karlstadt, who hadn't understood the man's name, said cautiously to Valentin. And she continued, 'I don't know why he makes me suspicious – he looks rather like a tramp.'
>
> When the tramp, in spite of his sinister appearance, was let in, he turned out to be the poet Bert Brecht, who in those days still called himself Bertolt and whose avant-garde play *Drums in the Night* was

> just about to be performed at the Kammerspiele in Augustenstraße. Brecht had come on behalf of the director to book Valentin for a post-show performance. (Riegler 1961: 36–37)

The anecdote needs to be taken with a large pinch of salt and has undoubtedly been subject to some retrospective revision (Brecht was already well-known to both Valentin and Karlstadt at this stage, so the idea of the young playwright appearing as a stranger is inconceivable), but it does rather reveal Karlstadt's antipathy to Brecht, who largely ignored her contribution to Valentin's success,[10] in the portrayal of him as the poorly dressed director's messenger boy.

The reason why Brecht recruited Valentin and Karlstadt to perform at *Die rote Zibebe* is not difficult to fathom. Brecht was experimenting in bringing the aesthetics of the *Kleinbühne* (small stage) to the grandeur of the Kammerspiele and there was no bigger name on the Munich scene than Valentin, nor any performer with such proven versatility. The reason why Valentin was keen to get involved in the venture is less certain. It is likely, though, that Valentin saw an opportunity here to reach out to a new audience and perform in a new type of venue and was prepared to overcome his antipathy towards the theatre for it. It may simply have been the attraction of the artistic challenge, but more likely Valentin was also hoping to expand his audience base (and potential engagements) at a time of economic uncertainty, not least for those working as popular performers. This was Valentin's opportunity to break into the legitimate theatre and he used the opportunity to develop his artistic range.[11]

Die rote Zibebe

There are a number of descriptions of the events at *Die rote Zibebe* on 30 September and 1 October 1922, but Hans Otto Münsterer's account of the second performance is probably the most detailed (1998: 104–106). It seems that at the rear of the stage was set a semi-circle of cabins, rather like beach huts, with a curtain in front of each. The first half was entitled 'Der Abnormitätenwirt' (The Landlord of Monstrosities) and Max Schreck[12] played the character of Old Grubb, the landlord of Die rote Zibebe, a role that he had played in the preceding play. As such, he adopted the role of a dumb *conférencier*[13] and, in turn, pulled back the curtain of each of the cabins, behind which was a performer, who 'trundled stiffly out like an automaton and sang or declaimed his piece' (Münsterer 1998:104). The description seems to anticipate the singing style adopted by Brecht a few years later in 1928 for *Die Dreigroschenoper* (*The Threepenny Opera*). Among the performers was Brecht himself as the character Klampfenbenke (literally, Benny the Guitarist), which, as Denis Calandra proposes (1974: 87), suggests that he sang to his own accompaniment (perhaps the same songs that had gone down so badly in Berlin earlier in the year). Other actors from the play stepped forth and read poems by Brecht. Kurt Horwitz played a *Virginiaraucher* (Virginia-smoker). Although not mentioned by Münsterer, other commentators indicate that Liesl Karlstadt played the Loreley[14] and Joachim Ringelnatz made an appearance as Kuttel Daddeldu the Sailor, a persona he had recently created for his cabaret performances. Valeska Gert performed *Canaille*, with which she had scandalized Berlin audiences earlier and in which she plays the part of a prostitute.[15] The poet Klabund also performed some of his own poems, which Münsterer found 'dreadfully tedious' (1998: 105).

The second half consisted, it seems, of two items by Valentin and Karlstadt.[16] The first was 'a penny-farthing sketch', which, according to Völker, 'Brecht had devised for Valentin' (1979: 61). If this was the case (and it seems entirely conceivable), then what Brecht did was to sketch out the scenario around which Valentin and Karlstadt improvised. There appears to have been very little by way of dialogue and everything seems to rest upon the physical performance and delivery of the actors for comic effect:

> Liesl Karlstadt played the impresario, and announced: 'Act One, three times round the stage on a penny-farthing.' Valentin clambered laboriously onto his antiquated vehicle and circled the stage three times. 'Act Two, three times round the stage on the penny farthing, with bells.' The

> same thing happened again, but this time accompanied by Karlstadt swinging a cow-bell. 'Third and Final Act, the death-defying journey through dark and murky night.' After a short but sinister silence – the tension was mounting – Karlstadt set up two poles with a paper banner bearing the legend 'dark and murky night'. Then Valentin wobbled cautiously back and forth a few times, before, eventually, he took a run and burst through the banner. Valentin was crowned with a laurel wreath to tumultuous applause, while Karlstadt presented the paper tatters to the audience as if she were an executioner displaying a guillotined head to the baying crowds. (Münsterer 1998: 105–106)

Reading Münsterer's description, it feels very much like a Valentin sketch (even the character of the penny-farthing cyclist is one that appeared elsewhere in Valentin's repertoire[17]), but it is also very Brechtian with its use of the *Spruchband* (banner) and its conscious drawing of attention to its own theatrical artifice. As brief as the description is, it holds for us some important indicators concerning the nature of the performance.

Attention might be drawn to the various direct interactions with the audience, ranging from Karlstadt's announcements, to her distributing of the paper tatters among the audience at the end. There is no direct reference to Valentin himself addressing the audience here, but it's inconceivable, for example, that he would not have acknowledged the applause, elicited by Karlstadt, when receiving the laurel wreath. This moment of audience participation is a key moment, as it turns the normally passive audience of the Kammerspiele into the popular audience of the cabaret, becoming co-creators and actors in the performance themselves.

One can also imagine any number of looks and gestures exchanged directly with the audience, as Valentin prepared for his supposed feats of daring. This kind of direct interaction with the audience was not unusual in the noisy, beery atmosphere of the *Singspielhalle* – in fact, it would have been absolutely necessary to do so in order to maintain their attention – but it was perhaps less usual within the hallowed walls of the Kammerspiele, where the theatrical convention of the 'fourth wall' was already well-established. For performers like Valentin and

Karlstadt, emerging directly from the cabaret tradition, this was not a case of their breaking the fourth wall, or even willfully ignoring it, but rather a case of their not even recognizing or being aware of its existence in the first place.

The second piece was *Das Christbaumbrettl* (The Christmas Tree Board), a one-act play that Valentin and Karlstadt had recently premiered at the Germaniabrettl on 1 July 1922 and had been well-received (Dimpfl 1996: 49).

Das Christbaumbrettl

If, as Völker maintains, the main purpose of *Die rote Zibebe* 'was to pay tribute to Valentin' (1979: 62), then the performance of *Das Christbaumbrettl* was the main feature and purpose of the entire enterprise, because it represented a double innovation: it was an innovation for Brecht in that it brought the *Kleinkunst* that he so loved into the mainstream theatre and it was innovative for Valentin and Karlstadt because it allowed them to bring their performances to a more mainstream theatre audience. The innovation for both was the synthesis of two types of theatre, two types of performers and two types of audience and for both it played an important role in developing their practices and careers. For Brecht it also contributed towards the evolution of his theoretical thinking about theatre and for Valentin and Karlstadt it allowed them to develop the longer-form sketch or playlet as part of their repertoire.

The action of *Das Christbaumbrettl* takes place in a family living room-cum-kitchen. It is Christmas Eve and the Mother (played by Liesl Karlstadt) is awaiting the return of her husband (Karl Valentin) with the Christmas tree. When he does, he has failed to procure a board or stand for the tree and so he is sent out again for some wood. When he finally returns he has brought two oversized planks which he proceeds to saw up in a display of complete incompetence. Once the tree is standing in the room, however, the children (one of whom is played by a dwarf) are summoned in for an exchange of gifts and the room begins to fill up. A Chimney Sweep (played by a giant) then arrives and further chaos ensues and all sense of order breaks down, when Valentin begins to cycle around the room, the sweep sits in the cake and the children start screaming. It finally transpires that it is not Christmas Eve after all, but the middle of June. Valentin has simply forgotten to tear off the leaves of the calendar.

Das Christbaumbrettl as social commentary

On one level the play follows a straightforward formula of blending incongruity and the central character's incompetence for comic effect to tell a story of a descent into chaos, where all sense of social order and decency disintegrates. The clown, in his role of outsider who fails to understand and comply with the accepted and expected behaviours of society, is the unwitting engineer of anarchy, innocently leaving a trail of destruction in his wake. However, *Das Christbaumbrettl* offers a more complex and nuanced variation on this theme and one that is deeply rooted within the social and political context of early 1920s Munich. It is inarguably a play of the 'now', rooted in the present moment.

At the beginning of the play we are immediately given a sense that this is not a scene of domestic bliss and stability, but rather this is a family that is already struggling to cling onto its respectability. The furniture is old, everything is crammed into a single room and even the crockery on the sideboard is broken. The 'wretched' room is in a state of 'colourful mess' (Valentin 1978: 322). The scene opens with Karlstadt, dressed in a shabby housecoat, sitting weeping into her hands. So the play does not tell the story of a journey from stability to chaos, but rather from instability into anarchy, very much reflecting the political reality of living in Munich at the time. As Brecht and Bronnen wrote of the play, 'it caught the era and the people of the era in the mirror of comedy' (quoted in Sackett 1982: 115). If the family in the play is representative of Munich society itself (or at least the part of Munich society represented in the audience), then this is a society that is stressed to breaking point and Valentin happily exploits the comic potential of this to draw attention to the social and political conditions that prevail.

Persona and character

Sackett argues that *Das Christbaumbrettl* works as an act of *Schadenfreude*, articulating 'the need of frightened middle-class people in Munich to find someone or some group whose inferiority appeared to guarantee the security of their own places in society' (1982: 118), with Valentin and Karlstadt taking on the roles of outsiders with 'their ability to pose as laughingstocks, in effect as miserable but funny proletarians' (119). It is entirely credible that *Das Christbaumbrettl*, with its exposition of the social and economic fragilities of the time and use of comedy to deal with them, served to help people survive through impoverished and uncertain times, although this may be because it represented a safety valve for the representation of their own anxieties and precarious state, rather than reassuring them that they had not sunk to the bottom of the social hierarchy. While Valentin's character may well be an outsider whose inability to engage effectively with the rules of society (his absurdity is often based on an extreme form of rationality that exposes social conventions as being equally absurd), he is an outsider version of the audience, it could be argued, not a scapegoated other.

What is particularly interesting about the characters played by both Valentin and Karlstadt (but especially Valentin) in *Das Christbaumbrettl* is that they are performed as variations of the comic stage personae that they had carefully created for themselves for the cabaret stage. What we have here then is an interweaving of performer identity and role: this is not Karl Valentin the actor playing the role of the Father, but Karl Valentin in his role of Valentin the cabaret persona, playing the role of the Father, in a way that both the Father and the comic persona are simultaneously visible. In this way we are seeing not only Valentin as Father/Karlstadt as Mother, but also Father as Valentin/Mother as Karlstadt.

The cabaret persona that Valentin created for himself consisted principally of two key components. First, the use and delivery of language to create 'social confusion and mayhem through the literal interpretation of language – a kind of logic *in extremis*' (Double and Wilson 2008: 215) and the use of wordplay, especially involving Bavarian dialect words; second, the use of his own physicality to create an embodied comic language.

The use and delivery of language

The linguistic aspect of Valentin's comedy first manifested itself in his 1908 sketch *Das Aquarium* (The Aquarium) (Valentin 1978: 13–14), the performance of which represented his breakthrough moment and secured him a paid contract at the prestigious Frankfurter Hof.[18] This kind of use of language and extreme logic is rife throughout *Das Christbaumbrettl*, such as in the following exchange:

> **MOTHER:** This one doesn't have a Christmas tree board with it. Have you lost it? I specifically said that you should get a tree with a board!
> **FATHER:** Yes, this one doesn't have one.
> **MOTHER:** I can see that it doesn't have one!
> **FATHER:** How can you see it, if there's nothing there?! (Valentin 1978: 323)

We might also at this point discuss the novelty of Valentin's style of delivery of speech, which was innovative and unlike that of other cabaret performers, including Karlstadt's. Unfortunately, no recording of *Das Christbaumbrettl* exists, but between 1913 and 1941 Valentin was also a prolific filmmaker. Many of those films include the performance of sketches that were originally written for stage and almost forty still survive. Of course, this material needs to be handled with some caution as it was produced for cinema, not live performance, but a key audience for these commercially produced films would have been audiences who had already seen Valentin perform, so we can reasonably expect that the sketches were restaged with a large degree of similarity in order to meet audience expectations. Furthermore, some of the filmed sketches are staged within a mock cabaret venue, presumably to give the audiences a sense of an 'authentic' cabaret experience. In addition, like many comedians of his generation, Valentin made extensive audio recordings of his material, some for radio broadcast and some for sale as gramophone records.

So, while we have no recordings of Valentin performing live, we are fortunate enough to have plenty of examples of his recreating those performances in the film or recording studio, and one defining feature of those is the remarkable style with which he spoke. The nature of the cabaret venue had necessitated the development of a declamatory style of delivery and recordings of other comedians of the time bear this out. There is little attempt at a naturalistic style of delivery, but instead lines are half-shouted, the pace is often slowed down, the articulation of words is stylized, clear and precise, and punch lines are often signposted through emphasis of certain words, or underscored by a physical gesture. This is common enough in popular performances where audiences are engaged in noisy social behaviours during the performance event itself. Liesl Karlstadt herself delivers her lines in such a manner, albeit in a less pronounced way than some of her contemporaries. Valentin, on the other hand, is noteworthy in the way that his manner of speaking is so understated, so *underperformed*, it could be said. He speaks quietly, sometimes even muttering, hesitating and repeating himself. It sounds fresh, unrehearsed and without artifice. One might even say that there is a kind of ultra-realism to his verbal delivery at times. It is the improvised and everyday manner of speech of someone who is struggling to comprehend the illogicality of the world in which he is living.

This particular tone, which we can assume was adopted at least to some degree for the performance of *Das Christbaumbrettl* (and which Brecht would have witnessed) has a number of effects. In the first instance it brings the everyday onto the stage, thus resisting the notion of the theatre as a place of escape from the harsh realities of life and locating the performance more securely in the present moment and drawing attention to the character's social condition. Significantly, though, it also contrasts both with the more mannered delivery style of Karlstadt (and other characters who may appear from time to time) and with Valentin's own physical appearance, often made all the more extreme through costuming, the use of wigs and the addition of prosthetic noses and so signposting the play's own theatrical nature. Thus it operates as a kind of *Verfremdungseffekt*, making the everyday appear strange and out of place and thus drawing attention to its absurdities. The realism of Valentin's persona and his understated delivery style demonstrate that his character's own troubles are not exceptional and are a direct consequence of the society through which he is destined to navigate.

Physicality and physical contrasts

Equally significant was Valentin's exploitation of his own physicality. It is said that it was Ludwig Greiner, with whom Valentin was lodging in Munich in 1907, who first suggested that he might use his thin, lanky appearance for comic effect, while Frau Greiner fashioned a costume out of an old athletics kit, which was tight-fitting and short in the arms and legs to accentuate his physicality. This aspect of the persona was established in the slightly earlier sketch *Ich bin ein armer magerer Mann* (I am a Poor Skinny Man)[19] (Valentin 1978: 14–15). It was an image that suited Valentin well, as he developed his career prior to the outbreak of the First World War, but would also have acquired a particular resonance in the years immediately following the War, when hunger was a daily peril among the working classes in Munich.

It was also an innovation that marked Valentin's increasing interest in physical contrasts and extremes. It was reputedly Liesl

Karlstadt's contrasting short, round physique that attracted Valentin to the young actress Elisabeth Wellano, when he first met her at the Frankfurter Hof in 1911 (see Riegler 1961: 15–23). This in turn led to a continued use by Valentin of contrasting physicality in his work.[20] As Michael Schulte says, 'He loved abnormality and contrast on the stage' (1982: 129). His use of a giant (as the chimney sweep) and a dwarf (as one of the children in *Das Christbaumbrettl*) is an early example of this, but further instances can be seen throughout his career, perhaps most notably in the film[21] of his sketch *Im Fotoatelier* (In the Photography Studio) (1932) in which Valentin plays the role of a portrait photographer and Karlstadt his young (male) assistant, who attempt to take a wedding photograph of a bridegroom and his young bride, both played by (male) giants, who tower over Valentin and Karlstadt.

This use of extreme physicality is not only a vehicle for comedy – the size of both Valentin and, especially, the Chimney Sweep, as well as the length of the planks are instrumental in causing the onstage confusion and chaos – but they are also ways of referring to the performance's sense of its own theatricality, an aspect of cabaret performance that particularly excited the young Brecht. Further examples include the opening scene, when, in a theatrical disruption of real time, the Mother (Karlstadt) speaks to the Father (Valentin) on the telephone to ask him to hurry back home. No sooner has she replaced the receiver, then Valentin arrives through the door:

> **MOTHER:** Ah, here is! I've only just been speaking to you on the telephone and you're here already!
> **FATHER:** Yes, I just hung up and started running!
> **MOTHER:** Yes, that's right. (Valentin 1978: 323)

Furthermore, as a means of drawing attention to both the dramatic irony and incongruity of the Christmas music that is playing on the gramophone and the beautiful sunny spring weather outside, when Valentin arrives through the door with the Christmas tree, he does so with his shoulder covered in snow that is 'auffallend künstlich' (conspicuously artificial). In this way it deliberately and unambiguously signposts its own theatricality and artifice.

One of the effects of this self-conscious theatricality is that it serves continually to remind the audience of the 'liveness' of the event and its location in the 'here and now', which in turn invites the audience to read the performance as current political and social commentary. For example, as Robert Eben Sackett rightly points out, when Valentin remarks that he has had to visit two different Christmas tree factories in order to get a tree, it is not only comic because of the absurdity of Christmas trees being made in factories (i.e. of course, before artificial Christmas trees were mass-produced), but would have had particular resonance with a generation of workers and tradespeople who had moved into the city to find work in the factories and 'who felt that too much had been taken over from the traditional workshop by mass production' (Sackett 1982: 115). Likewise when Valentin offers to hold the tree upright instead and Karlstadt replies that he can hardly stand there until Twelfth Night holding up the tree, he responds, 'Why not? I've got nothing else to do. I'm unemployed' (Valentin 1978: 324), in a way that clearly references the economic situation prevalent in Munich at the time.

As the play progresses, the breakdown of domestic order increases and with it the breakdown of social order too. It transpires that the presents that the children have acquired for their parents are stolen, but instead of admonishing them, the parents instead praise them for their skill, ingenuity and instinct for survival. 'There's a good child,' says the Mother, 'Everything's so expensive these days, you can't buy anything anymore' (Valentin 1978: 328). The Father even requests that they next go out and steal him a Mercedes. This is a world in which bourgeois morality has been turned upside down by economic circumstances and the point would not have been missed by a Munich audience caught right in the middle of hyperinflation in the autumn of 1922. As the curtain falls on a scene of domestic chaos and anarchy, it is merely a reflection on the social reality of Munich at the time.

Conclusion: The significance of *Die rote Zibebe*

There can be little doubt that Valentin and Karlstadt's performance at the Kammerspiele in *Die rote Zibebe* was a significant moment for Brecht in the development of the aesthetic of epic theatre. It was his first serious attempt to bring the worlds of the established high-brow theatre and the low-brow irreverent *Kleinbühne* together and its success must have been an encouragement to Brecht to make further experiments. The grounding of the performance in the social commentary of the present, the use of direct engagement with the audience, the interlacing of the identities of performer and character, and the use of novelty in terms of verbal delivery and physicality, are all features of popular performance that Brecht found exciting and which he incorporated into his later work. In the meantime it led to further collaborations with Valentin, Karlstadt and other cabaret performers, including the film *Mysterien eines Friseursalons* (Mysteries of a Barber's Shop) (1923) and a through line can also be traced to *Die Dreigroschenoper* (1928).

For Valentin too this was a moment of great importance. It was the moment that he broke through to a new, more respectable (and monied) audience. As Theo Riegler says:

> It was the great leap upwards. Through the engagement at the Kammerspiele, Valentin's comedy was endorsed for its 'literary worthiness' and declared fit for the salon. Even the harshest critics had recognized that he was no cheap pub comedian, swinging a mallet, but a subtle tragi-comic clown, who by rights belonged in the theatre. (Riegler 1961: 37)

According to Monika Dimpfl, Liesl Karlstadt kept an anonymous review of the evening proudly in her scrapbook. It concluded:

> The house was sold out and was passionately enlivened by laughter and protests. Everyone expected a wonderful evening and wanted to get their money's worth. (Dimpfl 1996: 51)

Furthermore it undoubtedly encouraged Valentin to innovate further with the longer form sketch (or short play) and helped him overcome his antipathy towards, and anxieties about, the theatre. By the end of the year he was already discussing a residency at the Kammerspiele that would ultimately lead to the staging of his hugely successful anti-war play *Die Raubritter vor München* (The Robber Knights Outside Munich). At the same time, by contrast, his main rival in the *Singspielhallen* of Munich, the arch conservative Weiß Ferdl, was the headline act at that year's Christmas party for the recently formed National Socialist Workers' Party of Germany (NSDAP). When Valentin and Karlstadt premiered *Die Raubritter vor München* in April 1924, the period of hyperinflation may have been over, but it would be in the aftermath of the failed Beer Hall Putsch by Hitler in November 1923 and the play's anti-militaristic message would have acquired a new relevance and poignancy.

Notes

1 See Double and Wilson (2004) for a full translation of the script.
2 These included *Die Hochzeit* (A Respectable Wedding) which centres around a party hosted by a newly married couple who have had to furnish their new home entirely with home-made items. As the party progresses, the furniture all starts to fall apart, resulting in a scene of complete anarchy, culminating in the marriage bed collapsing when the exhausted couple finally go to bed.
3 According to Klaus Völker, '"Die Junge Bühne" was not a commercial undertaking. It was one of the so-called lunch-time theatres (*Mittagstheater*), which had no home of their own and usually gave guest performances on Sunday mornings in other theatres. All those taking part worked for nothing' (1979: 54).
4 Schulte is scathing about Raupach's abilities as a playwright in general. Ernst Raupach (1784–1852) wrote 117 plays in total, which Schulte describes as 'a life's work whose quality stands diametrically in contrast to its astonishing quantity' (1982: 43).
5 Kurt Horwitz (1887–1974), one of the cast members of *Trommeln in der Nacht*.
6 In the twenty-five years from 1882 to 1907 the population of Munich had doubled from 250,000 to 500,000 (Double and Wilson 2006: 44) due to

the city's industrialization. Most of the population rise was due to families moving into the city from the surrounding Bavarian countryside.

7 *Die Elf Scharichter* (The Eleven Executioners) ran for three years between 1901 and 1904 in the backroom of Zum Goldenen Hirsch (The Golden Hart) in Türkenstraße. The venue seated 100 people and the programme, which was changed monthly, ran three nights per week. Among the 'executioners' were Frank Wedekind (1864–1918) and the same Otto Falckenberg (1873–1947) who was directing *Trommeln in der Nacht.*

8 *Simplicisssimus* was the name of a satirical weekly magazine (1896–1967), whose contributors included Wedekind (who was sentenced to several months in prison in 1898 on account of his satirizing the Kaiser), Heinrich Mann (1887–1950), Hermann Hesse (1877–1962), Hugo von Hoffmanstahl (1874–1929) and Erich Kästner (1899–1974). The *Simplicisssimus* cabaret was set up in 1903 by Kathi Kobus (1854–1929) in the 'Alter Simpl', also in Türkenstraße. Today this *Künstlerkneipe* has been restored to its former glory and is adorned with photographs of the many poets, singers and comedians who performed there, including Joachim Ringelnatz (Hans Bötticher; 1883–1934) and Erich Mühsam (1878–1934).

9 Valentin also parodied the very *Volksänger* tradition from which he emerged in the early Valentin-Karlstadt sketch *Aplensängerterzett* (Alpine Singers Trio) (Valentin 1978: 279–84).

10 As indeed did most of the press. In 1929 Karlstadt complained in a newspaper interview for the *Süddeutsche Sonntagspost*, 'Up until now the newspapers have only written about him and have totally forgotten about me' (quoted in Dimpfl 1996: 51).

11 Calandra (1974: 86) makes reference to both a letter of 14 March 1920 in which Brecht talks of seeing Valentin perform *Tingeltangel* at the Charivari Cabaret and also a description by the director Bernhard Reich of going with Brecht to see the same piece at the Kammerspiele. In 1920 Valentin was performing regularly at the Charivari (also known as the *Germaniabrettl*, because of its location at the Hotel Germania), but Reich may be referring to another, later performance of the same piece, performed at the Kammerspiele after Valentin had signed a contract to make regular appearances there. Monika Dimpfl suggests that the

piece was being performed at the Kammerspiele early in 1923, which would make sense as Brecht had not yet left for Berlin at that time (1996: 48). Certainly Reich suggests that Brecht returned time and again to see Valentin perform the same sketches 'because he was collecting observations and studying the plays as well as the acting technique of this extraordinary man'; Calandra (1974: 86).

12 Max Schreck (1879–1936), who went on to achieve international recognition in Paul Murnau's *Nosferatu* (1922), also collaborated with Brecht and Valentin the following year in the film *Mysterien eines Friseursalons* (Mysteries of a Barber's Shop).

13 Schulte (1982: 104) suggests that Valentin took this role.

14 This could possibly have been Valentin's own composition (1978: 181–82).

15 For an appreciation of the work of Gert (1892–1978) in the context of Weimar Germany, see Kolb (2007).

16 It is not entirely clear from Münsterer's description of the evening as to whether the first of these sketches was performed as part of the first half or the second half, but it would make most sense for it to have formed part of the second half, which was, in any case, given over entirely to the pair.

17 See, for example, *Der Radfahrer* (The Cyclist) in Valentin 1978: 202–3).

18 Up until that point Valentin had been working as a *Nachständler* at the *Baderwirt*, performing free floor-spots at the end of the evening's entertainment to establish himself on the circuit.

19 For an English translation of the sketch, see Double and Wilson (2008: 215–16).

20 Valentin's interest in 'dicke Frauen', it seems, was not purely professional. According to Schulte (1982: 139) Valentin possessed an enormous collection of pornographic photographs featuring well-proportioned women.

21 By the time that Karl Ritter (1888–1977), who later became a well-known propagandist for the Nazis, directed this short film, *Im Fototelier* was already an established favourite in Valentin and Karlstadt's repertoire and it appeared on the bill in 1929 when Valentin was establishing himself in Berlin at the Kabarett der Komiker (Schulte 1982: 139).

Bibliography

Budzinski, Klaus (1985), *Das Kabarett*. Düsseldorf: ECON Taschenbuch Verlag.

Calandra, Denis (1974), 'Karl Valentin and Bertolt Brecht', *The Drama Review*, 18 (1): 86–98.

Dimpfl, Monika (1996), *Immer veränderlich: Liesl Karlstadt (1892 bis 1960)*. Munich: A1 Verlag.

Double, Oliver, and Michael Wilson (2004), 'Karl Valentin's Illogical Subversion: Stand-up Comedy and Alienation Effect', *New Theatre Quarterly*, 79, 20 (3): 203–15.

Double, Oliver, and Michael Wilson (2006), 'Brecht and Cabaret', in Peter Thomson and Glendyr Sacks (eds), *The Cambridge Companion to Brecht*, 2nd edn. Cambridge: Cambridge University Press, 40–61.

Double, Oliver, and Michael Wilson (2008), '"I am a Poor, Skinny Man": Persona and Physicality in the Work of Karl Valentin', *Studies in Theatre and Performance*, 28 (3): 213–21.

Hayman, Ronald (1983), *Brecht: A Biography*. London: Weidenfeld and Nicolson.

Kolb, Alexandra (2007), '"There Was Never Anything Like This!!!": Valeska Gert's Performances in the Context of Weimar Culture', *The European Legacy*, 12 (3): 293–309.

Münsterer, Hans Otto (1998), *The Young Brecht, 1917–1922* (trans. Tom Kuhn and Karen Leeder). London: Libris.

Riegler, Theo (1961), *Das Liesl Karlstadt Buch*. Munich: Süddeutscher Verlag

Sackett, Robert Eben (1982), *Popular Entertainment, Class and Politics in Munich, 1920–1923*. Cambridge, MA: Harvard University Press.

Schulte, Michael (1982), *Karl Valentin: Eine Biographie*. Hamburg: Hoffmann und Campe.

Thomson, Peter (2006), 'Brecht's Lives', in Peter Thomson and Glendyr Sacks (eds), *The Cambridge Companion to Brecht*, 2nd edn. Cambridge: Cambridge University Press, 22–39.

Valentin, Karl (1978), *Alles von Karl Valentin* (ed. Michael Schulte). Munich: Piper Verlag.

Völker, Klaus (1979), *Brecht: A Biography* (trans. John Nowell). London: Marion Boyars.

4

Packed From Pit to Ceiling: The Kingston Empire (1910–1955) and British Variety

Adam Ainsworth

On the evening of Monday, 24 October 1910, a magician known as The Great Raymond took to the stage of the Empire at Kingston upon Thames. This was the theatre's opening night and Raymond, who was the 'top of the bill', proceeded to conjure hot coffee from cups filled with confetti, pluck pigeons from thin air with a net swung high above the heads of those watching him and perform a number of other relatively small tricks before wheeling on to the stage a cabinet designed to represent Noah's Ark. As the Empire's resident orchestra struck up a composition that evoked a terrific storm, Raymond revealed to the audience that the ark was empty and yet as the storm raged he promptly released a flock of twenty pigeons from a small door in its side. These were followed in turn by a dog, several cats, two rabbits, a parrot, a dozen geese, a monkey, a goat and, perhaps inevitably, three of the magician's assistants (*Era*, 29 October 1910).

In addition to The Great Raymond, who interchanged 'Noah's Ark' with a number of other grand illusions including 'The Hand of Fate', 'Metempsychosis' and 'El Baul Misterioso' (*Surrey Comet*, 22 October 1910), eight other unrelated 'turns' were included on the bill and this line up was presented in its entirety, twice a night, for the remainder of the opening week. The 'twice nightly' format, that would be applied throughout much of the Empire's forty-five-year history, was becoming standard practice in music halls by the late nineteenth century and was but one of many entrepreneurial innovations, instigated both by public demand and the need to increase profit margins, that changed music hall irrevocably by the turn of the twentieth. Indeed the social and economic circumstances that instigated the implementation of these 'refinements', explored in detail by Bailey (1987: 154–75), Double (2012: 37–50) and Russell (1996: 61–85) among others, resulted in a new, theatrical form that was defined by *The Times*, in an article published less than a year before the Empire opened to the public, as

> entertainment, presented in luxurious and sometimes beautiful theatres, at which an audience of men, women, and even children, all in their best clothes, could enjoy cleverness and fun and spectacle of many kinds, without hearing a word and scarcely catching a hint of ribaldry, and without being asked, or in some cases even allowed, to take a drop of alcoholic drink. (*The Times* 1910)

Described by Russell (1996: 61) as a 'hybrid', combining characteristics of the music hall and the legitimate theatre, it became known commonly as variety theatre, or simply variety, and as Russell observes 'it contained within it the seeds of many of the most successful elements of twentieth-century popular culture'.

These seeds were sown for the first time in Kingston on Thames by one Clarence Sounes (1855–1921) and his Empire epitomized the variety theatres identified in *The Times* (1910). Built as it was to plans produced by the renowned theatre architect Bertie Crewe (1860–1937), the Empire was designed ornately, furnished luxuriously and capable of seating 1,795 people. As such it was intended to attract and accommodate the sizeable, middle-class, family audiences to which *The Times* alluded. This was also the kind of clientele to which the Empire's repertoire was oriented. Sounes assured prospective patrons repeatedly that he would only provide entertainment of an 'inoffensive character' (*Surrey Comet*, 26 October 1910) and that 'the slightest attempt at vulgarity [would] be immediately suppressed' (*The Era*, 24 October 1910). While there is no evidence to suggest that he was ever compelled to do so, there is much to demonstrate that he engaged the wide assortment of clever, fun and spectacular acts that, as *The Times* implies, defined variety theatre. In its first year alone the Empire hosted inter alia acrobats; aerialists; animal acts; bioscope presentations, a blind pianist named Mendel; comedians; dancers; equilibrists; facial contortionists; fire dancers; human statuary; impressionists; instrumentalists; inventors; jugglers; juveniles; lecturers; magicians; military bands; minstrels; rifle shooters; siffleurs; singers of various styles; sketch comics, strongmen and trick cyclists, not to mention Dr. Wilmar and his Spirit Paintings; Madamoiselle Dalmere's Table Circus; Maurin's Marvelous Fountains (in which 20,000 gallons of water were poured on to the stage while being illuminated by powerful electric light), the Spiridion Trio; Briff, Braff and Broff; Olgar, Elgar and Eli and Pipfax and Panlo's Humpsti Bumpsti act.

None of these piqued the interest of Kingston's local press as much as an Annie Abbott act that topped the bill at the Empire throughout the week of 25 September 1911. According to Harrington and Harrington (2010: 9–13), this kind of act can be traced to one Dixie Haygood (1861–1915) who invented the Annie Abbott stage persona in 1889 and also began to use that name as her own, both publically and privately, shortly afterwards (Harrington and Harrington 2010: 31). As such, Haygood is an interesting example of ways in which a performer can become interlaced with her role, one of the threads that run through this book, and yet she was not the only performer to adopt or adapt this persona. Nor indeed was she the only one to assume the stage name, 'The Little Georgia Magnet', which she also invented and used when performing alongside Richard Abbey (1852–1927), her manager and husband, in an act that they claimed demonstrated Abbott's 'electric, spiritualistic, electro-biological [and] odic power' (*The Stage* 1891). Although these assertions were debunked and lampooned repeatedly by sceptics, tabloid journalists and opportunist performers who insisted that the act was made possible by a combination of misdirection, legerdemain and a working knowledge of fulcrum mechanics (Harrington and Harrington 2010: 53–55), the impact of Haygood's creation was such, as Harrington and Harrington (2010: 153–54) explain, that it would be appropriated for the next thirty years by a succession of turns on both sides of the Atlantic. Each of these took on a variant of the fictional persona of Annie Abbot, claimed to possess similarly enigmatic powers and 'demonstrated' these facilities by utilizing variations of the tricks that comprised Haygood's original act.

It was one of these Annie Abbotts who topped the bill at the Empire with an act that was described at length by the *Surrey Comet* (1911). As a consequence it is possible to infer that both the performer and the Annie Abbott role she took on were intertwined in interesting ways and that her performance demonstrated skill rather than magical ability. What is abundantly clear however is that the act was rooted firmly in the present moment and that it relied on a direct connection between the performers and the audience. As such, while this Annie Abbott act would appear to be consonant with each of the methodological concerns explored throughout the book, the primary focus of the following examination will be the ways in which Abbott and her manager, who orchestrated proceedings from start to finish as Abbey had with Haygood, not only both established very quickly and sustained a meaningful connection with the audience but also incorporated them into the performance.

Speaking directly to the audience from the outset, Abbott's manager explained that 'The Little Georgia Magnet' was so called because she was imbued with a supernatural power that among other things had prevented the strongest men of the time from lifting her off the floor even though she weighed a mere 98 lbs. Not even Abbott understood the precise nature of this facility, he continued, and yet it enabled her to bring under the influence of her will anybody with whom she established 'flesh contact' (*Surrey Comet* 1911).

Providing the audience with this kind of introductory exposition is common practice in stage magic, as Henning Nelms (2012: 6) indicates, and although neither Abbott nor her manager were billed as magicians or illusionists, their act clearly did not demonstrate the magnetic power they claimed Abbott possessed. Rather it comprised a succession of tricks that appeared to do so. In short, the act was an illusion, and according to Jim Steinmeyer (2006: 43), its success would have been dependent to a large extent on the skillful way in which the performers placed its constituent elements within a coherent context that seized the audience's attention and sustained their interest. Outlandish claims and intriguing references to inexplicable magnetism, to flesh contact and to the failed attempts of the world's strongest men to prevail against a woman of such slight build were designed to establish this 'false reality' in the minds of the audience. Nelms (2012: 6) refers to this as creating meaning, and as Anette Hill (2011: 482) proposes, it encourages the audience to 'tune into the magic of the moment'. However for Nelms (2012: 6) it also serves a more practical purpose. Creating meaning arouses the spectators' attention by inviting two very simple and connected questions: will the illusionist substantiate her claim and if so how?

Having introduced the ostensibly magnetic star of the show, Abbott's manager revealed that she would demonstrate her particular ability in a number of ways and that each required the assistance of members of the audience. These participants, he continued, would take to the stage to form a 'committee of inspection' and the members of the committee would not only test the veracity of the performers' claims but also pit their strength and guile against Abbott, both individually and collectively, in a series of challenges (*Surrey Comet* 1911).

Incorporating participants into the performance in this manner, which ensured that audience's involvement with the exploits on stage was by proxy both direct and instant, was not without risk, as is indicated by an item published in *The Stage* (1910) a year before Abbott brought her act to the Empire. Referring to a mishap that occurred at the London Pavillion on Tuesday, 6 September 1910, the piece describes the way in which 'one of the twelve gentlemen who undertook to serve upon the "committee" fell into the orchestra whilst crossing the gangway from the stalls to the stage' and goes on to note that 'what might have been a serious accident was treated as a huge joke by the spectators'. This brief account illustrates the way in which a single moment of a performance can arouse a unified response from an audience, and while it should be assumed that neither Abbott nor her manager orchestrated this apparent accident, they certainly did incorporate into their performance at the Empire moments that were intended to bring the audience together in a similar way. As Hill (2011: 482) demonstrates, these moments are not uncommon in stage magic wherein the relationship between performer and audience is akin to that which exists between a conductor and an orchestra. The illusionist and the audience commit to participate in the same creative process, as Hill explains, and they construct illusions collaboratively even though the former 'conducts' the latter. At times the illusionist will require participants to perform solos, at others they will need to contribute to an orchestral section and at key moments all those involved will be brought together simultaneously.

This is exactly the relationship that was established between the performers and the spectators during Abbott's performance at the Empire. Initially, individuals attempted unsuccessfully to pull a billiard cue from Abbott's hands. They then tried and failed to lift the performer off her feet. Thereafter their contributions became increasingly strenuous and collaborative. In one test a 'heavy-weight' spectator was asked to sit on top of a billiard cue held down by a group of men, but in spite of their efforts to resist her, Abbott not only lifted man and pole with one hand but also carried them across the stage 'with a following of struggling humanity'. In another, the same men formed a queue and 'pushed and writhed and sweated' in a failed attempt to press Abbott flat against a wall. Observing that Abbott remained unmoved 'in the two senses of the word' while the men collapsed on to the stage in 'tumbled heaps', the *Surrey Comet* (1911) suggests that the success of the act was due at least in part to moments such as these when the image of the slight, impassive and inscrutable Abbott was juxtaposed with that of the straining and sweaty participants drawn from the audience.

However, on one occasion Abbott was affected – or at least she appeared to be. For the finale of her performance on Wednesday, 27 September, a prizewinning tug-of-war team was invited to the stage and while Abbott purported to transfer her power to her manager by establishing flesh contact, members of the team made a concerted effort to pull a length of rope from his grip. Initially each of the competitors wore the heavy boots they used in a typical tug of war contest and when this strategy proved fruitless they removed their boots. The performer's grip did not waver in either case.

It should be noted that this was not the only tug-of-war contest the performers used to close the act in dramatic fashion. Earlier in the week they competed successfully against a team of heavy dray horses employed by the town's brewery. A regular feature of the act, which necessarily added even more local interest, this trick was also potentially risky. Earlier in the year, when it had been attempted during a performance at the Hippodrome in Warrington on Friday, 2 June, one of the horses, weighing approximately 800 kilograms, slipped into the orchestra pit. *The Stage* (1911) reported that members of the orchestra had sensed the impending danger and jumped clear; however the panicking animal not only damaged the footlights but also smashed many of the instruments. The response of those who witnessed this incident was much the same as that of those who saw the gentleman fall into the London Pavillion's orchestra pit and, as *The Stage* noted, it was some time before order was restored in the auditorium.

There was no such calamity during the week of performances at the Empire. Nevertheless, all the members of the audience were brought together in a similar fashion at the end of the tug-of-war contest introduced above when Abbott appeared to lose consciousness. The *Surrey Comet*'s description of the incident assumes that her collapse was brought about by the strain of transferring to her manager the power necessary to withstand the efforts of those hauling on the rope. This of course is possible. However, it is rather more likely that Abbott's blackout was another example of her ability to manipulate the audience's reception of the act. As such it would be consistent with the 'tiny lies, in words and deeds' (Steinmeyer 2006: 42) that stage magicians use to support and protect an illusion by embellishing the 'false reality' introduced at the outset. Whatever the explanation, Abbott's collapse was certainly a moment that united the audience who, according to the *Surrey Comet* (1911), responded with loud applause.

This bill-topping performance at the Empire occurred as Abbott reached the end of a year-long tour of the UK that had begun with a month of performances at the London Pavilion and subsequently included a lengthy engagement with Moss Empires. Established in 1899, when three smaller chains of theatres owned by H. E. Moss (1852–1912), Richard Thornton (1839–1922) and Oswald Stoll (1866–1942) were amalgamated, Moss Empires had become the largest theatre enterprise in the world by 1906 (Davis 1996: 121). As such it was the most important of the 'combines' to emerge at the end of the nineteenth century. Although between them these syndicates controlled a significant proportion of Britain's variety theatres by the early twentieth century, a small number were owned independently and, operated as it was by a succession of small limited companies, the Kingston Empire was one of these. For more than half of its history it was owned by Kingshot Theatres which, as the name suggests, was also responsible for the operation of the Hippodrome at Aldershot. The company was directed by Stanley Watson, who had managed both theatres under Clarence Sounes, and his tenure coincided with a period in which variety reached the peak of its popularity and profitability. Described by Double (2012: 51–69) as variety's golden age, this period began in 1928 when George Black (1890–1945) took on managerial responsibilities at the General Theatre Corporation and made an audacious yet ultimately very successful attempt to not only revitalize the fortunes of London's Palladium, the company's flagship theatre, but also to resuscitate variety from a lengthy period of decline in which it had struggled to compete with rival forms of entertainment such as revue and radio. This he achieved by fostering mutually beneficial relationships with revue and the various broadcast media but more importantly by programming celebrated turns of the highest quality and implementing lasting innovation.

Stanley Watson was also not averse to this kind of investment and innovation, albeit on a decidedly smaller scale. A year before the Empire celebrated its silver jubilee, *The Stage* (12 July 1934) recognized that the theatre was overseen by what it described as a 'live management', suggesting that Watson was an animated manager with an awareness of current events in the world of variety. This appraisal was not only offered in response to the costly alterations Watson had made to the stage and auditorium but also to the news that he planned to change the repertoire by staging 'cabaret-variety'. In this 'new experiment in variety presentation', Leslie Weston, who was to be employed as the resident compère-comedian, would preside over a show that was divided into two discrete sections. The first of these would be devoted to variety, while the second would be given over to cabaret. This innovation certainly altered the format of an evening's entertainment. However, it had very little impact on what was performed with the only obvious difference between the two sections being a greater number of musical numbers in the second half. Nevertheless, it proved very popular for a short time (*The Stage* 1934) although it did not have a lasting impact on the Empire's repertoire and Watson reverted to a more typical variety format relatively quickly.

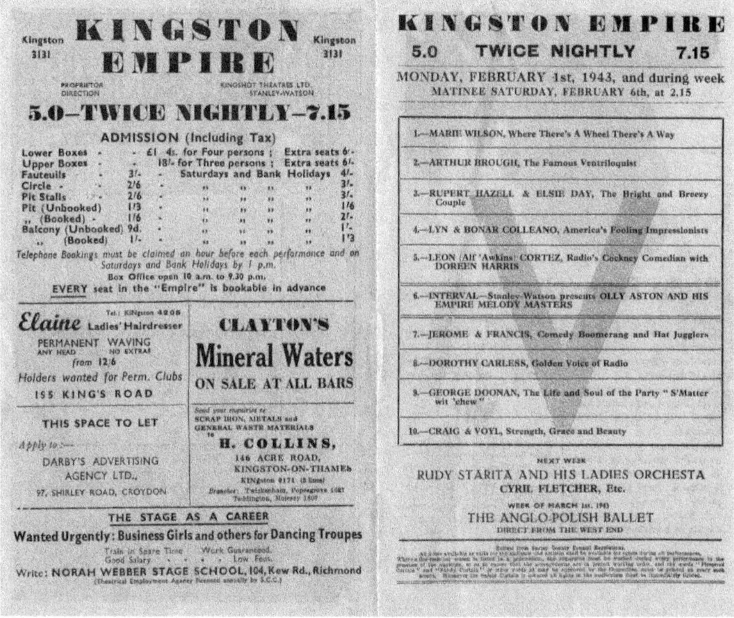

Kingston 3131 KINGSTON EMPIRE Kingston 3131

PROPRIETOR KINGSHOT THEATRES LTD.
DIRECTION STANLEY-WATSON

5.0—TWICE NIGHTLY—7.15

ADMISSION (Including Tax)

Lower Boxes	£1 4s. for Four persons ;	Extra seats	6/-
Upper Boxes	18/- for Three persons ;	Extra seats	6/-
Fauteuils	3/-	Saturdays and Bank Holidays	4/-
Circle	2/6	,, ,, ,, ,,	3/-
Pit Stalls	2/6	,, ,, ,, ,,	3/-
Pit (Unbooked)	1/3	,, ,, ,, ,,	1/6
,, (Booked)	1/6	,, ,, ,, ,,	2/-
Balcony (Unbooked)	9d.	,, ,, ,, ,,	1/-
,, (Booked)	1/-	,, ,, ,, ,,	1/3

Telephone Bookings must be claimed an hour before each performance and on Saturdays and Bank Holidays by 1 p.m.

Box Office open 10 a.m. to 9.30 p.m.

EVERY seat in the "Empire" is bookable in advance

Tel.: KINgston 4206
Elaine Ladies' Hairdresser
PERMANENT WAVING
ANY HEAD NO EXTRAS
from 12/6
Holders wanted for Perm. Clubs
155 KING'S ROAD

CLAYTON'S
Mineral Waters
ON SALE AT ALL BARS

THIS SPACE TO LET
Apply to:—
DARBY'S ADVERTISING AGENCY LTD.,
97, SHIRLEY ROAD, CROYDON

Send your enquiries re
SCRAP IRON, METALS and GENERAL WASTE MATERIALS
to
H. COLLINS,
146 ACRE ROAD,
KINGSTON-ON-THAMES
KINgston 0171 (3 lines)
Branches: Twickenham, Popesgrove 1087
Teddington, Molesey 1807

THE STAGE AS A CAREER
Wanted Urgently: Business Girls and others for Dancing Troupes
Train in Spare Time Work Guaranteed.
Good Salary . . . . Low Fees.
Write: NORAH WEBBER STAGE SCHOOL, 104, Kew Rd., Richmond
(Theatrical Employment Agency licensed annually by S.C.C.)

KINGSTON EMPIRE

5.0 TWICE NIGHTLY 7.15

MONDAY, FEBRUARY 1st, 1943, and during week
MATINEE SATURDAY, FEBRUARY 6th, at 2.15

1.—MARIE WILSON, Where There's A Wheel There's A Way
2.—ARTHUR BROUGH, The Famous Ventriloquist
3.—RUPERT HAZELL & ELSIE DAY, The Bright and Breezy Couple
4.—LYN & BONAR COLLEANO, America's Fooling Impressionists
5.—LEON (Alf 'Awkins) CORTEZ, Radio's Cockney Comedian with DOREEN HARRIS
6.—INTERVAL—Stanley-Watson presents OLLY ASTON AND HIS EMPIRE MELODY MASTERS
7.—JEROME & FRANCIS, Comedy Boomerang and Hat Jugglers
8.—DOROTHY CARLESS, Golden Voice of Radio
9.—GEORGE DOONAN, The Life and Soul of the Party "S'Matter wit 'chew"
10.—CRAIG & VOYL, Strength, Grace and Beauty

NEXT WEEK
RUDY STARITA AND HIS LADIES ORCHESTRA
CYRIL FLETCHER, Etc.

WEEK OF MARCH 1st, 1943
THE ANGLO-POLISH BALLET
DIRECT FROM THE WEST END

Figure 4.1 Programme from the Kingston Empire, Monday, 1 February–Saturday, 6 February 1943 (author's collection)

This format, examined by Double (2012: 12–20), Wilmut (1985: 84–86) and others, was organized in accordance with very specific conventions in order to create 'a nicely balanced bill' (Double 2012: 20). The preceding illustration indicates the way in which such a bill was arranged at the Empire throughout the first week of February in 1943, and to some extent it is consistent with Alan Chudley's description of the components of a typical Empire bill. Chudley was an assistant electrician at the Hippodrome in Aldershot during the 1940s and when interviewed by Claire Jones (2000) he explained that because the Hippodrome was the Empire's sister theatre, he was occasionally required to operate the lights during matinee performances at Kingston. Here, he notes, a show would always begin with an overture performed by the resident orchestra. During Chudley's time, the Empire's orchestra, which would also entertain the audience during the interval, as is indicated on the programme from 1943, was known as the Empire Melody Masters and it was led by Olly Aston. Following the overture, the opening act would usually be performed by dancers or acrobats. However, as both her bill matter and footage of her act reveal, Marie Wilson was neither a dancer nor an acrobat but rather a novelty cyclist (British Pathé n.d.). The remainder of the first half also differs subtly from the typical arrangement that Chudley remembers. Usually, he claims, the opening act was followed by the first comedian's act, presented by a lesser known comic; a speciality or 'spesh' act; and the interval act which was performed by the second biggest name on the bill. However the programme demonstrates that in this instance a well-known ventriloquist, a pair of eccentric musicians and an impressionist performed before cockney comedian Leon Cortez and his partner Doreen Harris presented the interval act.

The second half of the programme outlined in the illustration aligns more neatly with the kind of bill that Chudley recalled. At the end of the Melody Masters' second spot, the second half would begin with an act that Chudley refers to as 'the bar turn'. This, as he remembers, was used 'to get the people out of the bar', and to ensure that the audience didn't miss anything as they returned to their seats, it would rarely be performed by one of the featured acts. If the bar turn was not followed by a second spot for the artist who had performed the earlier interval act, it would usually be a musical act or a singer, such as Dorothy Carless; but whatever kind of act it was, its purpose was to pave the way for the top of the bill. Running for about thirty minutes, the top of the bill's act would be the longest in the programme, and while it would seem to make sense to end the show with a performance by the most popular act, in a typical variety programme, the top of the bill was followed by one last turn. At the Empire this was known as the 'chaser act' and it was short spesh act, often performed by acrobats such as Craig and Voyle. According to Chudley, the chaser act served much the same purpose as the bar turn except that in this instance it was programmed so that the audience could leave the theatre in time to catch their buses home and yet not miss any of the more well-known acts (Jones 2000).

The Empire's chaser act throughout the week of 5 October 1936 was a pair of aerialists known as Le Pomme and Sister, and among the acts that preceded them on the bill were the silent comedian Chaz Chase; Bob and Alf Pearson who performed duets at the piano; a troupe of speciality dancers called the Harum Scarum Girls and Wilson, Keppel and Betty. The last of these contributed an act called *Cleopatra's Nightmare* that was described by *The Times* (1936) as 'a broad burlesque of Egyptian dancing', and having made their British debut at the London Palladium some four years earlier (*The Stage* 1932), they had become both the most well-known spesh act in the business and established stars of variety and revue.

Jack Wilson (1894–1970), Joe Keppel (1895–1977) and Betty Knox (1907–63) began working together in 1928 when Knox was drafted in to provide an extra dimension to an act that Wilson and Keppel had conceived while performing as The Bus Boys on the North American vaudeville circuit (Stafford 2015: 45). The pair's vaudeville career had begun in 1920 with a clog dancing number they had developed while working in Australia for Colleano and Sole Brothers' Huge Circus and Menagerie.[1] Eight years later this had been superseded by a routine comprising singing, dancing, elements of physical comedy and an opening in which one of the duo peddled on to the stage a miniature bus while the other tap danced on the top deck (Stafford 2015: 44). Initially this material changed very little after Knox joined the act. Indeed the work with which Wilson, Keppel and Betty became associated would take some time to emerge and the characteristic Egyptian styling was barely formed when they made their way to Britain for the first time. It is however very much in evidence in each of the recordings of the trio at work. These videos, a number of which are available online, and reviews of their performances reveal that the act which ensured this celebrity status comprised a changing series of short scenes, underscored with unconventional arrangements of orchestral works with a broadly 'oriental' flavour,[2] in which the performers, wearing stereotypical attire (tunics, fezzes and Betty's various *bedlah* ensembles), danced and played musical instruments in front of backdrops upon which were painted various cartoon depictions of Ancient Egypt. As this description suggests, *Cleopatra's Nightmare* was a novelty, which is one of the recurring themes of this book; however this should neither imply that it was especially topical nor that its appeal was fleeting. While it was one of a number of notable cultural products of the early 1930s to appropriate the history, myths and iconography of Ancient Egypt,[3] thereby both reflecting and benefitting from the prevailing 'Egyptomania' that was brought about primarily by the excavations at Tell el-Armana during the 1920s and 1930s,[4] these temporary cultural preoccupations cannot have been solely responsible for the lasting appeal of an act that was one of the most popular in variety for well over a quarter of a century.[5] A more reasonable explanation, and one that centres on a subtly different definition of novelty, is that its sole purpose was to entertain. This it did with considerable success. Indeed, less than a year after their British debut, *The Stage* (1933) noted that Wilson, Keppel and Betty 'possesse[d] in a marked degree the art of keeping an audience interested and amused'. The way in which Wilson and Keppel achieved this is examined in the following analysis of the sand dance (Sterkens), a piece of work lasting a little under two minutes that *The Guardian* (1959) acknowledged quite correctly as their 'masterpiece'. However, Betty's relationship with the audience differed from Wilson's and Keppel's in significant ways, and as she did not perform in the sand dance, her work will be explored with specific reference to a solo contribution to the act (Hotun 2010).

In this recording, the material that was originated by Betty Knox was performed by her daughter, Jean Patricia, 'Patsy' Knox (1923–84) who replaced her mother in 1942 and performed alongside Wilson and Keppel until 1956. The way in which she presents the gymnastic choreography, which is the most significant feature of this number, epitomizes the self-expressive mode of performance defined by Bert O. States (1987: 160–70). In this mode the performer seems to say to the audience: 'See what I can do' (161), and although Betty remains silent throughout the dance, she commands the audience's attention and indicates when they should express their appreciation of her acrobatic ability by orienting her virtuoso performance to them directly. This she does from the outset by looking to the audience as she makes her entrance, crossing the stage with an occasional pirouette, and at a number of judicious moments thereafter. The remaining scene is given over to three sequences of increasingly demanding cartwheels. In the first of these Betty uses both hands, while in the second she uses only one, and in the third, which comprises six aerial cartwheels performed at twice the tempo of the preceding choreography, she places neither hand on the floor. At the end of each of these sequences Betty raises both hands above her head, and looking directly to the audience, sashays downstage in a manner that makes clear to the audience that an appreciative response is required. As such Betty's act embodies Marvin Carlson's (2003: 3) attempt to explain what makes performing arts performative in that it requires the physical presence of a trained and skilled performer whose performance is predicated upon a demonstration of skill.

Wilson and Keppel address the audience in much the same manner during the sand dance when, standing side by side, they look into the auditorium and raise their arms aloft in time with the final two beats of the orchestral accompaniment to indicate the end of the act and to cue a round of applause. However, prior to these final moments, their relationship with the audience is generally rather less explicit. This is because their contribution to the act differs from Betty's. As *The Stage* (1936) suggests, the success of *Cleopatra's Nightmare* can be attributed in part to the way in which it combines skillful dancing with ridiculous comedy, and while Betty performed the 'more formal types of dancing' during which the audience could appreciate her skill as a dancer, Wilson and Keppel drew on their 'comical appearances and clever dancing skits' to elicit laughter. To do so they worked primarily in what States (1987: 170–85) defines as the 'collaborative mode' of performance, playing characters who live in a world that includes the audience and sharing their attitude to that world with the audience. This extraordinary world was established very simply, not only by the scenic elements and lively musical accompaniment outlined above, but also by the way in which Wilson and Keppel performed a number of antics, variously servile and ritualistic, with an attitude that was described by *The Guardian* (1959) as 'an immense pale dignity sustained in rather trying circumstances by two typically frail human beings of less than comely aspect'. *The Guardian* proposed that the pair's exaggerated solemnity held within it the act's comic essence and this analysis is consistent with Athene Seyler's assertion that the comic actor must both understand and believe in the truth of the character she plays even though she distorts that truth consciously through exaggeration. In other words, while the performer must acknowledge that a character becomes distorted when a particular characteristic is accentuated for comic effect, she must still present the character to the audience as a truthful likeness (Seyler 2013: 34). While this is neither the appropriate place to problematize Seyler's repeated references to truth, nor to speculate about whether or not Wilson and Keppel believed in their comic creations, it is clear that both performed the sand dance with what Seyler (2013: 61) describes as the 'mood of confidence that is … essential in gaining the confidence of the audience' and each committed wholeheartedly to his comic creation in a manner that demonstrated not only 'firm trust in the comedic quality of his part' but also the 'assured expectation that the audience [would] respond' in kind. This confidence helps to explain why, unlike Betty, Wilson and Keppel rarely indicate when or how the audience should engage with the work. In this respect too their work is aligned with Seyler's opinion that true comics should in some way stand outside the characters they play and the situation in which these characters are placed in order to point out their delight in certain aspects of one or the other (2010: 25). This, she points out, should not be confused with 'the vulgar wink across the footlights' employed by music hall comedians to tell an audience when they should laugh but should rather be understood as a desire to establish an 'intimate' and reciprocal relationship in which the performer acknowledges that it is her responsibility to draw the audience's attention to comical aspects of the performance while the audience accept that their role is to laugh at them (2010: 25). Acceptance of this responsibility is evidenced both in Joe Keppel's comically baleful mugging during the section of the dance in which he appears to hex his partner and again moments later when he responds to a gentler section of the orchestral accompaniment with an exaggeratedly affected facial expression. However, it is demonstrated most clearly during a vignette in which Wilson and Keppel turn to the audience, revealing clearly the dignified facial expressions they both establish at the outset and maintain throughout the performance, and positioned side by side, proceed to lift the front hem of their respective tunics so as to reveal consciously an extra inch or two of scrawny, male thigh. In these moments neither performer enjoins the audience to applaud their skill, as Betty does throughout her solo spot, nor do they signal, perhaps with a nudge or a wink, that those watching must laugh at the sight of two 'spectrally thin men in Egyptian costume' (Kilgariff 1999: 278–79) who remain inexplicably solemn and dignified even as they waggle their legs in a ridiculous fashion. Instead they invite the audience to share their comic creation by looking across the footlights while performing simplistic and eccentric choreography with an ebullience that not only reveals their evident enthusiasm for the roles they have invented but also demonstrates great confidence in their ability to entertain. This they did until they were well into their sixties, performing alongside numerous Betties throughout variety's golden age and, as Eric Midwinter (1979: 120) notes, considered by many to represent 'all that was most immaculate and most satisfying' about the business. However, as Midwinter suggests, recalling the time he 'saw their names low on a bill posted on a wall for a third-rate revue in a declining Lancashire mill town' they could not remain at the top of the profession forever and although '[t]heir act was unchanging, one might say as eternal as the sand they sprinkled for their sandals to grate and rasp upon ... suddenly there was really no place for it, and a torn poster on the derelict wall of a now declining, once humming textile centre told it all' (1979: 120).

Variety's decline was as swift as it was terminal and this was very much the case at Kingston upon Thames. At the end of 1954, the *Surrey Comet* (15 December 1954) forewarned its readership that the variety bill being presented throughout the week of 13 December could be the last to be seen at the Empire as the theatre was to be sold when a three-week run of *Red Riding Hood*, that season's pantomime, drew to a close. This prediction proved a little premature because although the Empire was put up for auction on 20 January 1955 it failed to meet the reserve price and remained open to the public until the end of March. Nevertheless, when the curtain came down at the end of the final performance of a revue called *La Vie Parisienne* it would not rise again. A representative of Kingshot Theatres, one W. L. Hodges, suggested to the *Surrey Comet* (1955) that the company had been forced to sell the theatre because its intangible assets had diminished to such an extent that the board of directors considered them financially worthless. 'The Empire was auctioned as a site rather than as a working theatre', Hodges explained, 'because a theatre is offered with its goodwill – and there is no goodwill'. The reason for this was clear, at least to Hodges, who told the newspaper (1955): '[p]eople just do not seem to like our form of entertainment nowadays ... they are more interested in television'. While this assessment is not unreasonable given that, as Barfe (2009: 65) observes, the percentage of Britons who owned a television increased by some 15,000 per cent between 1947 and 1953; the negative impact of 'the box in the corner' (Wilmut 1985: 208) was felt more keenly after commercial television was established in 1955 and the rot had set in at the Empire well before then. Indeed for Olly Aston, the Empire's musical director between 1934 and 1947, the increasing popularity of this new medium had no effect at all on variety's fortunes or those of the Empire.

> It's rubbish to say [variety] was killed by television … It was the laziness of the artistes that killed it … Big stars were coming to the Empire twice a year and bringing the same material with them every time. They couldn't be bothered to change their acts. They couldn't even be bothered to attend rehearsals. 'We'll have a quick run through five minutes before the curtain up' they used to say, and it wasn't good enough. (*Surrey Comet* 1955)

If artistic standards had started to slip at the Empire some years prior to its closure, as Aston claims, this slippage did not affect the quality of variety performances in a manner that ever exercised local critics. It is then hard to accept that any apparent lack of professionalism on the part of variety performers would have been evident to audiences and by extension that it would have been responsible for the Empire's demise. Moreover, the diligence of variety performers is not called into question in any of the literature exploring the factors that contributed to variety's decline. According to Baker (2011: 215–21), Barfe (2009: 74–80), Double (2012: 69–92) and Wilmut (1985: 208–19) the contributory factors included a widespread lack of investment in the infrastructure of the industry; a reluctance on the part of industry leaders to implement lasting innovation; the burden of an apparently punitive entertainment tax that was described melodramatically by *The Stage* (1955) as an 'intolerable incubus'; and the increasing allure of newly prevalent forms of entertainment such as rock 'n' roll, skiffle and pop, as well as extravagant musical theatre productions imported from the United States and nude shows. During the first few years of the 1950s these forms were included in the Empire's repertoire with increasing regularity while variety necessarily became less common. Indeed, during the Empire's final year of operation, only seven variety bills were staged.

By contrast, twenty different revues were presented, including *Comic Strip*, *Too Hot to Handle* and *Piccadilly Peepshow*, and while the content of the majority can be surmised by the titillating titles of these few, the local press were not uncomplimentary. Although the *Surrey Comet* (22 September 1954) admitted that these musical revues comprised very little variety, it did acknowledge they were responsible for introducing a number of fresh artists, notably new comedians, and that many of these possessed real talent. In addition to this, the newspaper was not only adamant that the revues performed at the Empire during this period were of a higher standard than 'the cheap and nasty shows which degrade many of the old-time theatres', but was also confident that by programming this kind of show, Watson was simply 'presenting the style of entertainment which seem[ed] to appeal to the greatest number of people' (*Surrey Comet*, 15 September 1954). Variety was then no longer popular in Kingston, or rather it was less popular than the kind of show that promised 'Girls! Girls! Luscious Girls!' (*Surrey Comet*, 6 October 1954) and the *Surrey Comet* (9 June 1954) insisted that a 'new Kingston Empire' was required that would offer entertainment, including stage plays, of a standard sufficient to maintain the existing audience while attracting new interest. This may have been Stanley Watson's intention, and his efforts to bring in audiences cannot be denied; however, the mixture of nude revue, plays described in one representative review as being 'clumsily presented [by] a cast that seem[ed] largely bewildered' (*Surrey Comet*, 9 June 1954) and one off extravaganzas such as *Rose Marie on Ice*, replete as it was with skating Mounties, did not prove sufficiently attractive. The Empire went dark at the end of March 1955, and when Kingshot Theatres eventually found a buyer, it was gutted and turned into a supermarket. For the *Surrey Comet* (1955), the Empire's sale represented the end of an age. '[V]ariety is dying all over the country, not just in Kingston', it lamented, 'and soon perhaps there will just be the memories – the tattered programmes, the dusty newspaper cuttings – as memorials of some very great popular entertainment'. As wistful as this prediction clearly was, it was also remarkably accurate. Having emerged at the turn of the twentieth century, variety had survived and indeed thrived at times, even as critics had proclaimed its demise continually, and yet as Wilmut (1985: 17) suggests, by 1960, a mere five years after the Empire's closure, 'the corpse was truly cold'.

Wilmut's analogy is particularly pertinent given that one of the reasons variety had been so entertaining for so long was that it was defined to a great extent by its 'liveness', and although to some extent each of this book's core concerns is examined in this chapter, it is this quality, predicated as it is on the copresence of performer and spectator and brought about by the current or charge that passed between them, that has been the primary focus. As the preceding case studies have demonstrated, while this relationship was always direct, immediate and collaborative, it was established, shaped and manipulated in different ways by different performers. Although Jack Wilson and Joe Keppel were highly skilled dancers, they shared their eccentric creations with audiences in much the same way as an actor performing comedy on the traditional stage might. Their act placed a succession of tightly choreographed eccentricities inside a simple comic frame constructed from cartoon backcloths and stereotypical props and costumes, and yet it was not the unconventional choreography that amused audiences but rather the exaggeratedly sombre attitude with which the dancing was imbued and the way in which the performers both invited the audience to witness their antics and encouraged them to share their amusement. By comparison, Betty's relationship with the audience was decidedly more emphatic, and both the arrangement and the articulation of her choreography indicated not only when a response was required but also what form it should take. However neither Wilson and Keppel's sand dance nor Betty's acrobatic solo spot incorporated the audience to the same extent as Annie Abbott's display of feigned magnetism. Here the audience were not only spoken to directly to ensure that they fully understood the nature and extent of the feats they were about to witness but also called upon to enter the stage and enable these feats to happen by allowing the star of the show to establish flesh contact. In this respect, as Anette Hill (2011) argues, the audience was the show.

Notes

1 Bonar Colleano, the third act on the bill shown in Figure 4.1, was one of these Colleanos.

2 One of these was *In a Persian Market* written by Albert Ketelbèy, the Empire's original orchestra leader.

3 Two key examples are Karl Freund's *The Mummy* starring Boris Karloff and Cecil B. de Mille's *Cleopatra* that were released in 1932 and 1934 respectively.

4 Brier (2013: 151–61), Day (2006: 19–63) and Lupton (2009: 23–46) among others have demonstrated that this obsession with ancient Egypt had a significant impact on twentieth-century popular culture

5 Jack Wilson and Joe Keppel performed the act with four different Betties until 1962.

Bibliography

'40 Years On And Happy As Sand Dancers: W & K's Resounding Tinkle' (1959), *The Guardian*. 26 June, 7.

Bailey, P. (1987), *Leisure and Class in Victorian England: Rational Recreation and the Contest for Control, 1830–1885*. London: Methuen.

Baker, R. (2011), *Old Time Variety: An Illustrated History*. Barnsley: Remember When.

Barfe, L. (2009), *Turned Out Nice Again: the Story of British Light Entertainment*. London: Atlantic.

'Born Yesterday at Kingston' (1954), *Surrey Comet*. 9 June, 5.

Brier, B. (2013), *Egyptomania: Our Three Thousand Year Obsession With the Land of the Pharoahs*. New York: Palgrave Macmillan.

British Pathe (n.d.), *Marie Wilson, 1941*. Available at http://www.britishpathe.com/video/marie-wilson/query/bicycle+marie (accessed 20 May 2015).

Carlson, M. (2003), *Performance: A Critical Introduction*. London: Routledge

'Chit-Chat' (1891), *The Stage*, 19 November, 11.

Davis, Tracy C. (1996), 'Edwardian Management and the Structures of Industrial Capitalism', in Michael R. Booth and Joel H. Kaplan (eds), *The Edwardian Theatre: Essays on Performance and the Stage*. Cambridge: Cambridge University Press, 111–29

Day, Jasmine (2006), *The Mummy's Curse: Mummymania in the English Speaking World*. London: Routledge.

Double, O. (2012), *Britain Had Talent: A History of Variety Theatre*. Basingstoke: Palgrave Macmillan.

'Empire to be Closed – Still Unsold' (1955), *Surrey Comet*. 5 March, 1

'Entertainments Tax' (1955), *The Stage*. 9 November, 20.

'Grand Opening: New Empire, Kingston' (1910), *Surrey Comet*. 22 October, 5.

'Good Humour in Revue' (1954), *Surrey Comet*. 15 September, 5.

Harrington, Susan J., and Hugh T. Harrington (2010), *Annie Abbott 'The Little Georgia Magnet' and the True Story of Dixie Haygood*. Georgia: Createspace

Hill, A. (2011), 'The Audience is the Show', in V. Nightingale (ed.), *The Handbook of Media Audiences*. New Jersey: John Wiley, 472–89.

'Holborn Empire, Mr. George Robey' (1936), *The Times*. 28 April, 14.

Hotun (2010), *Wilson, Keppel and Betty (Patsy) 1940s*. Available at https://www.youtube.com/watch?v=Bj7bOxpXf-o&list=PLp1mmoxU9titRF1L07G0pzbAfuHMeYdrI&index=1 (accessed 15 July 2015).

Jones, Claire (2000), *Remembering the Empire: Kingston's Variety Theatre, 1910–1955* (SI (792) JON).

Kift, D. (1996), *The Victorian Music Hall: Culture, Class and Conflict*. Cambridge: Cambridge University Press.

Kilgariff, M. (1999), *Grace Beauty and Banjos: Peculiar Lives and Strange Times of Music Hall and Variety Artistes*. London: Oberon Books.

'Kingston Empire: "The Little Georgia Magnet's" Extraordinary Power' (1911), *Surrey Comet*. 30 September, 7.

'Last Variety At Kingston?' (1954), *Surrey Comet*. 15 December, 5.

Lupton, C. (2009), 'Mummymania' for the Masses – Is Egyptology Cursed by the Mummy's Curse?' in Sally Macdonald and Michael Rice (eds) *Consuming Ancient Egypt*. London: Routledge, 23–47

Midwinter, E. (1979), *Make 'Em Laugh: Famous Comedians and Their Worlds*. London: George Allen and Unwin.

Nelms, H. (2012), *Magic and Showmanship: A Handbook for Conjurers*. Newburyport: Dover Publications.

'New Faces at Kingston Empire' (1954), *Surrey Comet*. 22 September, 5.

'New Empire' (1910), *The Era*. 29 October, 3.

Russell, D. (1996), 'Varieties of Life: The Making of the Edwardian Music Hall', in Michael R. Booth and Joel H. Kaplan (eds), *The Edwardian Theatre: Essays on Performance and the Stage*. Cambridge: Cambridge University Press, 61–85.

'Saucy But Funny' (1954), *Surrey Comet*. 6 October, 5.

Seyler, A. (2013), *The Craft of Comedy: The 21st Century Edition*. 4th edn. New York: Routledge.

Stafford, A. (2015), *Wilson, Keppel and Betty: Too Naked for the Nazis*. Coventry: Fantom Films.

States, B. O. (1987), *Great Reckonings in Little Rooms: On the Phenomenology of Theatre*. Berkeley: University of California Press.

Steinmeyer, J. (2006), *Art and Artifice and Other Essays on Illusion: Concerning the Inventors, Traditions, Evolution and Rediscovery of Stage Magic*. New York: Carroll and Graf.

Sterkens, J. (2011), *Original Video: Wilson, Keppel and Betty, Sand Dance, 1933, HQ*. Available at https://www.youtube.com/watch?v=j2fqjsijaMM&index=1&list=RDj2fqjsijaMM (accessed 15 July 2015).

'The Empire, Kingston' (1910), *The Era*. 24 October, 8.

'The New Empire: Crowded Houses at the Opening Performances' (1910), *Surrey Comet*. 26 October, 3.

'The Theatres: The Theatre of Varieties' (1910), *The Times*. 24 January , 4.

'The Variety Stage' (1932), *The Stage*. 11 August, 3.

'The Variety Stage' (1933), *The Stage*. 25 May, 4.

'The Variety Stage' (1934), *The Stage*. 9 August, 3.

'The Variety Stage' (1936), *The Stage*. 18 March, 3.

'Variety Gossip' (1910), *The Stage*. 8 September, 13.

'Variety Gossip' (1911), *The Stage*. 18 June, 13.

'Variety Gossip' (1934), *The Stage*. 12 July, 6.

Wilmut, R. (1985), *Kindly Leave the Stage!: The Story of Variety, 1919–1960*. London: Methuen.

5

Grock: 'Genius Among Clowns'[1]

Louise Peacock

Introduction

Using Grock[2] as an example, this chapter explores key features of the clown as a readily recognizable trope of popular performance. By exploring important aspects of clowning such as how costume and catchphrases contribute to the communication of Grock's personality, the importance of the clown double act and the skill necessary for clown performance, the chapter defines what clown performance is and can be within the broader field of popular performance. The existence of film footage of Grock,[3] while not perfect in relation to a mode of performance which often relies heavily on interaction with a live audience, does at least provide the opportunity to analyse how Grock typifies and extends a range of clown techniques. As Schecter suggests, 'an electronically recorded act is likely to lose some of its suspense, immediacy and interaction between actors and spectators' (Schecter 2003: 7) but the filmed performances of Grock do allow us to see the structure of the entrée, his looks to camera give some indication of where connection points with a live audience might have occurred and the level of skill involved in his performance. Two sequences will be used in this chapter to illustrate Grock's handling of persona, audience and skill. The first of these is the 'Drum' sequence taken from *Au Revoir M. Grock* (33:30–36:28) and the other, the 'Violin and Piano' sequence is found on both that film and *La Vie D'un Artist* created in 1931.

Adrien Wettach (1880–1959) was a performer who was and is difficult to label. It is tempting to claim that he was originally a circus clown who later made the transition to music hall and theatre but a thorough reading of his memoirs (much of which is reproduced by Remy and Disher) demonstrates that, while he had early contact with circuses, his initial performance experiences were in cafes and inns run either by his parents or other local proprietors, providing an experience closer to that of the music hall than the circus. In many of these performances the emphasis was on musical performances and on-stage acrobatics. He started his performing life as a musical eccentric, referring to himself as a 'freak instrumentalist'. He did not come from a circus background, though his father, who was at various times a watchmaker and an inn or café proprietor, had some experience as an acrobat. It appears that this influenced his son to pursue a life in circus performance. More importantly, from the age of seven, having seen a small travelling circus run by Wetzel, a friend of his father, his ambition was to be a clown, 'I realize that the longing to be an artiste took shape at this time' (Wettach 1957: 23). To pursue this dream he developed skills in a number of areas which would later become central to his act. He learnt to play several instruments, taught himself to walk the tightrope on a line set up in his back garden, practised acrobatics and contortion and learnt some magic tricks. The detail of Wettach's biography is, however, less important than the obvious sense in which he was self-trained, working on skills and strength in the hope that he would eventually have the opportunity to use them in the circus ring.

The skills and physical precision which he learnt when young remained with him and formed a cornerstone of his act throughout his life. His career stretched from the early 1900s to his final performance in Hamburg in October 1954. What becomes clear as we trace the history of Grock's performances is that he moved backwards and forwards between circus and music hall throughout his career. Both circus and music hall, as forms of popular performance, are 'concerned with the widest reach of audience available at a given moment or place' (in Mayer and Richards 1977: 263). Using Grock as an example, this chapter will identify and examine the conventions of clowning found in circus and music hall.

Grock's first performance as a clown is usually recorded as occurring in 1903 when he joined Brick. However Remy's chapter on Grock suggests that before working with Brick,[4] Grock worked in two circuses, the Circus Crateil for two years working as part of an act known as the Alfredianos and in the Circus Baracetta. In *Life's a Lark* (Wettach 1931), Grock suggests a more varied route, working as a duo with a clown called Massimo Spitz with a number of circuses including the Rattay Circus and the Moses Circus before reaching the Baracetta Brothers with whom he founded a circus. Remy and Wettach agree that Wettach joined the Swiss National Circus as a cashier. This may not have been a performance opportunity but it certainly allowed him to see the acts, including the clowns, in rehearsal and performance. It was while he was with the Swiss National Circus that he teamed up with Brick to form an eccentric double act. He may not have been born into the circus, but by 1903 Grock was clearly of the circus. There he remained until, in 1911, he and another clown, Antonet, played the Winter Garden in Berlin.

The central importance of the double act to clowning and Grock's development from junior to senior partner in such pairings offers a further example of an integral feature of clown performance which was adapted by Grock to suit his ambitions. It is common in clowning for clowns to work within a double act, pairing a whiteface with an auguste. The advantage of this pairing is that it supplies various binaries through which the performers can create humour. Brick and Grock encountered both success and difficulties while performing as musical eccentrics within a clown double act. In this double act both clowns were a form of the auguste. While Brick was the more experienced performer, onstage the status and look of the two clowns would have been very similar. This may have limited their comic interaction, as according to Remy 'the two performers … left the ring to general indifference' (2002, 388). The greater the distinction between the clowns, the more binaries there are for them to play with.

Images of augustes and clowns from the early 1900s (Wettach 1931, 1957; Remy 2002; Clair 2004) reveal clear conventions with regard to both costume and make up. This had the advantage of allowing the audience to recognize immediately the elements of the clown double act as the two clowns look very different. The whiteface's costume signifies his superior status and this is supported by the way in which he behaves towards the auguste. The whiteface is always in charge. In Grock's early career this was as true outside the circus ring as it was in it because of the way in which Grock was invited to join the more established whiteface to replace the departing auguste of the original double act. In this way Grock's role was to learn the act as it existed rather than to create new material. It appears that Grock accepted this as part of his training and career trajectory but when he separated from Antonet in 1913 he did not seek another whiteface to perform with. Instead, he took a step which was to shift the way in which clown circus and music hall clown partnerships operated, financially and creatively. Grock, the auguste or musical eccentric, became the hiring partner, taking on the first of many partners whose contribution to the new double act would be to act as Grock's straight man, contributing in the ways dictated by Grock to his now growing entrée. When Grock left Antonet and hired Lola, he became an innovator among augustes by hiring a clown as his stooge and by taking control of the development and rehearsal of the entrée. From this point on his partner's name is not included in any publicity relating to the act. He is always billed as Grock and partner, highlighting the importance of Grock over his partner. He toured Europe as a variety clown, with occasional appearances in circuses before returning to the circus for the final period of his career. By the end of his career his entrée often lasted longer than an hour, and Grock founded his own Variety-Circus in 1951 which allowed him to perform his extended entrée in a circus setting. Whether in music hall or circus he remained instantly recognizable as Grock. As a reviewer of Grock's performance at the Ardwick Empire, Manchester, in May 1919 acknowledged, 'it is too late by far to put Grock forward as a discovery … he is, beyond any question, one of the great men of the music hall'

(*Manchester Guardian*, 13 May 1919). His recognizability and the recognition of his talent rested on his ability to present a persona to his audience; one which allowed him to connect to them and to demonstrate a very high level of skill.

As Grock's career progressed and as he moved further away from a clown double act, reinventing himself as a solo performer, he continued to work with an onstage partner to feed the lines which allowed him to demonstrate his creativity and skill. This shift ensured that the comedy of the act rarely, if ever, derived from the actions of Grock's partner. The partner acted as a foil, creating the situations and offering the cue lines which allowed Grock to move from one section of his entrée to another. The partner dressed in evening wear and wore no clown makeup, looking more like a musician than a clown. According to Towsen, 'while Grock perfected the entrée form, he also turned it into a one-man show, his musical eccentricities existing virtually independently of the whiteface clown. His comic effects were derived from his many props more than from any dramatic conflict with the whiteface clown' (1976: 233). The status interaction of the duo therefore moves to one between Grock and his props. Of central importance is how that interaction is communicated to his audience, and the first step in Grock's process is the establishment and presentation of his clown personality.

Persona

Key to the notion of popular performance is the personality of the performer and the blurring of the distinction between the everyday personality of the performer and the persona of the role performed. Working in either circus or music hall, the persona of the clown can be communicated to the audience through costume, through complicité and through catch phrases. None of these is as simple as they might seem and each is worthy of exploration here. We shall begin with costume. Images of Grock throughout his career indicate that there were at least two major costumes which Wettach used consistently when performing as Grock plus additional costumes which may have been specific to entrées performed with partners when Grock was the junior partner (more on the junior/senior partner distinction to follow later in the chapter). These costumes remain constant whether Grock is performing in the ring or on stage. Clown costumes work very rapidly as signifiers to an audience of the kind of behaviour to be expected from the performer. Towsen (1976), following Perrodil, credits James Guyon with establishing both the character and costume of the auguste. According to Towsen, 'the early auguste usually wore misfit evening clothes … [and] a battered opera hat and white quilted gaiters' (1976: 210). This attire would have formed a strong contrast on stage with the more formal attire of the white face clown typified by much more stylized face make-up and a costume which was covered in sequins to catch the light. Davison suggests that the auguste costume is a parody of the ringmaster's and that as an imposter the auguste 'is not called upon to master any of the skills of the circus. This new clown can be as bad at anything as he wants' (2013: 71). Grock, however, was master of very many skills and in the analysis of three sections of his entrée which follow later in the chapter, it is evident that even when dressed in this parodic costume, his skill level is extremely high and the success of his act relies on his skill, precision and physical control. Grock's particular version of the auguste comprises of trousers which are loose at the waist (allowing him to get his arms stuck inside the trousers), a jacket with sleeves that are slightly too short, a battered hat and white shirt and a simple ribbon tied into a bow. On his feet he wears black elongated clown shoes. In some instances the breasts of his jacket are held together with a very large safety pin. He also wears white gloves. Elements of the costume are significant not only for the look and what they indicate to the audience but also because they can contribute functionally to the development of the act. In both the films of Grock performing, we see Grock remove his gloves, ball them together and proceed to create the illusion that he is juggling with just a single ball. He also makes the ball disappear from behind one leg only to reappear behind the other. Thus the gloves work visually to support the attempt at elegance represented by the evening clothes and they provide the opportunity for the demonstration of two skills: juggling and magic.

Later, as Grock asserts himself as the senior partner and builds his entrée around work he has done with other clowns and skills he possesses, he more commonly begins his act in his other main costume of baggy tartan trousers and an oversized coat, also in a different tartan. From the neck of his jacket we can see that Grock wears a white shirt and a black ribbon bow tie. He still wears the oversized clown shoes and white gloves. At some point Grock fixed upon his distinctive look in terms of make-up and baldness. A description of Grock's first appearance with Antonet mentions his 'bald head and pink face' and the bald cap is evident in images from 1907 onwards (see Wettach 1931). Later (though it is impossible from existing images to identify exactly when) Grock used make-up to emphasize his mouth. The area between the top lip and nose is filled in with white face paint, as is the area from the bottom lip to bottom of chin. His lips are picked out in a darker colour which is also used to define the edges of the area below his bottom lip. Most images of Grock are black and white so precise colours are hard to define, but in many images it also looks as if his cheeks are reddened where the white face paint ends. This makeup works in a number of ways: it draws attention to Grock's mouth, and through the direct contact with his audience of smiles or through allowing his mouth to drop open as if in shock, he establishes complicité.

Complicité was 'a term used by Lecoq to mean shared understanding between two actors or between actors and audience' (2009: 174). For Grock, as for all clowns, this connection with the audience is established by looks (for a more detailed consideration of looks, clock and drops, see Wright 2006), by direct address to the audience or by involving the audience in the performance in some way. Grock does not use this latter technique but there are many points in his entrée where he uses looks to the audience to punctuate the rhythm of the performance and to encourage the audience to feel more actively involved in the act of spectatorship. For Grock these looks are often combined with his two catchphrases. It is a signal of Grock's international appeal that his usual catchphrases exist in both French and German. One phrase translates simply as 'why?' In French it is 'pourquoi?' and in German 'Warum?' Both of these words can be extended beyond their usual length by emphasizing the vowels. This makes the catchphrase seem more important and highlights the childlike aspect of Grock in performance. His other catchphrase, 'nicht möglich/sans blague', is usually translated into English as 'no kidding' and once more the vowels can be extended to emphasize the phrase. In these moments Grock uses the catchphrases to communicate his difficulty in understanding the world to his audience. Often the lines are used in response to some information given to Grock by his partner about what is expected of him in the way of behaviour.

Taken together, Grock's costume, make-up and catchphrases create a clown persona which appeals to the audience equally well in the ring and on stage, through his seeming simplicity. His incomprehension of the world is signalled through all three of these elements. The childlike look of his make-up and childlike nature of his catchphrases encourage the audience to feel sympathy towards him and to be on his side.

Audience

The development of Grock's entrée from the 'usual 10–20 minute entrée in the circus' (Davison 2013: 10) to over an hour (Remy 2002: 407), made it difficult for the entrée to be contained within a standard circus programme which relied on a quick turnover of acts so Grock turned to music hall venues where he had much success from 1911 onwards. It will be useful, therefore, to consider the different expectations audiences may have had in the two locations and the different demands that the common performance venues of circus and music hall make on the performer. Grock alludes to the change in performance style necessary when he moved from circus to stage in *Life's a Lark* when describing an attempt made by Antonet and Grock to perform in a music hall in Berlin in 1911. 'It's one thing to have your audience all around you and another in front of you. Your turn in the circus ring must be bold and exaggerated … but a music hall turn must be altogether on a smaller scale, much more sharply defined' (Wettach 1931: 45–46). There are two key elements here: the arrangement of performer and audience and the level of playing required. Music hall stages position the performer end on to the audience. There is no need, as there is in circus, to play in the round taking into account an audience which virtually surrounds you. Also in a music hall theatre, the performer is normally on a stage above the audience in the stalls with no easy means of access to them. The performer also has to acknowledge those audience members positioned above him in the circle and upper circle. In the circus the performer begins on the same level as the ringside members of the audience. There is always the possibility that the performer may cross out of the ring into the audience. In terms of establishing a connection with the audience, looks can be directed to the audience more easily, but a potential downside of music hall performance (despite Grock's comment about the necessity of a smaller playing scale) is that the audience may be much further away from the performer than in the circus. Grock commonly performed at the London Coliseum (which opened in 1904 and rapidly became a leading music hall venue) which had an audience capacity of 2359. He also commonly performed at the Cirque Medrano which used a permanent circus building in the centre of Paris. The audience here would have been even larger than that of the Coliseum. The building (now known as the Cirque d'Hiver) originally held 3,900 seated in three concentric circles. Still this building had no stage and the ringside audience members would have been much closer to the performers than was possible in the Coliseum.

The entrées available to us from the film of Grock's work provide examples of Grock working the audience from both the music hall stage and the circus ring and the techniques used remain remarkably constant. The 'Drum' sequence shows Grock in the ring with Antonet. Grock enters from behind Antonet carrying a chair which he puts down and stands on. From this vantage point he looks at the audience and with this look begins to establish his connection with the audience. He extends the connection by smiling and by waving at someone. He acknowledges the existence of the audience far more than he acknowledges the existence of his partner. As the sequence progresses he begins to play on the drum he has with him and he smiles broadly at the audience as if he expects them to enjoy his playing. As the audience laughs more loudly, Grock turns, smiles at the audience and flops his hand around in pleasure. This is a clear example of connection with the audience in the here and now and the nature of the clown entrée means that either clown is free to respond, in the moment, to reactions from the audience, endowing the audience with an element of control over the speed at which the act continues.

The camera frequently pans away from the performers to show the audience reaction, but even when the camera is trained on Antonet and Grock it is often possible to see the audience behind the performers on the far side of the ring. Nonetheless, the act itself is played largely to the front, except for some moments when the performers appeal to the audience for a reaction. Antonet looks all around the ring when he is first interrupted by Grock in order to draw the audience into his frustration and Grock does it to a lesser extent when he smiles in response to the audience's laughter. Most important though is to note the way in which Grock uses regular looks, predominantly to the front, to engage the audience. The same technique for audience engagement is at play in the 'Violin and Piano' sequence.

This sequence is filmed as performed on a stage rather than in a circus ring, with Max Van Embden as his partner. Embden, wearing evening dress, is not presented visually or in performance style as a clown and does nothing to generate laughter. As the sequence opens, Embden is on stage and Grock enters from the wings carrying a large suitcase and a chair. He looks towards the audience, smiles and opens the suitcase and extracts a miniature violin establishing an early incongruity. He smiles at the audience again as he takes out the violin, drawing a laugh and strengthening his connection with them. He puts the case upstage near the backdrop and comes back to Embden smiling at the audience and looking very pleased with himself. As the sequence continues Grock grins at the audience a number of times. Each time he grins it serves to highlight a moment where Grock feels he has excelled himself and the look or grin usually provokes laugher from the audience. Turning away from Van Embden he adjusts the position of his chair with his violin sticking out behind him. Emden lifts the bottom of the violin and Grock kicks out behind him, knocking Emden's fingers away. Grock then tries to stand on the chair. This section of the sequence is an example of the paradox which lies at the heart of much clowning: the demonstration of incompetence but an incompetence which can only be displayed because of the great skill of the performer.

Skill

A number of key features have been identified in earlier works analysing clown performance by Peacock, Simon and Davison. Davison indicates that Grock's performance is 'a catalogue of odd behaviour: accidents, upsets, failures, surprising or unusual uses of objects, verbal misunderstandings, misbehaving bodies, bizarre yet logical thinking and sudden emotional shifts' (Davison 2013: 14). This list of elements is not so different from the list of deviations from the norm which I suggested in 2009 in *Serious Play.* These include behavioural deviance ('interacting with objects in ways which are not common in everyday life' [Peacock 2009: 26]); disruption of performance conventions and linguistic variation. I also suggest that clown routines and actions can be classified into types such as '"interruption of ceremony", "subversion and parody", "physical skill" … "incompetence", "interaction with objects", interaction with other clowns", "status", "food" and, more recently, "the exploration of the human condition"' (23). Not all of these elements are to be found in Grock's performance but a significant number are included. Grock interrupts ceremony by disrupting the attempted musical performance of his partner. He makes unexpected use of objects, for example, balancing his violin bow on his foot rather than using it as a bow. Indeed for Grock any item on the stage may be used in unexpected ways. The lid of the piano designed to cover the keyboard is pulled off to become a slide. In his memoirs he recounts how he stumbled upon this very successful business as a result of his spontaneous, frustrated response to Antonet who was performing badly having lost a lot of money gambling. Provoked by Antonet, Wettach explains how as Grock he tore the lid off the keyboard section of the piano and chased Antonet with it. Antonet fled and Grock went to place the lid back but realized it was easier to prop it up against the side of the piano. He let his hat slide down it and 'the great inspiration came! Why not toboggan down after my hat? I climbed up on to the piano, slid down the slope straight after my hat' (Wettach 1957: 86). Wettach created this sequence between 1911 and 1913 (when he stopped working with Antonet) and it is captured on film in 1931 and again in *Au Revoir M. Grock* in 1950. Wettach was able to respond spontaneously to the situation he found himself in and in so doing generated wonderful new material.

Grock also provides us with examples of incompetence. One instance of this is provided in his entrée when he gets his hands stuck inside his trouser pockets. Status and interaction lie at the heart of the entrée because it is the struggle for supremacy between Grock and his props which is one of the elements that provokes the audience's laughter. Linguistic variation or deviation is also a repeated feature of the entrée as recorded in both 1931 and 1950. Grock replies in several languages but misidentifies them, asking his partner why he is speaking Spanish when the partner is speaking English. When pushed to identify his own nationality he offers the word Catholic rather than saying he is Swiss. In the 1931 version of his entrée he gives his name as something which his partner cannot pronounce because it begins with a whistling sound that only Grock can make. This brief list demonstrates why Grock's entrée might provide a rich source for analysing the characteristics of clown performance. Consequently what follows is a more detailed analysis of the 'Drum Entrée' (already considered previously in relation to audience interaction).

This is a filmed reconstruction of an act from early in Grock's career with the older, more experienced Grock revisiting his earlier performance. Still it provides a valid example of the way in which the act would have been performed and thus affords the opportunity for the analysis of a number of elements of clown performance. As the entrée opens, Antonet, in typical whiteface makeup and costume, is playing the violin. He is upstaged by Grock's entrance, behind him, from the opening to the circus ring. Grock is wearing baggy tartan trousers, elongated clown shoes, a loose black overcoat and a battered hat. Immediately a visual contrast is established, one which also provokes expectations in the mind of the audience as to what may occur. As Grock enters, he is wearing a large bass drum, supported by shoulder straps, and he is dragging a chair behind him. He then proceeds to beat the bass drum and to sing in an inarticulate child-like way. The impact is one of noise rather than music, in contrast to the beautiful playing of Antonet. Antonet stops playing, turns and stares at Grock who continues to play before slowing to a stop and looking at Antonet in surprise. Antonet puts his violin to his chin and as soon as he begins to play Grock beats his drum. At this point, Grock is fulfilling the role of the typical auguste. He appears not to understand the convention which dictates that he should not disrupt his partner's playing. This is reinforced by the fact that Grock's beating is now more enthusiastic. This suggests the possibility of conflict or some kind of statue tussle between Grock and Antonet. Antonet stops him again. Grock explains that he is trying to serenade his love and, as he makes this claim, the spotlight picks out a woman in the audience, suggesting that she is object of his affections. Antonet tells him that he should serenade using a violin or a mandolin, but with a typical auguste's disregard for the norm Grock tells him simply that his love favours the drum, as if it should have occurred to Antonet that this might be the case. In a show of his higher status position, Antonet makes Grock take the drum off. Grock puts the drum down and makes a great show of throwing the beater and straps to the ground, and in doing so he is responding to the laughter from the audience. Grock suggests that he might sing and Antonet offers to accompany him. Grock sings sweetly, wringing his hands a little and creating a pathetic impression. His facial expressions are exaggerated which reinforce the clown nature of his persona. As the song comes to an end Grock takes several steps backwards, waving his arms gently in time to the song. He stumbles and crashes backwards onto the drum. The skin breaks and Grock ends sitting in the drum, unable to get out. This is an example of clown incompetence or failure. The singing had been going well but as soon as the auguste appears to be in some way competent that competence has to be fractured and the auguste is brought, literally in this case, crashing down to earth. Some elements of Grock's musical skill were in evidence in this entrée in that Grock sings well but beyond that this entrée represents a fairly simple example of the way in which a clown double act entrée might develop between a conventional whiteface and auguste combination.

Grock's skills, both physical and musical, are foregrounded in the 'Violin and Piano' sequence. In this there is a moment shortly after his entrance when Grock tries to stand on the chair but his foot slips off. This generates the first laugh from the audience, supporting the notion that there is a pleasure for clown audiences in feeling superior to the clown. Next he lifts his right foot onto the chair with his hand and tries again to stand on the chair. He slips again but manages to turn the slip into balancing on the chair which tips from side to side (controlled by Grock just as it looks as if he is losing control). He gains his balance and smiles at the audience. He then balances his bow upright on the tip of his shoe. Neither object is intended to be used in the way Grock uses them but, in misusing them, he displays great skill in balance. Embden tries to take the bow but Grock controls it, takes it and looks pityingly at Embden. Grock then scrapes his chin with the violin as if shaving, again using an object against its purpose. Grock positions the bow in his right hand ready to play but as he lets go of it, it slips through his fingers. He catches it at the point that it would slide through his hand to fall to the floor. He grips the tip with his left hand only for it to fall again. He repeats this for a third time. Repetition is often used in this way in a clown entrée to assist in structuring the act and in building and controlling audience expectations. Finally he grabs the bottom of the bow firmly and proceeds to tune the violin. He takes a balloon from his pocket, blows it up and holds it so that air escapes making a high pitched squeal. He then plays a note on the violin which is very close to being in tune with the balloon note.

He looks extremely pleased with himself. With some difficulty he puts the still squealing balloon back in his pocket. Throughout this Embden stands looking slightly bewildered. When Grock finally begins to play, two things become clear: despite its size the violin is perfectly playable and despite his incompetence up to this point Grock is an extremely talented musician. He ends by sliding down onto the chair and spinning the violin round and round on the end of his bow. Both he and Embden look surprised. Grock then stares at the spinning violin in concentration before intercepting it to stop it. This sequence is representative of clown performance in that it demonstrates an unusual approach to the world and to the props that make up the immediate world of the performer. It also allows Grock to demonstrate his skills, physical and musical, while establishing a strong connection to the audience.

It is not possible to leave Grock without considering one of his most popular tricks. This might even be considered his signature, as much a signifier of Grock as his catchphrases. The sequence comes towards the end of his entrée after the 'Violin and Piano' sequence. It begins with Grock standing on a chair playing his concertina. The chair seat gives way and Grock falls through. He looks at the audience to register the event. He then gathers himself and jumps back up so that he lands in a sitting position on the back of the chair with his legs crossed, the supporting foot resting on the outside edge of the chair seat. He looks at his audience again and readies himself to play. There is much to unpack here. The level of skill involved is high, likely to impress his audience, particularly as he could still achieve this trick in 1950 at seventy years of age. He punctuates the demonstration of skill with looks to the audience which signal first that this is a mishap from which he must extricate himself and second that he is proud of having done so in such a skilful way. His solution would be a surprise to anyone who has not seen the trick before as there are more obvious ways for him to get out. For anybody who knows what is coming next, there is a moment of anticipation before a feeling of delight at witnessing such skill. Many circus clowns were highly skilled but Grock is perhaps unusual in having such a range of skills. He was an innovator in the way he developed his entrée.

Conclusion

Grock's career is marked by his ability to adapt and refine the nature of clown. He developed and innovated, moving between circus and music hall in a way unusual at the time. While his clown persona remained constant, certainly from 1911 onwards, Grock refused to be limited by expectations and, as a result of his skill, developed a level of fame and wealth which allowed him to extend the limits of the traditional clown entrée to the extent that it can be seen as the template which allowed clown theatre to develop subsequently. In Grock's entrée the whole act revolved around him and invited the audience into the world that he created. Clowns since have continued to adapt and innovate in ways which echo Grock. Slava Polunin occupies the pivotal position in *Slava's Snowshow* (a title like that of Grock's performances which does not acknowledge the names of other performers). In addition, Polunin extended the scope of the entrée to include a more overtly theatrical setting than Grock's. Polunin's show, like Grock's, seeks to communicate something about the nature of existence. In a 1919 review of Grock, the reviewer ventures, 'one wonders whether his "turn" is not the considered expression of a view of life which sees us all as children very much bewildered by the perplexity of life' (*Manchester Guardian*, 13 May 1919) and in doing so he identifies the universal appeal of Grock's clowning which plays equally well to adults and children; to royalty and to ordinary people and to audiences of all nationalities. In this, Grock may be claimed to be a genius among clowns and represents a comprehensive example of this form of popular performance.

Notes

1 'The Coliseum', *Times* [London, England] 7 May 1918: 3. *The Times Digital Archive*. Web. 21 August 2014.
2 Grock is the name given to the clown created by Adrien Wettach.
3 *La Vie D'un Artist* (1931) and *Au Revoir M. Grock* (1950).

4 Brick was the stage name of Marius Galante who earlier performed as part of an August double act with a partner name Brock.

References

Billon, Pierre (dir.) (1950), *Au Revoir M. Grock*. https://www.youtube.com/watch?v=SlEI5YjkMus (accessed 27 September 2015).

Boese, Carl (dir.) (1931), *La Vie d'un Grand Artiste*. https://www.youtube.com/watch?v=SNm4JJDYipY (accessed 15 September 2015).

Clair, Jean (ed.) (2004), *The Great Parade: Portrait of the Artist as Clown*. New Haven: Yale University Press.

Davison, Jon (2013), *Clown: Readings in Theatre Practice*. Basingstoke: Palgrave.

Disher, Maurice Willson (1925), *Clowns and Pantomimes*. London: Constable.

Lecoq, Jacques (2009), *The Moving Body*. London: Methuen.

Mayer, David, and Kenneth Richards (1977), *Western Popular Theatre*. London: Methuen.

Peacock, Louise (2009), *Serious Play: Modern Clown Performance*. Bristol: Intellect.

Remy, Tristan (1997), *Clown Scenes*. Chicago: Ivan R Dee.

Remy, Tristan (2002), *Les Clowns*. Paris: Grasset.

Schecter, Joel (2003), *Popular Theatre: A Sourcebook*. London: Routledge.

Towsen, John (1976), *Clowns*. New York: Dutton.

'Variety Theatres' (1919), *Manchester Guardian*. 13 May, 8.

Wettach, Adrien (1931), *Life's a Lark*. London: Heinemann.

Wettach, Adrien (1957), *Grock: King of Clowns*. London: Methuen.

Wright, John (2006), *Why Is That So Funny? A Practical Exploration of Physical Comedy*. London: Nick Hern.

6

Something Wicked: The Theatre of Derren Brown

Michael Mangan

Introduction: The live and the mediated

This essay will explore contemporary stage magic by focusing on the work of Derren Brown, drawing on analyses of some key recent performances, his own published writings, his contributions to social media, and interviews that he has given both to myself and others. Brown is a particularly good case study for the purposes of this volume and this chapter for three reasons. First, his performances encapsulate many of the things that are typical of stage magic now and in the past. Second, in other respects he is also a rather unique performer, not only in being one of the best and most successful of contemporary British magicians, but also in exploring the boundaries of this form of popular performance. Third, because he is a high-profile performer, he is well enough known for his work to be accessible, even familiar, to most readers – if not from live performances, then from recorded television broadcasts of those performances, or from thematic TV 'specials' (both of which are documented online).

The choice of such a high-profile performer, though, raises certain issues for the analysis of 'popular performance'. Like many forms of popular performance, magic exists on a number of professional and amateur levels. At one end are a small number of well-known 'personality' performers, primarily those who have made their names on television. However,

> it's a tip of the iceberg thing. There is only a tiny percentage of magicians who are known … At least, there is a very huge number who are very well known *amongst the profession* … But you couldn't list ten magicians who are very well known [to the general public]. (Brown 2014b)

There are thousands of less well-known professional, semi-professional and non-professional magicians plying their trade throughout the UK. They spend most of their time on close-up magic and 'working the room', doing tricks with cards, coins, silks, ropes and everyday objects; performing mentalist routines, sleights of hand, physical feats such as escapology and so on. They buy equipment from specialist magic shops and websites, they form both online and real-world communities and they hold regular meetings to support each other, develop skills and promote the art. They work as children's entertainers, as street buskers, as featured acts on variety bills, at corporate events, weddings and private parties, typically charging between £150 and £400 per hour (Reyes 2013). So while we will be focusing on one high-profile performer, it is important to acknowledge that magic continues to flourish as a form of performance that is 'popular' in that other sense of having a widespread grassroots-level presence. But that grassroots presence also serves as a reminder that the relationship between liveness and mediatization in popular performance is a paradoxical one (see Auslander 1999). A distinguishing feature of much popular performance – a feature that in part defines this present collection of essays – is that it is rooted in the present moment, directly acknowledging the reality of the performance situation, its venue and its audience, with whom the performer establishes a direct connection. All of which, of course, are potentially compromised by mediatization.

Even so, all forms of popular performances since the early twentieth century have had to embrace, first, the recorded and broadcast media, and then more recently digital and social media. Magic, more than most, needs television and the internet to maintain its position as a genuinely popular form rather than a niche activity for hobbyists. From this has developed a complex symbiosis between the live performance and the digital/broadcast performance. And so Derren Brown's live shows sell out regularly because of his established TV presence, both in edited versions of his stage shows and in documentary-style television 'specials', such as *Apocalypse* (2012), which often take the form of elaborate practical jokes. Conversely, the appeal of his TV shows is enhanced by the fact that he is also known as a live performer: all his recent live shows have been filmed, then broadcast in an edited form after the event; the presence of a live audience offers a sense of immediacy and an implied guarantee (on one level at least) of the 'authenticity' of the performance. At the same time these shows themselves have incorporated video, digital and social media. In 2005–6 *Something Wicked This Way Comes* featured a complex finale using video cameras and playback. In 2015–16, as *Miracle* continues to tour, Brown's website blog asks readers to send videos 'that capture a special event or moment in your life' (Brown 2015a), while his Twitter account asks his followers to 'Please tweet any word using #DerrenMiracle & be part of tonight's show' (Brown 2015b).

But while these media can be incorporated into the magician's routine and utilized, they also pose a threat. Increasingly sophisticated film, video and digital technologies have led to increasingly sophisticated viewing audiences, for whom the pleasures of witnessing the impossible have become almost commonplace. At the same time, a simple Google search will bring up any number of explanations and video demonstrations of how various effects are achieved. Part of the job of the contemporary conjuror, consequently, has been to restore a sense of naïvety – hence the inevitable disclaimers reassuring us that 'No actors or stooges were used in the making of this programme and there has been no prior preparation with any members of the audience' (Brown 2013–14). The broadcast audience has, for the most part, accepted this implied contract, and as a result television magic shows can still command reasonable, if not astronomical ratings. Of the live shows which are discussed later, edited television versions of two – *Svengali* (2011–12) and *Infamous* (2013–14) – have been broadcast by Channel 4 and are, at the time of writing, available for viewing online. No digital record in the public domain currently exists of the third, *Miracle*, which is touring until July 2016.

Miracle (1): The secrets of magicians

At the start of *Miracle*, and in the accompanying printed and digital promotional material, the audience is repeatedly asked not to reveal to anyone else what goes on in the performance, verbally, pictorially or otherwise because 'it is important that the show's content remains secret' (Brown 2015–16; see also Billington 2014; Rudin 2015; Whitehouse 2015).

Magicians are famously secretive about their art – and for good reason. The relationship between what the audience sees, or believes it sees, and the methods which are used to create an effect, lie at the heart of most magic acts. And while in theory it is possible for a magician to copyright or patent a particular effect under the intellectual property legislation of many countries (traditionally by classing it as a performance narrative such as a pantomime), the paradox remains that in order to register such a copyright, the jealously guarded details have to be put into the public domain via the copyright or patent office concerned! No wonder then, that individual magicians guard their performance secrets fiercely, or that the magicians' fraternity upholds a code of secrecy which it takes with great seriousness.

Yet this 'secrecy' is also itself partially a matter of smoke and mirrors. All the great magicians, from Robert-Houdin to Harry Houdini, from Blackstone to Blaine and Brown, have cashed in on their fame by publishing works which let the general reader in on *some* of the tricks of the conjuror's trade – sometimes, it must be admitted, rather well-worn ones, but genuine techniques nonetheless (see Robert-Houdin 1881; Houdini 1927; Blackstone 1985; Blaine 2002; Brown 2010). The secrets of other illusions can be bought over the counter in many a specialist magic store or through commercial and personal websites and blogs. The magicians' code of secrecy is woven in glamour, but it has a pragmatic economic base to it.

Even so, a performing art which takes as one of its axioms that its techniques should be kept secret offers certain problems in terms of academic research and publishing. And in the light of this, courtesy, research ethics and academic rigour come into conflict: having been specifically asked not do so, how appropriate is it to talk about *Miracle* while the live tour continues?

But the question itself may be a meaningless one. One of the major secrets that Brown himself reveals is that

> [a]t least half of any trick happens after it is over … This finishing process occurs as the spectator reconstructs the trick, ready to tell his friends; as he edits and deletes all the errors and bias of personal memory; as he ensures the trick sounds impressive enough to enthuse others and save him sounding too easily duped. The magician plants all the seeds needed to ensure that this inevitable process works in favour of a true miracle. (Brown 2010: chapter 2)

This revelation that 'at least half of any trick happens after it is over' might trouble some of the usual expectations of the scholar of popular performance, since it runs counter to our sense of the importance of the moment of 'presence': that which happens at the immediate point of engagement between the performer and the audience. And it is true, of course, that if the magician cannot carry off an effective illusion in that moment, then no amount of post-show reconstruction or mental re-editing will turn a clumsy routine into a miracle. But Brown's 'confession' that much of the work is being done for the magician by the audience after the event rings true: social and perceptual psychologists are only too aware of the amount of misperception and misreporting that goes on in our everyday lives. Still, if what Brown says is true, the injunctions to secrecy at the beginning of *Miracle* and many of Brown's other shows is … what? Reverse psychology? Misdirection?

Svengali: Mentalism and magic

Although he himself is (understandably) not fond of the term, Brown is best known as a 'mentalist'. Mentalism is a branch of stage magic which includes a range of activities apparently involving mind-reading, hypnotism, psychokinesis, telepathy and a range of occult or psychic powers. It should be emphasized, however, that all these are still, essentially, a form of conjuring or stage magic. Most successful conjurors try out various branches of the art early in their careers, and then specialize as they develop their own 'voice' and persona. Brown's own early professional act included a wide range of (fairly) standard card tricks, with his own variations on classic routines. His later career has focused more on 'mind control' and mentalist routines; but all this remains within the field of magic, and many of Brown's 'mind control' routines overtly use the same techniques that he explains in *Confessions of a Conjuror* in terms of card tricks (Brown 2010: chapter 2). To be sure, mentalism has its own specialist techniques, just as tricks with coins or cards or grand levitation or disappearance illusions have their own specialist techniques; and some practitioners specialize in one thing and others in another. However, most of the principles of the mentalist's act are the same as those of any other branch of stage magic; it relies on basic techniques of conjuring: misdirection, dexterity, palming, specialist doctored equipment, forcing, substitution and so on.

To say this is not to give away any deep secret of Derren Brown's, or any other mentalist's art: standard books on mental magic, such as Theodore Annemann's *Practical Mental Magic*, Marc Lemezma's *Mind Magic* and Brown's own *Tricks of the Mind*, detail how such-and-such a routine, which appears to 'demonstrate your wonderful powers of telepathy,' is actually effected by means of a substitution effected by 'cross-cut force' or some similar standard technique of legerdemain (Lemezma 2003: 33, 35; see also Nelms 1969: 8).

It was during the so-called Golden Age of stage magic in the nineteenth century that mental magic rose to prominence, as a result of a concatenation of circumstances. With the advent of telegraphy, telephony and, later, wireless broadcasting, science and technology had established that 'invisible' communication was not only a theoretical possibility but an everyday reality. At the other end of the cultural spectrum, there was a growing interest in psychic phenomena and in the possibility that a sufficiently sensitive person might be able to tune in both to messages from the spirit world and to 'telepathic' communications from living persons – either with or without the consent of the sender. Somewhere between the scientific and the spiritual lay the development of clinical hypnotism – popularized by the well-qualified but not entirely respectable Franz Anton Mesmer. A man of medicine, Mesmer was also a showman and a charlatan. Nonetheless, he was onto something; and while many of his peers believed his theories of 'mesmerism' (hypnotism) and of 'animal magnetism' to be completely fraudulent, the therapeutic claims of his theory could be evidenced, and he laid the foundations of medical hypnosis used by leading 'alienists' of the nineteenth century and thereby to Freud's investigation of the subconscious.

The rise of the mentalist act shows magicians doing what they had always done: seizing on an idea that was already rooted in the popular imagination and exploiting it for their own ends, taking it to extremes to frame their effects within a narrative which – to an audience of the time – would both make sense in terms of that audience's existing picture of the world ('invisible communication is a reality according to the laws of nature') and also leave room for the wonder and amazement that is an essential response to the magician's performance.

But if magic can absorb and appropriate current ideas, events and ideologies, it can also be damaged by them. Stage hypnotism itself underwent a drastic decline at the beginning of the twenty-first century following a series of court cases, such as *Howarth v Green* (2002), relating to incidents in which subjects claimed to have suffered real-life psychological disturbances as a result of being hypnotized on stage. Brown has distanced himself from the term, explaining that

> I'm not using formal hypnosis ... [And] there are all sorts of problems if you're known as a hypnotist in terms of getting gigs and all sorts of legal issues. I use it covertly, but at that point it ceases to be hypnosis, it becomes ... suggestion, or waking hypnosis, or something that isn't strictly speaking hypnosis per se. (Carpenter 2003)

Instead, he began to define a form of mentalist act which reinvented old routines for a new generation, and which became known by the name of the early television shows: *Mind Control*. *Mind Control* combined two key elements: there was the traditional magician's mind-reading act – but this was now framed, not as a demonstration of occult or psychic powers, but as the consequence of Brown's advanced understanding of social and personal psychology. The explanation of the effects, we are assured, lie in Brown's ability to read body language, to understand and predict how an individual will react to certain stimuli and to influence his subjects' thoughts, not through occult 'powers' but with the aid of science, by planting subliminal images which manipulate the mind at an unconscious level. The mentalist act is framed and explained in terms of rational scepticism, and current scientific psychological models. Nor is this altogether a deception: after all, one reason why so many academic psychologists are interested in magic is the fact that *all* magicians use and exploit an understanding of our regular habits of perception and of the ways in which we construct reality. They use this to guide us towards the response they most want, to misdirect our attention while a substitution takes place, or to force a particular card on us (see Lamont and Wiseman 1999). There *is* an element of 'mind control' in even the most traditional of card and coin tricks.

The relationship between mentalism and other forms of magic is nicely illustrated in the routine with which *Svengali* opens: Brown, wearing only one shoe, enters in the high-energy persona of a crass TV game show host in order to challenge the audience to a 'game' of 'Where's Derren's Other Shoe?' – a particularly frivolous version of the eternal classic conjuror's routine known variously as the Cups-and-Balls, or the Shell Game. This is, literally, one of the oldest tricks in the book and certainly one of the oldest for which we have any kind of reliable visual evidence: Hieronymus Bosch's painting *The Conjuror*, which shows the Cups-and-Balls routine being performed by a street-corner trickster, dates from c. 1480. (It has also been claimed, although more contentiously, that visual archaeological evidence from a tomb dating back to 2500 BC demonstrates that it was popular in ancient

Egypt [Dekker 1993: 123–24; see also Wilkinson 1878].) The Cups-and-Balls routine is often regarded as one of the fundamentals of good conjuring: the great Robert-Houdin, doyen of conjurors in the Golden Age, devoted a whole chapter to it in his foundational text on conjuring (Robert-Houdin 1868). It employs all the classic techniques of the conjuror: sleight of hand, physical misdirection – and control of the audience's perception through well-judged 'patter'. The basic idea is simple: the audience (or, when played for money on street corners, the 'mark') is invited to guess under which cup a ball is hidden. The audience will always guess wrong, of course – and in Brown's version of the game, which scales the objects up so as to involve three shoeboxes and his right shoe, the same rule applies: the magician is always one step ahead of the audience.

It is one of the commonplaces of the conjuror's art that effective use of patter is one of the keys to making a simple routine effective. It frames the sleight of hand, it diverts attention from the palmed object, it disguises the fact that the equipment may not be quite what it appears to be. In his 'Shoes and Boxes' version of this classic routine, Brown's patter draws attention to the very techniques of psychological manipulation and 'mind control' on which he built his early reputation. He starts the game by offering the audience as a whole the opportunity to vote, by the volume of their applause, as to which box the shoe is under; and when we inevitably get it wrong, he acknowledges (perfectly truthfully) that 'It's not too difficult to manipulate an entire crowd, but the fewer of you there are, the more of a challenge it is' (Brown 2011–12). And so he homes in on individual audience members.

A randomly chosen couple are challenged first: but before they are given the chance to choose Box #1, #2 or #3, they are told to remember that they have 'a completely three choice'. The audience giggles to itself – and was that a gesture with three fingers that Brown made there? We've spotted how the trick is done, haven't we? Isn't it that auto suggestion, the 'subliminal advertising' thing that we have seen him doing before, on TV specials such as the original *Mind Control* programmes, or in live shows such as *Something Wicked This Way Comes* (2005–6). He has even explained it in the past – this is how advertisers manipulate us, through words and pictures that we half-perceive, by subliminal suggestions that sneak in under our conscious controls and nudge us in the direction of buying one product rather than another (Mangan 2007: 178–80). So, planting the idea of Box #3 in the minds of the couple by saying 'three choice' instead of 'free choice' is … Well, actually, isn't it too obvious? Surely we can't have spotted it that easily?

And the way that the patter develops demonstrates that indeed we can't. A further series of other manipulative tricks are dangled in front of us, each implying a rational explanation of how Brown can 'control' the minds of his subjects.

> I'm going to want a joint decision from you … and what's interesting is this. Ian is on the left, Louise is on the right, so Ian will be naturally drawn to box number one, the one on the left and Louise will be naturally drawn to box number three, the one on the right … So if between them they go to number one, we can presume that Ian is the dominant partner in this relationship because Louise will have submitted to his natural instinct; and likewise if they go for number three we can presume the Louise is the decision-maker in this household. Is that clear Ian and Louise? We *ARE* judging you (Brown 2011–12).

Again, the manipulation is so obvious that the audience laughs. And again, whatever the subjects guess, they get it wrong. Another audience member is challenged and subjected this time to a high-speed and extremely confusing lecture both on the psychology of bluffing and double-bluffing and also on the unlikely statistics of why changing your mind is always a good idea – before she once again chooses the wrong box.

And of course we know that she *will* choose wrongly. If she gets it right, the show is as good as over – so the laws of theatre demand that she get it wrong. The question the audience is invited to ask itself is, *why* does she get it wrong? Everything about Brown's patter insists that it is because he is controlling her mind, through logic, through argument, through force of personality, through sharper intelligence, through his ability to confuse, through some kind of psychic force … At which point it is worth repeating: the majority of the mentalist's effects are brought about by the traditional skills of the stage magician: dexterity, palming, specialist doctored equipment, forcing, substitution, misdirection and so on. The skill of a practitioner as brilliant as Derren Brown lies in his ability to make us forget that, even as we suspect it to be true.

Infamous: Persona and performance

One of the most important elements of a magician's show is the persona he creates, and 'with the *persona* you create, there's a sort of narrative that comes with it' (Brown 2014b). And usually, of course, that persona is a complete fabrication. After all,

> magicians lie by the very nature of what they do … Magicians lie about their origin, their nationality, their education … Magicians tell you their equipment came from some exotic flea market, from their ancestors, from the attic of a haunted house. Lies, more lies. They talk about fantastic feats they have performed. Still more lies. And when they retire and write their memoirs, they lie there, too. (Crasson 1999)

These lies, and the 'dishonesty' that Brown talks about in the epigraph to this chapter, are nowhere more apparent than in the elaborate personae that conjurors have traditionally created for themselves. Extravagant names, tag lines and overblown PR were all part of the act for performers such as 'Professor Anderson – The Great Wizard of the North', 'Houdini – The Handcuff King', 'Mysterious Mahendra', 'Hermann the Great', 'Newmann the Great' and so on. Fashions in dress as well as fashions in nomenclature have come and gone. Early modern conjurors (or jugglers as they were called) tended to portray themselves as exotics. By the nineteenth century, Robert-Houdin's advice to the would-be magician that 'the ordinary dress of a gentleman is the only costume appropriate to a high-class conjuror' (Robert-Houdin 1889: 36) was being widely heeded, and the (usefully multipocketed) tail suit and (easily gimmicked) top hat became de rigueur. Harry Houdini inherited that tradition, but then broke the mould by taking most of his clothes off and displaying his naked and vulnerable (but admirably muscled) body for many of his most famous effects. The majority of Houdini's contemporaries such as Harry Kellar (1849–1922), Howard Thurston (1869–1936) and their followers continued to follow Robert-Houdin's advice and repeatedly referenced all the signs of the perfectly socialized nineteenth-century gentleman – although the imagery of orientalism and the exotic retained its popularity too. Some performers, such as Alexander ('The Man who Knows'), combined the two, wearing both a turban – again, handily gimmicked to aid his mentalism act – and white tie and tails.

The contemporary magician tends to eschew such outdated imagery, and the revival of magic in the age of television has led to a greater variety of available images. The traditional top-hat-and-tails is still to be seen occasionally, but the persona of the stage magician is now far less dependent on the semiotics of either class or race. (The semiotics of gender, on the other hand, remain comparatively stable, since the profession continues to be dominated by men.) But while the details might change, the persona remains an important part of the magician's toolkit, both onstage and off. Just as magicians blur the boundaries between reality and illusion in a performance, so they have traditionally maintained a continuum between the stage persona and the offstage self in everyday life. It is in keeping with one of the basic principles of magic – that the real work takes place before the audience is even aware that the trick has started, and keeping up a sense of mystique even when not apparently 'on duty' can be valuable in enhancing the effectiveness of the performance itself. However, in an age of commodified celebrity, where questions of whether (and if so, how) to keep some kind of distance between the public and private spheres are always problematic, this may also put a particular strain on the performer.

Brown has addressed this continuum between the stage persona and the private individual directly. In 2007, in his mid-thirties ('really late', as he himself puts it) he came out as a gay man, announcing the fact in an interview for *The Independent* (Brown 2014a; see also Alexander 2014). Talking about this relationship between the performing and the private selves he said:

> I've never really seen the question of sexuality as part of what I do. It's not central to it, it's just me ... I came out really late, and it's just not worth doing it that late, you miss a lot of time ... I don't 'not talk about' [my personal life], I don't want to be too precious about it! But I was snapped walking down the road with my partner, and the headline was 'the look of love: Brown clearly adores his partner' ... it's nothing negative, it just leaves a bit of a nasty taste in your mouth, and feels a bit intrusive. I understand you have to put up with a certain amount of it ... but when it's about your relationship, or judgments being made about what you do and what your tastes are, you have to draw a line. (Brown 2014a)

This is, perhaps, pretty much the conventional discourse of celebrity. But Brown has also woven his own personal life into his stage show, in a way that problematizes that discourse.

Brown has developed a stage persona with two main aspects to it. First, there is the traditional fast-talking showman, bantering and joking with the audience. But alongside this is another persona: that of the intellectual and scholar. In many of his recent shows Brown has delivered what appears to be a learned paper on the history of magic or related topics. Thus in *Svengali* he bases much of the second half of the show on a history of the automaton; in *Miracle* he gives a talk on faith healing. This 'intellectual' side of his persona, in fact, has something of a contemporary Renaissance man about it: Brown's live shows typically include a range of references to disciplines such as philosophy, psychotherapy, cultural history, social psychology, fine art, the psychology of perception, the history of religion and (one is encouraged to suspect) more or less anything else to which he decides to turn his hand. As theatre critic Michael Billington put it, Brown is 'a sharp-brained figure who can do old-fashioned card tricks and, at the same time, quote the philosopher David Hume' (Billington 2014).

One doesn't need to dig much deeper, though, to come across a third element – one which is unusual among magicians at any level of the art: a scepticism, a sense of embarrassment, even, he tells us, a 'potential for self-loathing', at the idea of magic itself, which

> comes from the unavoidable problem that one is engaging in a childish, fraudulent activity: although it has the capacity to delight and amaze, the performer is also a hair's breadth from being justifiably treated like a silly child. It is, after all, just tricks. (Brown 2010: chapter 1)

This element of the personal is there, too, in the stage performance. In the opening lines of *Infamous*, for example, Brown – seated on a chair in the middle of an empty stage – immediately enters a mode in which he both lectures and confides in the audience:

> We are all trapped inside our own heads. And our beliefs and understandings about the world are limited by that perspective. I came out when I was thirty-one. I presumed that I was gay since I was a teenager so that fifteen, sixteen years of pretending that that huge part of you doesn't exist. (Brown 2013–14)

It may not be a moment of revelation itself (Brown is talking several years after the interview with the *Independent on Sunday*, after all) but there is something undeniably intimate about this opening. This intimacy increases as the audience realizes that Brown's subject is not so much his own sexuality as his feelings about hiding or revealing it.

> And then many years later you realize that you have to come out, you have to tell people about it at some point ... And then when you do if you have any secret whatever it is, anything that you carry around with you, and you think you couldn't possibly tell people – when you finally do – when you finally summon up the courage to get this *big* thing off your chest you realize – people don't care. (Brown 2013–14)

One of Brown's own favourite quotations, to which he refers frequently, including in this show, is from David Foster Wallace's cult novel *Infinite Jest*: 'You will become way less concerned with what other people think of you when you realize how seldom they do' (Wallace

1996: 203). In *Infamous* he goes on to talk about the typical patterns that social psychologists have identified in peoples' life-course, and he explains that 'if I were a psychic – which I am not; or if I claimed to have special powers – which I really don't – I could use that kind of information to seemingly know a lot about you, or give somebody a powerful reading' (Brown 2013–14).

There is a well-known classical psychological experiment which Brown has used in one of the programmes in the third series of *Trick of the Mind* and about which he talks openly in his book of the same title. The original Forer Experiment was written up in detail in an academic article entitled 'The Fallacy of Personal Validation: A Classroom Demonstration of Gullibility' (Forer 1949: 118–23; see also Brown 2006: 322–53). It demonstrates how a series of generic statements descriptive of character, appropriately packaged and presented, will be read by the great majority of subjects as if it applies to them and them alone. Long before Forer conducted his experiment, though, the same routine was being practiced by conjurors, stage psychics and confidence tricksters under the name of 'cold reading', exploiting the fact that 'Everybody is identical in their secret unspoken belief that way deep down they are different from everyone else' (Wallace 1996).

'So imagine you've come to see me and I'm a stage psychic', continues Brown. By now the lecture in social psychology is on its way to becoming the launch pad – and the framework and the mode of misdirection – for a series of routines in mental magic that reference traditional techniques used by stage psychics, fortune tellers, confidence tricksters and mentalists alike. One of these involves a parody of a fake psychic who bears an uncanny similarity to Paul O'Grady's Lily Savage and who becomes a running gag throughout the show:

> Alright love, I'm getting your grandma – she's coming through … She's giving me a phone number as proof that she's coming through. Alright – she's saying … she's giving me an 0. She says there's an 0 at the start of the number – is that right? (Brown 2013–14)

The blatant absurdity of this 'proof' raises laughter in the audience, as do further supposed proofs: 'She says there's a number in your phone number – it's *like* a 5 or a 3 or a 9, is that right?' and 'There's not a triple two in the middle is there, love? 222? No? No that's what she's saying – that there's *not* a triple two in the number' (Brown 2011–12; see also Brown 2010: chapter 2). Like the blatant manipulation of the audience's 'three choice' in *Svengali*, Brown's humour here is deceptive. For a magician, a joke may be just a joke but it also frequently constitutes a form of misdirection, since it serves to confuse and distract: it disrupts or interrupts the spectator's logical train of thought, making it that much harder for him or her to infer the method from the effect. The human mind can only concentrate on so many things at once, and a spectator who is busy laughing is less likely to spot a secret move or uncover the deception.

Here, the comic 'take' on stage spiritualism also paves the way for the rest of the show. This has two main elements: there is a series of 'reading' effects and memory feats accompanied by a psychological patter, drawn both from academic psychology and from popular books on improving your mental power (e.g. Buzan 1989), which appears to explain the techniques by which these are achieved, but which turns out to explain nothing at all. And there are further *exposés* of the trickery of charlatans past and present. Brown's targets range from mediumship and telepathy to homeopathy and Filipino shamanic healing, all of which he demonstrates, debunks and then re-presents on a different level. The theme of the show is the relationship between scepticism and belief, or between open-mindedness and gullibility. 'Being open-minded', he reminds us, 'doesn't mean believing *everything* because you'd like it to be true' (Brown 2013–14). And so the audience is repeatedly educated in the ways of deception – and then we are deceived anyway.

This pattern, of apparent explanation followed by further deception, is typical of a contemporary trend in magic, not just a technique of Derren Brown's. The present-day magician is faced, as we have said, with an audience which is immersed in both the technology and the ideology of late-capitalist culture – an audience that in consequence typically thinks of itself as more sophisticated, sceptical and secular than its predecessors; an audience which may well have seen it all before on television and the internet and which certainly has greater access to the magicians' secrets than did previous generations. Living in an information age, the contemporary magician needs a different strategy, one which understands that access to 'how to' is a given and which plays along with and exploits the audience's sense of sophistication and scepticism, showing or suggesting how a trick is done – and then doing it again in a completely different way, staying one step ahead of the audience in order to amaze after all.

Miracle (2): Scepticism and belief

Brown, then, operates within a recognizable genre of contemporary magic – one which, to draw an analogy from mainstream theatre, effectively disposes of the illusory 'fourth wall' of classical naturalism in order to draw up a *new* contract which enables the audience – willingly or unwillingly – to suspend disbelief in a fresh way. In Brown's case, though, there is more to it than that. His recent live magic acts are also lecture-demonstrations on the subject of ideology and philosophical relativism; they are about the limitations of our own habits of perception, about our willingness to be fooled – and most importantly about the willingness of others to take advantage of that. It is an angry attack not just on bad science and snake-oil medicine, but, more importantly, on those who would use these to exploit and profit from other peoples' loss and grief.

In this, Brown aligns himself with a further historical tradition – that of the magician-turned-sceptical 'investigator' of paranormal claims.. Several eminent practitioners have followed this path, most notably John Nevil Maskelyne and Harry Houdini. Indeed, in the years following the First World War, Houdini's repeated attacks on the claims of fraudulent spirit mediums took on the character of a crusade (see Maskelyne 1912; Houdini 1920). In 1988, James 'The Amazing'

Randi retired from the stage in order to found the Committee for Skeptical Inquiry and the James Randi Educational Foundation, subsequently offering a million-dollar prize to anyone who could demonstrate occult, psychic or psychokinetic powers under agreed laboratory conditions (James Randi Educational Foundation 2015).

In *Miracle* (2015–16) Brown takes scepticism even further, creating a performance which is structured around an *exposé* of Christian faith healers. Like earlier shows, this contains plenty of smaller and more light-hearted routines, but there is no mistaking the seriousness at the heart of *Miracle*'s debunking of the techniques of the evangelical pastors whose considerable personal fortunes are made at the expense of the vulnerable. Two television specials on a similar theme, *Messiah* (2005) and *Miracles for Sale* (2011), had already attacked 'the wickedness in the world of faith healing . . . [where] if you want to be cured you are encouraged to dig deep and donate' (Brown 2011).

Questions of faith, belief, fundamentalist ideology and mental and emotional manipulation have different cultural implications in the early twenty-first century from those of the early twentieth, and the subject matter of Brown's performance seems to align him with current high-profile humanist sceptics and in particular with Richard Dawkins, whom Brown frequently quotes approvingly and on whose television programme *Enemies of Reason* he has appeared. There is, though, something more openly personal, and also something less evangelical, in the tone of Brown's approach to this than there is in Dawkins's dogmatic rationalism. Brown, who 'grew up Christian, [and] once went to a religious camp to be "cured" of his homosexuality, but is now an atheist' (Brown 2014c) lacks Dawkins's contempt for the believers as well as for the belief. Perhaps his professional understanding of how easily the mind can be tricked makes him more humane, more compassionate towards the believer or the victim – and more contemptuous towards the exploiter of belief.

In *Miracle* he both performs his own 'miraculous healings' live on stage and also develops the theme from the opening moments of *Infamous*: that we are trapped inside our own heads – but that once we understand that, we are able to take control of our own minds and emotions and live fuller, happier lives and respond to the actual miracle that is our everyday existence. It is the sort of message that one can read in the wisdom literature of many religious and philosophical traditions – and in many a contemporary book on 'positive psychology', mindfulness or self-help – and indeed, one of Brown's ongoing projects at the time of writing is an 'anti-self-help book' (Brown 2014b) on the theme of happiness. Out of context, this kind of positive message can sometimes appear naïve, sentimental or over-simplistic. Encountered as one strand within a complex narrative of magical illusions, however, it becomes something rather more complex.

While Brown's work embraces skill and novelty in ways that are typical of mainstream popular performance, there is more to it than this. Expert conjuror though he is, Brown's engagement with popular culture encompasses more than just his ability to produce increasingly impressive stage illusions. In his most recent work, rather, the illusions seem to be a means to an end rather than an end in themselves.

The trajectory of Derren Brown's most recent work seems to be a search for new relationships between form and content in popular culture – and not just popular performance, now, but including too those modes of popular science, popular psychology and popular philosophy which have entered the public sphere. It is not, I think, that Brown is attempting to transcend the popular, or to leave it behind. On the contrary, he appears to be travelling deeper into its heart, using the formal characteristics of popular performance as a vehicle for new explorations.

And it is the formal elements of popular performance that enable these explorations. The direct connection between stage and spectator which popular performance traditionally establishes, and its insistence on the present moment and the apparently unmediated presence of the performer, establish a framework in which the spectator's active role in meaning-making (often erroneously!) becomes a central element of the meaning of the performance itself. At the same time, performer and role become interlaced in the playfully ambiguous persona which

Brown presents/performs: part showman and part shaman, part comic and part academic, part intimate *confidant* and part enigmatic conman. Between them, these ambiguities set up an unstable relationship with the audience in which form and content work together to destabilize the everyday. Brown's routines (like the routines of all good magicians) repeatedly offer us 'logical' explanations, only to cast doubt on these. In the process, these routines bring us up experientially against the limits of our own habitual ways of perceiving and against the limits of our ability to interpret those perceptions. What makes Brown stand out from many of his conjuring colleagues is that he suggests, through his performance, that to experience these limits and thus to recognize that 'we are all trapped inside our own heads. And our beliefs and understandings about the world are limited by that perspective' (Brown 2013–14) might be the most important thing that a popular performer can do.

Bibliography

Alexander, Ella (2014), 'Derren Brown on the Disappointment of Coming Out', *The Independent*, 24 November 2014, http://www.independent.co.uk/news/people/derren-brown-on-the-disappointment-of-coming-out-it-s-not-that-people-react-badly-to-it-they-really-9879967.html (accessed 22 November 2015).

Annemann, Theodore (1983), *Practical Mental Magic*. Mineola, NY: Dover.

Auslander, Philip (1999), *Liveness*. London and New York: Routledge.

Billington, Michael (2013), 'Derren Brown *Infamous* – Review', *The Guardian*, 28 June 2013, http://www.theguardian.com/stage/2013/jun/28/derren-brown-infamous-review (accessed 20 November 2015).

Blackstone, Harry with Charles and Regina Reynolds (1985), *The Blackstone Book of Magic and Illusion*. New York: Newmarket Press.

Blaine, David (2004), *Mysterious Stranger. A Book of Magic*. London: Channel 4 Books.

Brown, Derren (2005–6), *Something Wicked This Way Comes* UK Tour. Edited broadcast 29 December 2006, E4.

Brown, Derren (2006), *Tricks of the Mind*. London: Channel 4 Books.

Brown, Derren (2010), *Confessions of a Conjuror,* Kindle ed. London: Channel 4 Books.

Brown, Derren (2012), *Apocalypse* [Two-part TV programme] 26 October, 2 November, Channel 4.

Brown, Derren (2011–12), *Svengali* UK Tour. Edited broadcast 18 September 2012, Channel 4.

Brown, Derren (2013–14), *Infamous* UK Tour. Edited broadcast 22 September 2014, Channel 4.

Brown, Derren (2014a) 'Interview: Derren Brown on Coming Out, Russia, and His Pet Parrot', *Pink News*, 11 February, http://www.pinknews.co.uk/2014/02/11/interview-derren-brown/ (accessed 15 November 2015).

Brown, Derren (2014b), interview with Michael Mangan, 14 October, London.

Brown, Derren (2014c), 'Interview: Coming Out Is a Let-Down', *Telegraph Men*, 25 November. http://www.telegraph.co.uk/men/the-filter/11252337/Derren-Brown-Coming-out-is-a-let-down.html (accessed 18 November 2015).

Brown, Derren (2015a), 'Your Videos Please … *Miracle* Tour 2015/16', *Derren Brown Blog*, 12 August. http://derrenbrown.co.uk/blog (accessed 30 November 2015).

Brown, Derren (2015b), 'Please Tweet any Word Using #DerrenMiracle in the Next 10 mins for My London Show. Thanks All', *Derren Brown @ DerrenBrown*, 28 November. https://twitter.com/DerrenBrown?ref_src=twsrc%5Egoogle|twcamp%5Eserp|twgr%5Eauthor (accessed 30 November 2015).

Brown, Derren (2015–16), *Miracle* UK Tour.

Buzan, Tony (1989), *Master your Memory*. Newton Abbot: David & Charles.

Carpenter, Ian (2003), 'Magic Profile: Derren Brown', *Magic Week*. http://www.magicweek.co.uk/magic_profiles/magicprofile_0033_derren_brown.htm (accessed 27 October 2015).

Crasson, Sara (1999), 'Magic History and Magical Myths: The Historian's Challenge', *Magical Past-Times: The On-Line Journal of Magic History*. http://illusionata.com/mpt/view.php?id=77&type=articles (accessed 20 January 2006).

Dekker, Wolfgang (1993), *Sports and Games of Ancient Egypt* (trans. Allen Guttman). Cairo: The American University in Cairo Press.

Forer, Bertram R. (1949), 'The Fallacy of Personal Validation: A Classroom Demonstration of Gullibility', *Journal of Abnormal and Social Psychology*, 44: 118–23

Houdini, Harry ([1927] 2001), *Houdini's Book of Magic*. Amsterdam: Fredonia Books.

Houdini, Harry (1920), *Miracle Mongers and their Methods*. New York: E. P. Dutton.

Howarth v Green (2002), All ER (D) 331 (November).

James Randi Educational Foundation (2015), 'JREF Status', http://web.randi.org/home/archives/09-2015 (accessed 23 November 2015).

Lamont, Peter, and Richard Wiseman (1999), *Magic in Theory. An Introduction to the Theoretical and Psychological Elements of Conjuring*. Hatfield: University of Hertfordshire Press.

Lemezma, Marc (2003), *Mind Magic*. London: New Holland Publishers.

Mangan, Michael (2007), *Performing (Dark) Arts: a Cultural History of Conjuring*. Bristol: Intellect.

Maskelyne, John Nevil (1912), *The Fraud of Modern 'Theosophy' Exposed. A Brief History of the Greatest Imposture Ever Perpetrated under the Cloak of Religion*. London: George Routledge; New York: E. P. Dutton.

Nelms, Henning ([1969] 2000), *Magic and Showmanship: a Handbook for Conjurors*. Mineola, NY: Dover.

Reyes, Dominic (2013), 'How Much do Magicians Charge? Setting a Price', *Merchant of Magic. Advice and Training for Magicians*. http://blog.magicshop.co.uk/2013/01/how-much-to-hire-magician.html (accessed 17 September 2015).

Robert-Houdin, Jean Eugène (1881), *The Secrets of Stage Conjuring* (trans. and ed. with notes by 'Professor Hoffmann' [pseudo. Angelo John Lewis]). London: Routledge.

Rudin, John (2015), 'Review: Derren Brown's *Miracle*, Sunderland Empire', *The Journal*. http://www.thejournal.co.uk/culture/arts-culture-news/review-derren-brown-miracle-sunderland-9338064 (accessed 13 October 2015).

Wallace, David Foster (1996), *Infinite Jest*. Boston: Little, Brown.

Whitehouse, R. (2015), 'Review: Derren Brown: *Miracle* @ Theatre Royal, Plymouth', *West Briton*, 21 April. http://www.westbriton.co.uk/REVIEW-Derren-Brown-Miracle-Theatre-Royal/story-26364265-detail/story.html (accessed 27 October 2015).

Wilkinson, J. G. (1878), *The Manners and Customs of the Ancient Egyptians, Volume II* (new edn in 3 vols, rev. and corrected by Samuel Birch). London: John Murray.

Wygant, Ann (ed.) (2007), *The Meanings Of Magic. From the Bible to Buffalo Bill*. New York and Oxford: Berghahn.

7

Performing the Burlesque Body: The Explicit Female Body as Palimpsest

Lynn Sally

Setting the *mise-en-scène* at a prototypical American burlesque show

It is past 10.00 pm in the darkened room. Friends cluster around cabaret tables chatting and drinking, eagerly anticipating the start of the show. A few patrons stand to the side of the tables near the velvet-curtained windows that span two floors; others sit in the back of the intimate room in the 'playpen', a slightly raised platform area with bar-stool height seating. On the second floor, an ornate wrought iron fence surrounds the balcony allowing spectators to see the action from above. On the weekend, the venue will fill to standing-room-only capacity as some spectators arrive hours before the advertised start time of the show to ensure a good seat. Tonight, a comfortable fifty or so patrons litter the room for the Wiggle Room, one of several weekly burlesque shows at The Slipper Room, a burlesque and variety arts venue on the Lower East Side of New York City. The Slipper Room has a decadent, Victorian feel, with flowered wallpaper, dark wood trim, and curtains and paint in burgundy and gold. At the apex of the proscenium stage, a red spotlight illuminates a woman's face as surreal video montages are projected on the red velvet curtains. The curtains, now shut tight, will open and close between each act, giving a theatrical flair to the evening's performance.

A drum roll sound cue dramatizes the commencement of the show. The audience, intoxicated from the alcohol and the delayed start time, hoot and holler in response. The curtains part slightly as Sir Richard Castle, the host of the show, slips through the opening and steps onto the small go go platform – a nod to the Minsky Brother's introduction of the runway to American burlesque audiences in the 1920s – that extends from the front of the stage. Castle is clad in a tuxedo, his jet black hair slicked back with a sharp part and a painted-on white stripe. Castle is played by talented actor, writer and sketch comic Bradford Scobie whose many other characters include 'Dr. Donut', a mutant evil superhero who espouses the virtues of preservatives while donning a very large, removable éclair in front of his genitals, and 'Moisty the Snowman', a whiney-voiced, sexually ambivalent snowman fabricated from the dirt- and garbage-filled snow of New York City streets. Sir Richard Castle is a slightly delusional, dandy-esque British bloke played, as with all of Bradford Scobie's characters, with cartoon-like exaggeration.

'Welcome to the Wiggle Room. I am Sir Richard Castle', he announces in a fake British accent, bowing deep at the waist. He flashes a large painted on gap between his front teeth to the audience in an exaggerated greeting. He then stands upright, his arms outstretched inviting applause. The crowd obliges in the first of many opportunities throughout the night to show their enthusiasm – and participate in the performance – through applause and verbal response. Noticing the curtains are still slightly parted behind him, Castle breaks character and screams backstage: 'Close it, close it, close it!' The stage curtains, operated by one of the less than a handful of performers in the show, close behind him.

'Fuck me. What a shit show', he jokes. 'Welcome to the Slipper Room', he booms, rolling his tongue and prolonging the 'sl' of Slipper. 'A fine-oiled show business machine. Showing you we can be wildly entertaining without the dull drudgery of rehearsal.' Opening a show by acknowledging 'mistakes' is a refreshing way to draw the audience in as part of the fun at a burlesque show is expecting the unexpected.

Through sarcasm and humour, the host highlights burlesque's unique approach to performance which celebrates an 'anything goes' spirit. Neo-burlesque utilizes some of the conventions of traditional theatre, including the use of a proscenium stage, lights and music to enhance the performance, choreographed movement and other traditional theatrical conventions. Yet counter to a traditional performance model (prevalent in much theatre, dance and music) where rehearsals lead, hopefully, to a seamless performance, burlesque prefers to capitalize on the surprise of live performance as one of its defining characteristics. Burlesque subverts the canon of the traditional proscenium stage through its whimsical and exaggerated presentation and style. The traditions of theatre, so revered in other contexts, become the butt of a joke in burlesque, one which pokes fun at institutions as a whole. This becomes evident in Castle's hosting as he draws the audience into the show while subverting the audience's expectations of a theatrical performance.

Burlesque celebrates and is rooted in the present, and it is this 'in the moment' liveness that makes burlesque exciting for the audience and performers alike. The actor playing Castle speaks to the audience directly, and the audience is invited – and encouraged – to respond. At this moment, a strict division between spectator and performer dissolves, as does the proverbial fourth wall of traditional theatre. In fact, interaction between the audience and the performer is highly celebrated in burlesque through call and response, audience participation and direct address. This direct address to the audience occurs often in response to what may be deemed 'mistakes' – stuck costume pieces, misremembered choreography, props that go awry. Rather than 'covering up' those unplanned moments, the (seasoned) burlesque performer acknowledges and exaggerates those mishaps for comedic effect through physical or verbal commentary. The bodily and facial physical responses represent what Dodds (2011: 124) characterizes as performers' 'choreography of facial commentary': 'they wink suggestively, flick their eyes to heaven, pull coy faces, fabricate mock shock, and offer smiles of pleasure and collusion as a self-reflexive performance strategy.' The choreography of facial commentary allows for performer and spectator to acknowledge what's happening in the live, lived experience of popular performance. Perfection, as in hitting all one's 'marks' in a highly choreographed dance or playing all the notes in a classical composition, may come second to another set of performance criteria in burlesque: remaining 'in the moment', staying connected to the audience, and 'going for it'. By acknowledging mistakes and mishaps, burlesque celebrates the (often) nonsensical whimsy of popular performance, so clear to the audience yet which in traditional theatrical and performance mediums may go unacknowledged.

This essay's notion of burlesque as popular performance is indebted to Dodds's (2011: 47, 64) defining and contextualizing of popular dance as 'an approach' rather than a fixed site. The 'popular' has been categorically dismissed as 'mere entertainment' that caters to the 'lowest common denominator' (4), a dismissal that misses its productive qualities. As the popular is rarely subsidized, it's often produced at low cost by the same entities who create the work (63). Creators of popular dance are often both artists and producers, a duality evident in much neo-burlesque, which contributes to the creation of close-knit communities and creative autonomy. As Dodds (2011: 119) points out, 'the neo-burlesque scene propagates a popular dancing body valued for its creative autonomy, corporeal diversity, and strategies for audience access and inclusion'. Reading burlesque as an approach that 'takes place under a range of conditions' (5) helps illuminate some of the productive qualities of burlesque as a popular performance.

In this essay, the 'range of conditions' of popular performance oscillates around four major categories. First, popular performance is rooted firmly in the present and its in the moment liveness which, in burlesque, is marked by the celebration of the unexpected. Second, the strict division between spectator and performer has been eradicated and replaced with active participation from the audience on numerous levels; going beyond simple audience applause or response, the spectator-performer interaction is central to understanding burlesque as what I term 'a participatory sport'. Third, novelty is celebrated, and that which is read as nonsensical or frivolous in other contexts is highly regarded as emblematic of the creativity and artistic commentary celebrated in much neo-burlesque performance. Fourth, the performer and the character are interlaced in such a way that the characters created and performed – often with separate identities, histories and performance modes than the actors – become synonymous with the performer. This last characteristic, in particular, opens up the potential for burlesque performers to transgress social norms, an argument that will be examined in more detail in a close reading of one particular neo-burlesque act performed by MsTickle. The opening scene of this article, then, sets the stage for unpacking burlesque as popular performance through readings grounded in performance practices and theories around those practices to better understand the way the explicit female body on the neo-burlesque stage is written and in turn writes counter-narratives of gender representation and desire. I offer the idea of the explicit female body as palimpsest, one that's able to rewrite these narratives, yet which is always marked by the textual renderings of patriarchal culture.

Burlesque undone: Histories, contexts, theories

This article's opening with a description of the mise-en-scène at one particular venue is being replayed at venues across the country and, increasingly, around the world as the neo-burlesque movement has gained in popularity. The new or neo-burlesque movement emerged in the mid-1990s as an underground, anti-status-quo performance art movement that references the historical antecedent of the 'bump n' grind era' of burlesque (1940s–1960s) (Shteir 2005) while recontextualizing it with modern themes (Baldwin 2004). New burlesque is a live performance art medium comprised of short, vignette-style narrative acts that stage and play with notions of sexuality, gender and social expectations through the employment of multifarious strategies that may include self-authorship, humour, over-the-top presentation of self, transformation, storytelling, cultural parody and camp to poke fun at and potentially destabilize cultural norms. Nally (2009: 635) aligns burlesque performance 'with camp, with a heavy criticism of hetero-normative genders, and ultimately with the queering of identities'. Central to this 'camping' includes an over-theatrical presentation of femininity which allows the burlesque performer to 'disrupt norms of femininity by parodying them in her excess' (Roach 2008: 87).

According to Susan Sontag (2002: 63) in her often-cited 'Notes on Camp', one of the primary vehicles for the delivery of camp sensibility is comedy: 'Camp proposes a comic vision of the world.' While an extended discussion of burlesque's indebtedness to campy humour is outside the scope of this article, I want to briefly tease out burlesque's use of camp humour to disrupt notions of femininity and gender. New York based boylesque performer Tigger (2015) identifies humour as one of the three defining characteristics of burlesque in his 'burlesque equation': 'burlesque = sex + humor + self-expression'. Alluding to the difficulties in definitively codifying a fluid and constantly charging art form, Tigger (2015) jokes 'If it has those three elements – sex + humor + self-expression – it's probably burlesque.' The simultaneous application of humour and tease to a wide range of cultural references contributes to burlesque's unique ability to make social commentary. As Dodds (2013: 80) puts it, 'Humor acts as a means to parody, satirize, or ridicule traditions of female representation, while tease enables a self-reflexive mode of performance.'

Through this knowing wit, what some scholars (Allen 1991; Buszek 2006; Nally 2009; Sally 2009) have identified as performers 'aware of their own awarishness', burlesque has an uncanny power to upend – and even dismantle – striptease from its historical and performative connotations. In neo-burlesque, the striptease has become a performance and political strategy of social transgression; put another way, burlesque uses the tease to subvert (some of) the social meanings of the strip. The primary performance mode of neo-burlesque, the striptease, then, 'offers performers a multitude of creative possibilities through which to present' their original ideas (Dodds 2011: 113). This multitude of creative possibilities is clearly represented in the diversity of topics, narratives and performance styles at a typical burlesque show and, in turn, contributes to burlesque performers' strong sense of agency. On the surface, this may seem like an unnerving paradox that striptease, traditionally understood as a symbol of women's oppression, can be used to transgress social expectations and even oppression.

Recently, scholars (Buszek 2006; Liepe-Levinson 2001; Nally 2009; Roach 2007; Ross 2009; Sally 2009; Willson 2008) have begun to unpack this seeming contradiction that burlesque striptease can be liberating. In her study of commercial striptease culture inspired by her friend's decision to drop out of graduate school to become a stripper, Roach (2007) embarks on a journey to better understand her subject – from the dancers' motivation to the operations of strip clubs – as well as the larger trend towards 'raunch culture' (Levy 2006) and 'striptease culture' (McNair 2001). The burlesque version of sexuality on stage seems to poke fun at rather than simply reinscribe raunch culture. Though parody – the *burla* of burlesque – and striptease as performance strategies, burlesque puts forth a positive portrayal of women's sexuality on stage. As Roach observes, 'Sex-positive feminism, as exemplified in the neo-burlesque movement, is a parody of patriarchal norms' (Roach 2008: 112). In a Brechtian presentational (not representational) way, burlesque performers present hyper-stylized and hyper-sexualized images of women as a form of social commentary.

To understand how striptease can be used as a form of social commentary that parodies patriarchal culture invites us to shift our gaze to live performance practices. As Robert Allen (1991) suggests in his quintessential study of nineteenth-century burlesque, *Horrible Prettiness*, studying burlesque as popular culture requires a case history rather than an exhaustive historical approach. As culture is difficult to quantify and define, the case history 'attempts to make a problem intelligible without requiring that historical comprehensiveness or conclusive proof' (Allen 1991: 41). The knowledge produced from such an approach is always tentative and open for revision (ibid.). As a living, popular art form, studies of burlesque must be open to this type of continual revision as the art itself constantly morphs and changes, making even the seemingly simple tasks of defining and describing it difficult. The remainder of this article, then, will focus on a case study, namely a close reading and analysis of MsTickle's Super Star/Blowup Doll Act, to flesh out the meanings of this act as a cultural artifact on its own, in the context of neo-burlesque, and, even more broadly, as it fits into a larger narrative of the display of female bodies in popular performance. Here I argue that the explicit female body serves as a palimpsest whereby traces of historic renderings of the body remain, but the burlesque performer is able to 'rewrite' her own image on top of those remnants, a reinscription that has the potential to scream volumes in its transgression of social norms.

Reading to read: Layers as/of 'uncovering' in MsTickle's performance

MsTickle is a New York-based performer and designer who began performing in the 1990s in New York City's underground nightclub scene as a solo performer, go go dancer and a member of the 'Bombshell Girls,' a troupe she formed with former burlesque performer and producer Lady Ace. Through the years, MsTickle has gained a reputation as one of the most respected and innovative neo-burlesque performers, known for her stunning costuming and props (which she designs and fabricates herself) and cutting-edge, conceptual acts. The description of her performance that serves as the basis of my unpacking of burlesque popular performance is based on a video recording of a performance at the 2011 Burlesque Hall of Fame (BHOF) competition for the title of 'Reigning Queen of Burlesque', though I witnessed this act dozens of times live in large and small venues alike.

MsTickle enters the stage wearing an extravagant red velvet cape, her left arm extending in front of her, fingers reaching for the light. As she walks slowly across the stage, a long red fabric unfolds behind her, her own runway carpet attached to her body, literally (and figuratively) creating the space for her own celebrity. A strobe light flickers on and off, mimicking light bulb flashes of the paparazzi. A woeful moan can be heard over the electric, bass-heavy music. Right before the lyrics begin, MsTickle removes her red cloak and red carpet runway and presents herself as an iconic Hollywood starlet – replete with a blond Marilyn Monroe-esque wig and a plastered smile – as she struts around the stage waving and blowing kisses to her hypothetical fans. She wears a gold, sequined 'wiggle' gown – a form-fitting design with fishtail curved bottom that exaggerates a woman's curves – opera-length red satin gloves and a red bolero jacket. The back of the dress features a large bow covered with rhinestones that glitter in the stage lights.

MsTickle's movement gains meaning when juxtaposed against the song's longing lyrics. MsTickle removes one glove slowly and then her bejewelled necklace as the lyrics lament mortality and what it takes to achieve celebrity: 'If I could live forever/I wouldn't ask what price: fame' (Kinzie 2004). MsTickle struts for a few beats and then removes her other glove to the chorus: 'I want to be a superstar/I want to have a house on Sunset/you'll only see me afar.' She wraps the gloves around her wrists and lifts her arms in pseudo-bondage, wiggling her body in mock seduction as she faces the audience, front and centre. Her face is expressionless, fixed on a one-note smile that hints at the superficiality of celebrity culture.

At an instrumental break in the song, MsTickle leans forward and lets the red bolero jacket fall off of her body. While stooped over at the waist, she unzips her gold gown, steps out of it, removes her blond wig and peels off the mask featuring the fixed-smile painted face. MsTickle stands upright again, pausing in mid-pose, her arms bent at her sides, hands reaching towards the audience. Here the audience sees that underneath the Hollywood starlet mask is another mask and another iconic figure: that of a blow-up doll. Wearing a full body plastic blow-up doll suit with exaggerated lips sculpted into a permanent phallus-receptive 'O', MsTickle's movement changes from the beautiful, fluid gestures of the Hollywood starlet greeting her fans to the mechanical, stilted and explicit gestures of the blow-up doll come to life. The lyrics contribute

Figure 7.1 MsTickle performing at the Burlesque Hall of Fame, Las Vegas, NV in 2011 (photo © Ed Barnas)

to her message: 'I'm public property sacrifice me/let there be no mystery you have made me/I am the main attraction kept in a gilded cage' (Kinzie 2004). MsTickle teeters around the stage with unstable physicality, pausing numerous times to execute several obscene gestures, including fellatio, fisting and exaggerated, mechanical masturbation.

Next MsTickle literally peels herself out of the blow-up-doll suit and mask to reveal thigh-high boots, a tiny thong and pasties fabricated from baby bottle nipples giving her real breasts a cartoonish feature. She celebrates her liberation from the confining artifice by rubbing her hands seductively on her skin, flipping her (natural) hair and luxuriating in her own body. She digs into her tiny g-string, removes a lipstick which she uses to touch up her makeup before turning it onto her own body to writes on her exposed midriff: 'For Sale'. She waves to the audience and blows kisses, returning to the physicality of the Hollywood starlet image from which she began the act.

MsTickle's performance is very much a commentary on mainstream culture's obsession with celebrity culture as well as a startling reminder of the continued commodification of women's bodies in our society. MsTickle (2013) has identified the 'layers' in this act as a process of 'uncovering'. Underneath the masks and beneath the layers are more layers – shocking, unexpected, explicit – suggesting that a core essence might be unattainable. MsTickle (2013) says she added the runway effect in her act for the Burlesque Hall of Fame competition partially to 'take up more space' but also to help 'set up the narrative', a narrative that, according to her, plays with the 'icon of glamour and vanity, all the stuff we are taught to admire and aspire to'. MsTickle (2013) specifically used the 'blow-up doll as sex object' to suggest that 'underneath all that glamour begs the question: how much are we selling ourselves for?' Underneath the female body as sex object is another layer 'that is a real body but it's still stripper-esque' (MsTickle 2013), suggesting that women are unable to escape from the signifying practices of a sexualizing patriarchal culture. MsTickle consciously choose this theme of sexual display as a commentary on objectification, and ultimately identity, by asking: 'When we strip down the layers, what's underneath?' (MsTickle 2013). She answers this question, to some degree, in the final moments of the act by writing her message, literally, on her bare body: For Sale. In the context of the narrative of this act, this simple message has, like the layers removed, layers itself.

This description of MsTickle's act comes from a performance at the Burlesque Hall of Fame (BHOF) competition, a large-scale, 'high-stakes' show that occurs once a year in Las Vegas, Nevada. Although this type of radical performance art is, for many, what's compelling about and representative of neo-burlesque acts, it is unlikely that MsTickle's act would normally be accepted to compete in the 'Reigning Queen of Burlesque' category at BHOF. At BHOF, if an act diverges from classic burlesque, it tends to be in the realm of variety acts, which celebrate skill-set diversity more so than body, race, age and performance-style diversity. MsTickle was guaranteed a highly coveted performance spot in 2011 because the prior year she had won the 'Best Newbie' category at the competition. Upon winning, MsTickle (2013) says she 'knew instantly' she wanted to do her blow-up doll act the next year: 'Especially coming from New York City where [burlesque] used to be commentary, political, cutting edge … I wanted to represent my work, and represent people doing interesting, conceptual stuff.' MsTickle says she considered it her 'duty' to represent the performance art side of burlesque, the type of burlesque that bubbles up in venues like the Slipper Room described at the beginning of this article, where the 'anything goes', in-the-moment liveness encourages performer experimentation and audience participation alike.

Dodds (2011) argues that artists in 'smaller'-scale venues 'prove far more radical' while more 'commercially' successful burlesque performers put forth a more 'conservative image'. I agree with Dodds that radical burlesque often is located in small-scale venues that provide the potential to circumvent traditional narratives of desire and sexuality. (A quick survey of fringe and underground art throughout the decades clearly suggests that art tends to lose its edge when it becomes commodified and packaged for a mainstream audience.) As Dodds sums it up: 'the less the performance disturbs, the wider the audience it attracts' (2011: 113). MsTickle's act on the BHOF stage simultaneously proves and complicates Dodds' argument. Taken out of the context of a small-scale venue and placed on the stage of the BHOF competition, MsTickle's act gains new meaning as a direct commentary on the beauty ideal embedded within the pageant structure of the competition. Dodds understandably aligns radical performance with small-scale venues, and that's likely where MsTickle's act was born. But maintaining this strict division between commercial and small-scale burlesque seems to limit rather than expand burlesque's radical potential and opportunities for gender expression. By removing the possibility of political efficacy in commercial burlesque, or by containing radical burlesque to small-stage cabaret venues, we lose some of burlesque's radical potential. We lose the playful juxtaposition of serious issues with trivial theatrics.

We lose the pleasure in the delightful absurdity of competing for the 'Reigning Queen of Burlesque' as a giant blow-up doll. And we lose burlesque's celebration of frivolity as central to its creative spirit.

MsTickle's act, then, becomes both a protest against and a celebration of the explicit female body, one that gains new meaning in the more 'commercial' context of the BHOF stage. MsTickle's performance specifically and neo-burlesque more broadly represents the new kind of gender expression that Jack Halberstam celebrates as 'Gaga feminism'. Gaga feminism is a 'symbol of a new kind of feminism' embodied in (but not reducible to) the pop figure Lady Gaga that has opened up a space for reinvented representations of gender. Halberstam (2013: xii) suggests that Lady Gaga is a 'loud voice for different arrangements of gender, sexuality, visibility, and desire', arrangements which similarly play themselves out on the neo-burlesque stage in challenging and provocative ways As Halberstam puts it:

> these feminists are 'becoming women' in the sense of coming to consciousness, they are unbecoming women in every sense – they undo the category rather than rounding it out, they dress it up and down, take it apart like a car engine and then rebuild it so that it is louder and faster (2013: xiii).

This metaphor of 'undoing' the category of 'women', 'dressing it up,' and 'rebuilding' it so that it is 'louder and faster' as an apt way to think about the performance of gender politics and the politics of gender performance on the neo burlesque stage.

Though it may initially seem an oxymoron, the exploitation of sexuality via the signifiers of gender normally ascribed to patriarchy can be used as a tool to unpack that same system. As Halberstam (2013: xi) puts it, Gaga feminism 'strives to wrap itself around performances of excess, crazy, unreadable appearances of wild genders; and gender experimentation'. This presentation of self manipulates preexisting iconography, but it is through that decontextualization and reconfiguration that gendered representations become self-authored. In the case of MsTickle's multilayered performance, she uses startling gender stereotypes to make a bold commentary about the continued oppression of women while telling a narrative of self-transformation. Femininity is heightened, exaggerated and put on display – so actively, vividly, completely – in performances that do not reduce women to one singular gender expression but rather open up the possibility that self-expression comes in many forms.

Through her 'excessive performance,' MsTickle 'dismantles the character of woman': the female body is literally 'taken apart' through layers and it is through and on her body that that narrative takes place. The layers in this performance – both literal and figurative – expose the fallacy that one is ever able to transcend what the female body signifies in our patriarchal culture. MsTickle's bare body serves as a canvas on which she writes her message of both political protest and artistic provocation: For Sale. The audience is forced to think about MsTickle's provocative message all while consuming her bare body in its power, beauty and sexual allure. Part of the productive quality in burlesque, according to Willson, comes from the performer who intentionally makes a spectacle of her desirable body: 'By looking at the spectator in the eye and smiling she is mocking, teasing, and challenging the spectator as well as pleasurably and actively affirming, "making a spectacle" out of her desiring/desirable sexual self' (Willson 2008: 113). In making a spectacle of her desiring/desirable body, MsTickle – as is true of many burlesque performers – gains delight in her body. That final liberation from her blow-up doll artifice unleashes a physical and psychic release. The performer gaining pleasure in her displayed body similarly invites spectators to consume her unveiled female form as a pleasurable delight and as a cognitive provocation.

And yet the material reality remains: MsTickle uses her body as a canvas to remind the audience that the same body she has put on display in spectacular and pleasurable way is ultimately a commodity 'for sale.' Here I would like to offer the concept of the explicit female body as a palimpsest to help think through this seeming contradiction. From the Greek 'palimpestos' which means 'scraped again,' a palimpsest is a writing surface on which the original writing has been erased to make room for new writing; despite the erasure, remnants of the original writing may bleed through and become part of the canvas of the new text. Ultimately, MsTickle's performance suggests that the remnants of patriarchy are still legible, even in self-authored contexts such as this one. By acknowledging that those traces of patriarchy are always already subtexts of public performance of gender, both staged and real, the explicit female body on stage as palimpsest offers a counter-narrative that flaunts, teases and throws those very same assumptions to the wind. This helps us understand the transgressive and liberatory potential of burlesque that, on the surface, may appear counter to feminist ideology.

Carolee Schneeman famously said 'I am both image-maker and image. The body may remain erotic, sexual, desired, desiring, but it is as well votive: marked, written over in a text of stroke and gesture discovered by my creative female will.' Halberstam (2013: xii) similarly argues that Gaga is a 'media product and a media manipulator', that she represents 'both an erotics of the surface and an erotics of flaws and flows'. Put quite simply, the female artist can be both subject and object; the creator of the image is author and product. The explicit female body serves as a palimpsest, and when those reimagined images get 'written over in a text of stroke and gesture', as Schneeman puts it, or rebuilt like a car engine, as Halberstam puts it, we still see the marks from that which has been erased. It is impossible to remove the explicit female body from what it represents, from what it signifies. And yet if we think about the explicit female body on stage as a palimpsest, that remainder is a necessary possibility for its very being. The question of whether burlesque oppresses or liberates becomes obsolete as a new reading of the productive possibility of popular performance comes centre stage in all its subversive potential and glamorous excess.

Bibliography

Allen, R. C. (1991), *Horrible Prettiness: Burlesque and American Culture*. Chapel Hill: University of North Carolina Press.

Baldwin, M. (2004), *Burlesque and the New Bump-n-Grind*. Denver: Speck Press.
Buszek, M. E. (2006), *Pin-Up Grrrls: Feminism, Sexuality, Popular Culture*. Durham: Duke University Press.
Desmond, J. (ed.) (2001), *Dancing Desires: Choreographing Sexualities on and off the Stage*. Madison: University of Wisconsin Press.
Dodds, S. (2011), *Dancing on the Canon: Embodiments of Value in Popular Dance*. London: Palgrave MacMillan.
Dodds, S. (2013), 'Embodied Transformation in Neo-Burlesque Striptease', *Dance Research Journal*, 45 (3): 75–90.
Halberstam, J. (2013), *Gaga Feminism: Sex, Gender, and the End of Normal*. Boston: Beacon Press.
Kinzie, M., F. L. Malcolm and W. Weichert (2004), 'Super Star' in *Stories by the Fireside*. n.p.: Spyralhead Lady.
Levy, A. (2006), *Female Chauvinist Pig: Women and the Rise of Raunch Culture*. New York: Free Press.
Liepe-Levinson, K. (2001), *Strip Show: Performances of Gender and Desire*. New York: Routledge.
McIntosh, B. (2011), *BHOF11 – Miss Exotic World8 – MsTickle.mp4*. https://www.youtube.com/watch?v=_Wkm1Bdi7nw (accessed 14 January 2014).
McNair, B. (2002), *Striptease Culture: Sex, Media, and the Democratisation of Desire*. New York: Routledge.
MsTickle (2013), Interview by author, 22 September.
Munoz, J. E. (1999), *Disidentifications: Queers of Color and the Performance of Politics*. Minneapolis: University of Minnesota Press.
Nally, C. (2009), 'Grrrly Hurly Burly: Neo-Burlesque and the Performance of Gender', *Textual Practice*, 23 (4): 621–43.
Roach, C. M. (2007), *Stripping, Sex, and Popular Culture*. Oxford: Berg.
Ross, B. (2009), *Burlesque West: Showgirls, Sex, and Sin in Postwar Vancouver*. Toronto: University of Toronto Press.
Sally, L. (2009), '"It is the Ugly that is so Beautiful": Performing the Monster/Beauty Continuum in Neo-Burlesque', *Journal of American Drama and Theatre*, 45 (3): 5–23.
Shteir, R. (2005), *Striptease: The Untold History of the Girlie Show*. Oxford: Oxford University Press.
Sontag, S. (2002), Notes on 'Camp,' in F. Cleto (ed.), *Camp: Queer Aesthetics and the Performing Subject: A Reader*. Ann Arbor: The University of Michigan Press, 53–65.

Tigger (2015), Guest Artist Talk. Lecture to Drama Department, New York University, 5 August.

Willson, J. (2008), *The Happy Stripper: Pleasures and Politics of the New Burlesque*. London: I. B. Tauris.

8

'Hiya Fans!': Celebrity Performance and Reception in Modern British Pantomime

Simon Sladen

A staple of British Christmas tradition, pantomime is an intrinsic part of the United Kingdom's cultural and theatrical landscape. Most towns and cities in England, Wales, Scotland and Northern Ireland will host at least one pantomime production between November and February each year, with the industry's annual box office worth an estimated £146 million (Celebrate Panto 2014).

The conventions and practices of modern British pantomime were crystallized in the late nineteenth century when music hall made Marie Lloyd, Dan Leno and Herbert Campbell into household names. Praised by critics and in demand at the box office, their popularity saw them play the largest venues in London, as well as tour the United Kingdom. Their yearly schedule would comprise appearing on a variety of bills and more often than not conclude in a residency at one of the country's largest theatres as the star name in that year's pantomime.

In London, the productions at Drury Lane under the management of Augustus Harris were seen as the cultural pinnacle of pantomime. Although not the first to do so, Harris popularized the use of well-known personalities in his productions capitalizing on their celebrity status. The Theatre Royal, Drury Lane engaged Leno in its annual pantomime sixteen times between 1888 and 1903, resulting in Leno's appearances shaping the show and culminating in 1902's *Mother Goose* being created especially for him by J. Hickory Wood and Arthur Collins. Leno's annual casting meant that he became part of and created certain traditions for the theatre, and due to Drury Lane's cultural status, other theatres and producers attempted to emulate Harris's successful business model by following suit.

Modern British pantomime can be defined as an interactive comedy production, utilizing a fairytale or similar fantastical narrative featuring musical numbers and slapstick, catering for a wide cross-section of society. Spectacle and celebrity were, and still are, two fundamental aspects of British pantomime, particularly for the commercial sector, whose producers rely on box office income to recoup their costs and make a profit. This chapter sets out to examine contemporary British pantomime's use of celebrity and to explore its enduring appeal. Why and how have celebrities become such an expected and anticipated aspect of commercial pantomime and in what way do they contribute to the production's creation and reception?

With its roots in Victorian pantomime, the practice of celebrity casting has since been embraced by producers and has become an anticipated aspect of mid- to large-scale productions. Celebrity came to define twentieth-century commercial pantomime, so much so that in 1981 pantomime producer Derek Salberg wrote, 'the most important engagements to be made were naturally those of the stars' (1981: 181). According to Gerald Frow, celebrity casting during this period led to more streamlined and understandable narratives and reduced performance times, while 'still permitting the stars sufficient artistic freedom to display their own personalities and talents' (1985: 182), thus contributing to the genre's success and popularity. A survey of pantomime history books reveals that the 1980s saw commercial productions 'awash with television names' (Lathan 2004: 60), with Lathan arguing that the decade was 'characterized by the arrival of Australian soap stars in pantos, primarily from *Neighbours* and *Home and Away*' (ibid.).

Alwyn W. Turner describes the 1980s as being shaped by, among others, 'Murdoch and Maxwell, Schwarzenegger and Stallone' (2010: ix), suggesting a period dominated by celebrities and the media. The expansion of commercial television as a result of the Broadcasting Act 1980 and the birth of gossip magazines contributed greatly towards the rise of celebrity culture in British society. Turner notes that popular US soap operas *Dynasty* and *Dallas* 'inspired the inflation of women's fashions and hairstyles' while 'tours by pop superstars became bigger and more lucrative and were individually branded to enhance their commercial potential' (ibid.). Celebrity had become a marketable commodity, with the celebrities themselves existing as cultural currency. David Giles (2000: 148) and Chris Rojek (2001: 97) argue that a rise in single-person households during this period led to individuals constructing relationships with celebrities – overt media personalities – as a way of combating loneliness (Giles 2000: 6). Being 'easily accessible through internet sites, biographies, newspaper interviews, TV profiles, radio documentaries and film biographies', Rojek argues that a celebrity's veridical self as a 'site of perpetual public excavation' (2001: 19) offered guidance, comfort and a sense of belonging and community to those in need.

In 1982, Nick Thomas produced his first pantomime at the Charter Theatre, Preston, later merging the production company with his Artist Management Group to form Qdos Entertainment Ltd in 1999, the same year in which the company purchased competitor E&B Productions. This heralded the start of the company's industry domination, and in 2003 Qdos Entertainment acquired Midas Productions, increasing their industry reach and producing pantomimes at many of the UK's largest regional theatres.

However, in 2005, the UK's largest commercial theatre company, the Ambassador Theatre Group, formed subsidiary company First Family Entertainment to provide eight of its regional venues with their Christmas pantomime. Prior to this, Qdos Entertainment produced over 10 per cent of the UK's pantomimes in the UK's large- and mid-scale theatres and went from staging thirty-two pantomimes in 2004 to twenty in 2005, losing around a third of their business. In creating a subsidiary company, the Ambassador Theatre Group brought its pantomimes in-house, regaining creative and economic control over the product and benefiting financially by retail retention.

Rather than emulate Qdos Entertainment's casting model of engaging light entertainment performers and family-friendly television personalities, First Family Entertainment's chief executive Kevin Wood, who had previously produced mid-scale pantomimes under Kevin Wood Productions, decided that the company's unique selling point, and one he deemed would be popular with Ambassador Theatre Group audiences, would be that of casting American celebrities and respected actors. As First Family Entertainment's mission statement on the company's website in 2015 claimed:

> FFE were also the first pantomime producers to entice American artists to appear in this very British genre, including Henry Winkler, Patrick Duffy, the late Mickey Rooney, Pamela Anderson, David Hasselhoff, Paul Michael Glaser, Steve Guttenberg and Priscilla Presley. Ground breaking casting and spectacular shows have secured high media attention, tremendous critical acclaim and box office records.

Often seen as the apex of the star system, Broadway and Hollywood stars cater to a wider and more diverse audience and it was this that First Family Entertainment hoped to capitalize on, in a similar way as the casting of stars, such as openly gay, camp comic Julian Clary had for Qdos Entertainment previously. As Martina Lipton writes in reference to the casting of non-white and gay actors, Qdos sought 'a new taste community for its product' (2007: 142) hoping to increase audience figures by casting 'a personality that connects the existing fans and attracts the new ones' (ibid.). In using non-British celebrities, First Family Entertainment sought to create a brand that honoured the traditions of British pantomime and thus retain loyal audience members accustomed to the Qdos brand they had previously seen at their local venue, while enticing new patrons to the pantomime for whom, by casting such names, the productions were now attractive.

In their first decade of operation, First Family Entertainment cast a number of international celebrities in their pantomime debut including Jerry Springer, Linda Gray and Barry Humphries's alter ego Dame Edna Everage. The performers had generally appeared in long-running American television series, such as *Baywatch* in the case of David Hasselhoff, were known for their long and sustained careers, such as

Mickey Rooney, or were famous by association, like Priscilla Presley. These performers were frequently unknown to pantomime's younger audience members and were seen to attract an adult, rather than family audience.

On 14 October 2009, it was revealed that Pamela Anderson would play the Genie of the Lamp in New Wimbledon Theatre's production of *Aladdin*. The pantomime followed a new casting practice for First Family Entertainment as four performers would share the role over the run. Pamela Anderson was engaged between the peak periods of 13 December–27 December, with comedian Ruby Wax, actor Anita Dobson and drag-act turned television presenter Paul O'Grady covering the remaining dates. 'We hope they will all bring something completely different to the role' (*Metro*, 14 October 2009), said a theatre spokesman, and in doing so conveyed the producer's intention that each casting would appeal to a different taste community.

Pantomime is a genre not practiced widely in America and to which Anderson had no prior exposure, but being scheduled as the second Genie meant she had the opportunity to witness the production once it was open and thus see how this peculiarly British form functioned with a live audience. As commented by producer Wood, 'When you introduce it [pantomime] to new people, and they come and experience it, and they see the audiences, and see how loved as an artform it is, they get it straight away' (*BBC News*, 15 October 2009). When Anderson's casting was announced, year-on-year ticket sales rose by 800 per cent (Lee 2009), the high increase an example of what David P. Marshall terms a celebrity's 'affective power' (1997: 50). As Michael Quinn states, there are 'compelling economic reasons and ideological uses for stardom' (1990: 154) as a star can 'guarantee the flow of investment by reducing uncertainty' (ibid.). With a venue capacity of 1,670, producers at this venue need to ensure that the pantomime attracts a sustainable audience to recoup its costs, especially as the New Wimbledon Theatre is situated a mere thirty-minute public transport ride from London's West End. In addition, competition from other forms of entertainment, such as television, has led to the commercial sector relying on the engagement of performers from these fields due to their existing relationship with the British public and increased opportunities for media exposure.

'The most powerful – and most downloaded – Genie in the world'

According to the independent communications industry regulator Ofcom, in 2015 97 per cent of UK households owned a digital television, with the average viewing time per day in 2014 for those aged above four years of age totalling 220 minutes. Television viewing is, therefore, a fundamental part of many British people's daily routine and constitutes their most oft-consumed form of entertainment. Marshall notes that 'television brought with it intimacy' (1997: 38), and due to the domesticated nature of viewing, Ellis Cashmore argues that, 'like radio, its precursor, television brought entertainment into the home' (2006: 119). The advent of on-demand services increases a user's control of broadcast media, with programmes being able to be viewed across a range of locations at any time via devices including laptop computers, iPads and mobile phones.

Between 1992 and 1997 Anderson played the role of C. J. Parker in US series *Baywatch*, a programme centred on a team of lifeguards in California and reported to have attracted a weekly audience of 1.1 billion viewers in 148 countries, where it was translated into 44 different languages (Abhishek 2013). The series is credited with launching Anderson's international profile, having already enjoyed a successful career as a *Playboy* model. In many ways Anderson's casting as Parker could be described as what Richard Dyer terms a 'perfect fit' (1979: 145), where 'all the aspects of a star's image fit with all the traits of a character' (ibid.) and are used to celebrate, in this case, Anderson's body. With its prime-time broadcast slot and international audience, *Baywatch* helped created a second generation of Anderson fans, who had previously been unexposed to her

Playboy career. However, both roles helped to construct, enforce and distribute Anderson's media personality with her role as the red-swimsuit-wearing C. J. Parker becoming part of Anderson's iconography. This iconography has since been embraced and parodied by a diverse range of performers including British comedy partnership French and Saunders and the Muppets' spoof *Bay of Pigswatch* featuring Spamela Hamderson, itself a pun on Anderson's, rather than her character's name.

The opportunity to witness a performer, usually consumed via a screen, live in pantomime, is therefore attractive as viewers can be in the unmediated presence of an individual about whom they already know a lot. In Anderson's case, her global exposure as a result of *Baywatch* led to what Graeme Turner calls her 'celebritisation' (2004: 8), the point at which media focus turns to the continual excavation of a celebrity's private life. Shedding their original ascension to fame, the goal of many a celebrity is to be, as Daniel J. Boorstin describes, 'well-known for their well-knowness' (1971: 58), and Anderson's appearances on reality television shows, cameos in films and charity work through her foundation and People for the Ethical Treatment of Animals (PETA) has ensured she remains in the public eye and is introduced to a third generation of fans. Her global appeal as the sex-goddess-cum-mother-cum-human, animal and environmental rights campaigner means she has great affective power, and it is this that producers want to capitalize on by making her available for public consumption via performance. Used in this way, a celebrity is both a marketable device and an invested sales-advisor offering proximity and closeness in a theatrical genre that thrives on immediacy and interaction.

'This isn't a performance – it's a personal appearance'

But what do celebrities do in pantomimes that makes their casting attractive to producers and audiences alike? How is the celebrity integrated and celebrated? What conventions do writers, designers and directors use to enhance an audience member's pleasure at witnessing the celebrity on stage? When reviewing Anderson in pantomime, *Guardian* critic Lyn Gardner (2009) concluded '[t]his isn't a performance – it's a personal appearance'. But such an observation ignores the complex layering of character, role and performer utilized by the genre. The first aspect to consider here is that of character construction and the aim to achieve Dyer's perfect fit. The utilization of stock characters, such as Dames and Villains, as part of pantomime conventions, and their correlation with celebrity types enables the effective integration of a celebrity and allows for creative interplay in a form of enforced ghosting. As Marvin Carlson argues, 'ghosting presents the identical thing they [the audience] have encountered before, although now in a somewhat different context' (2003: 7), and in the case of actors, 'will almost inevitably in a new role evoke the ghost or ghosts or previous roles' (2003: 8). To ensure certain ghosts are summoned, the pantomime audience is constantly reminded of the celebrity's presence via a series of overt signifiers that reflect the celebrity's public persona and career, ensuring the performer's past is not only part of the reception process, but the performance itself.

Given that Anderson's *Playboy* career and *Baywatch* casting relied heavily on the exposure of her body via topless photographs and the now iconic red swimsuit, it is no surprise that the role of the Genie was chosen for her. As defined by respected pantomime practitioner and Dame Christopher Biggins, Genies should be 'a glamorous woman, a large black man or anyone else, though glamour is an important aspect' (Pavia 2009). In theatre, as Carlson reminds us, the 'body dictates what an audience will accept you as' (2003: 53).

Figure 8.1 depicts Anderson's costume – an allusion to the C. J. Parker red swimsuit worn in *Baywatch*. The red sequins add glamour to the costume and a sense of magic as they reflect the light like rubies, signifying that although this is not the *Baywatch* costume, it is highly influenced by it. Anderson's body links the two and acts as the intersection of a metaphorical Venn-diagram in which the collision of circles

Figure 8.1 Pamela Anderson as the Genie of the Lamp in First Family Entertainment's pantomime *Aladdin*, New Wimbledon Theatre, 2009 (photo © First Family Entertainment)

is verified and validated by her presence; she unites and concurrently inhabits the two and it is through her that their meaning manifests.

Anderson made her first entrance from the theatre's fly floor singing Christina Aguilera's 'Genie in a Bottle', a highly sexualized song using the genie in a bottle metaphor for sexual intercourse. Not only does this reflect Anderson's past, in that in 1995 a sex tape was leaked with her then-husband rock musician Tommy Lee, but it also reflects her *Playboy* career where she was actively employed to be objectified. During her goddess-like descent to the stage, her exposed legs enter the performance space first, providing what Martina Lipton terms the 'voyeuristic titillation' (2008: 481) once reserved for the thigh-slapping cross-dressed female Principal Boy. As Lipton explains, 'In a society where glamour models adorn the pages of the tabloid press, producers have created a new figure that men in the audience can "objectify and fetishize"' (481). The anticipation at the sighting of celebrity is increased by the slow reveal and heightened by Anderson's voice with the lyric 'Come, come, come on in and let me out' helping to establish an air of mysticism and eroticism for the self-proclaimed 'most powerful – and most downloaded – Genie in the world' (Adams 2009). That the audience helped summon the Genie by revealing the lamp's whereabouts to Aladdin when trapped in the cave acts not only as a metaphor for celebrity power, but also empowers the audience, as because of them, Anderson is permitted onto the stage. But the Genie herself can also be read as a metaphor for celebrity, an individual controlled by others and worshipped when released; this dual empowerment of Anderson's reveal and the Genie's reveal reflects the structure of celebrity power, where the public help in the construction of celebrity and determine their longevity.

At certain points in a pantomime's narrative, audience members are required to assist the protagonist in their quest by revealing the whereabouts of Aladdin's lamp or warning Cinderella of the Ugly Sisters' wicked plans. In responding, the audience engages in dialogue with the characters and thus constitute what renowned pantomime Dame Clive Rowe terms 'the last cast member' (Sladen 2011). However, despite appearing spontaneous, as Millie Taylor argues, call and response conventions follow strict patterns of engagement and are often heavily scripted (2007: 123–33).

Although direct address is used by most characters at some point in a pantomime, it is primarily the Dame and Comic who engage in two-way communication with the audience. In addition to providing the production's slapstick and comic elements, the characters' primary function is to help establish a shared community in which audience members come to constitute their extended family and adopt the Dame and Comic's views, morals and ideals. This is achieved through opening spots in which the characters speak directly to the audience in a break from the narrative and establish certain call and response patterns, such as the salutation 'Hiya Wishee' to *Aladdin*'s Comic's call of 'Hiya Kids'. Call and response conventions between Audience, Comic and Dame represent allegiance, reliance and a sense of trust between the tripartite of 'characters' and are fundamental in establishing the pantomime's shared community for performance.

Although the role of the Genie has no interaction as such with the audience, the illusion of interaction is created, first by the scripted exchange between Aladdin and the audience to find the lamp and later by Anderson's direct address as the Genie. A simple 'Hello' encourages the audience to replicate the conventions already established by Wishee Washee, the pantomime's comic, and Dame Widow Twankey, whose function is to establish a shared community by eliciting a response to salutations and catchphrases. When introduced to Aladdin's mother and brother, the Genie remarks, 'Lovely to be here in Wimbledon with all of you', which resulted in whoops and cheers from the audience in acknowledgement of their identification. The text could be interpreted as referring to Wishee Washee and Widow Twankey; however, Ian Talbot's direction and Anderson's front-on position to the audience as a result of being suspended in a flying ring resulted in an interpretation that she was referring to either the audience alone or to the audience, Wishee Washee and Widow Twankey. As Taylor argues, 'These four characters, [C]omic, Dame, and Immortals [Fairy and Villain] are the characters who have the most interaction with the audience' (2007: 125) and are vital in creating and enforcing the notion of a shared community, as it is they who interact and, more importantly, react to the audience's actions, even though heavily scripted.

If, as Rojek argues, celebrities are 'elusive and inaccessible' (2001: 62), pantomime provides fans with the opportunity to encounter the celebrity through live performance. As outlined earlier, such an encounter appears to encompass active participation, but, as Millie Taylor suggests, the relationship merely 'gives the audience members a sense of involvement … and encourages them to believe they have shared a unique experience with the performers' (2007: 123). This mode of performance relies heavily upon the layering of illusion, the foundations of which are present in the construction of Role; a conflation of Character (Genie of the Lamp) and Performer (Anderson). Successful illusive performance results in audience members believing they are participating freely with Anderson when in fact they are participating with the Role, the illusion strengthened by textual and aesthetic allusions to Anderson's career and personal life incited by the Character.

The Role, therefore, provides an intersection between Anderson and Genie through which to excavate markers of familiarity. Such enforced ghosting works to actively trigger collective memory of the Performer's public persona and career, validated by their presence and verified by programme biographies and production posters, as well as the opportunity to meet them at the stage door. Heavily mediated, like pantomime's call and response patter, the presence of the performer's body provides the illusion that the audience is, in this case, witnessing the celebrity uncovered, un-airbrushed, unedited and free to perform as 'self'; but 'self' in Anderson's case is mediated via the Role and rarely manifests.

In Role, Performer Anderson is never fully exposed, the Character's costume and text act as distracters to ensure that 'self' remains elusive. Even if Anderson breaks the text, exposing the 'self' by responding to the audience in an aside, her costume acts as a shield, reminding the audience that the Genie has a function to play and preventing the discussions from continuing as the plot is swiftly resumed by the other characters continuing their dialogue. Such role construction aids to protect less experienced pantomime performers, as in the case of Anderson, who was heckled in a number of performances. As critic Charles Spencer reports,

> Kneeling before Aladdin in the cave, she [Anderson] sexily inquires, 'Master, what is your wish?' 'Tell her to rub your wick,' suggested a raucous voice from the stalls.

It is not surprising that audience members heckled Anderson. In a performance genre that breaks the fourth wall, audience members are afforded the opportunity for live interaction with people and characters who, prior to the event, have only be consumed via screen or publication. A heckle such as this, therefore, can be read as the externalization of an internal thought with the individual's goal being that of identification and acknowledgement. It is unclear whether Anderson reacted to this heckle, but another example shared via YouTube depicts the same scene and her response of 'Ain't that the truth!' when a male voice interjects after Aladdin asks, 'What can you show me in here [the cave] that I haven't already seen?' Heckling, therefore, attempts to disrupt the Role, forcing it to break into Performer and Character. In the above case, Anderson's immediate reaction appears to have constituted an excavation of 'self' (Performer). Her response, aimed directly at the audience, acknowledged their presence, but did not leave Performer fully exposed due to the existence of the costume, surrounding characters and set. Although disrupted, the construction of Role in pantomime ensures the equilibrium between Performer and Character can never be broken during performance, even when confronted with a heckler or an aspect of the production gone wrong.

Many aspects contribute to the creation of Role as well as aesthetic allusions, such as the *Baywatch* swimsuit and use of a surfboard for the Genie's transportation; comedy is an important factor and contributes to pantomime's enduring appeal. In the case of celebrities, comedy is almost always created by the juxtaposition of coincidence and irony, the acknowledgement of which results in a feeling of superiority for audience members. Scriptwriter Eric Potts's opening dialogue for Anderson as the Genie of the Lamp reveals one way this is achieved through the character's description of her function in the narrative:

> **Genie of the Lamp:** … to help them [people], to guide them, to run provocatively towards them in slow motion on the beach as the tide comes faster in than they expect.

The dialogue refers to the opening credits and the much-parodied sequences in *Baywatch* which have become an iconic aspect of popular culture. Comedy is achieved by the fact that Anderson is reciting the lines and that the Genie is unaware of their significance. In this sense, it is merely a coincidence that the Genie's actions should echo those of C. J. Parker's, but the presence of Anderson links the two Venn-like. With Anderson re-creating the run onstage and dressed in an evocative costume, enforced ghosting is employed with pleasure in the form of laughter achieved from the shared recognition of Anderson in the role.

But comedy is also used to help heighten pantomime's notion of the unique event, which itself stems from the fact that Anderson only appeared in Wimbledon for a short period of time. The following dialogue in which the Slave of the Ring and Genie of the Lamp meet while in the Enchanted Cave helps locate the production firmly in Wimbledon, while also mirroring the celebrity-fan relationship:

Genie of the Lamp: I've flown all the way from Beverley Hills and that's all I can do for you?
Slave of the Ring: I know Beverley Hills, her father's a butcher in Streatham.
Genie of the Lamp: I think it's a different Beverley Hills. I'm loving that top.
Slave of the Ring: Thank you great Genie. You can get two for ten pounds in Matalan.
Genie of the Lamp: Matalan? Is that the place on the strip between Gucci and Prada?
Slave of the Ring: Erm … I think I'm out of my depth here.

The contrast of high-street value brand Matalan against luxury brands Gucci and Prada distinguishes the Genie of the Lamp against the Slave of the Ring, with whom the audience are more likely to identify as the inclusion of local neighbourhood Streatham links the Slave of the Ring to Wimbledon. Further distance between the characters is created not only by the geographical contrast of Beverley Hills and Streatham, but also by the contrast in clothing choices which helps contribute to the Genie's superiority and one whose lifestyle reflects that of Anderson. But Anderson's celebrity profile does not only encompass luxury brands, her blonde hair and famous figure contribute towards a ditzy blonde persona, which was used to great effect in the following dialogue amended for the Liverpool transfer that also references *Baywatch*:

Genie of the Lamp: Would you like to travel on a magic carpet or off?

Aladdin: What's ever easiest for you. I can go on, but it's no hassle off.

Genie of the Lamp: Hasselhoff? That sounds vaguely familiar!

Aladdin: Isn't he playing Peter Pan in Wimbledon this year?

Genie of the Lamp: No, it's Captain Hook actually.

The punning of 'hassle off' with David Hasselhoff, Anderson's co-star in *Baywatch*, creates yet another reference to the television series, while 'this year' situates her performance in the present as part of the shared community of now. That the Genie of the Lamp recalls the name strongly suggests a link between the Genie and David Hasselhoff, via the role of C. J. Parker played by Anderson. The uncertainty also reflects Anderson's ditzy blonde persona as the Genie can't locate where or why she knows 'Hasselhoff' and therefore leaves the audience feeling superior on account that they have 'got' the pun.

But a feeling of superiority may also arise from the opportunity to witness Anderson's stage debut, which will encompass, as she writes in her blog, the first time she will sing in public (Monetti 2009). Turner argues that,

> Audiences place individual celebrities somewhere along a continuum that ranges from seeing them as objects worthy of desire or emulation to regarding them as spectacular freaks worthy of derision. Mostly celebrities attract one form of response rather than the other …, but it is possible to attract both from different constituencies – or even from the same constituency (2004: 55)

However, although Anderson controlled and facilitated the acknowledgement of her public persona through its visual and textual reference, it was also an opportunity for her to display lesser-known talents. In the Liverpool Empire transfer, the Genie entered the laundry playing a saxophone when meeting Wishee Washee and Widow Twankey for the first time. The audience's reaction was markedly different to that of her other entrances due to the saxophone's sound being heard before she was revealed. Audience members are likely to have presumed the saxophonist in the band was playing the musical instrument as part of the Genie's entrance music, but when it was revealed that Anderson was the saxophonist, after initial whoops at her sighting, the audience fell quiet, almost stunned to silence. As audience members began to appreciate Anderson's musical skill, or perhaps cynically avoided noise in the hope of hearing a mistake, whoops of encouragement were heard followed by wolf whistles. While sexually suggestive, the entrance displayed her musical talent and increased the nature of the unique event as the audience bore witness to a rare Anderson saxophone recital.

A survey of the production's reviews reveal that although, in the words of Charles Spencer, 'no one in their right mind, could describe her as a good actress' (2009), her appearance was, according to Lynn Gardner, 'perfectly genial' (2009) with Rhoda Koenig adding that 'Anderson is up to the demands of the role – cheerleader enthusiasm, harem-girl submissiveness, and a bit of pouting' (2009). Carlson discusses how audience members 'may experience a famous actor through an aura of expectations that masks failings that would be troubling in someone less celebrated' (2003: 59), and in Anderson's case, audience members audibly communicated their excitement and enjoyment at her appearance. The fact that her acting constituted what Gardner calls 'a personal appearance' (2009) rather than a performance is exactly the reason her fans attended – Anderson's fame overriding any disappointment of talent. But while fans relish the opportunity of the unique event to celebrate Anderson's presence, non-fans can equally enjoy Anderson's performance, relishing the opportunity to witness a celebrity struggling to perform to the same standard as her fellow actors. This duality of audience was particularly evident in Act Two during a musical number in which characters sing of other jobs they would like to do, usually more famous or glamorous than their current situation. This 'dream' builds until Anderson makes an unexpected entrance and participates with the lyric 'If I were not in Old Peking, someone else I'd rather be. If I were not in Old Peking, I'd still be me!' She then proceeds to body pop in a moment where certain audience members cheer and applaud *Baywatch*'s Pamela Anderson as the Genie of the Lamp while others laugh at the moment's absurdity.

'There is no doubt whom the audience is there to see'

Henry Hitchings, the *Evening Standard*'s theatre critic, wrote that 'there is no doubt whom the audience is there to see' (Hitchings 2009). With so many references to her career throughout the production, and with the pantomime's advertising centring on her casting, it could be successfully argued that Anderson's appearance warrants classification as a vehicle play, defined by Carlson as 'a work constructed precisely to feature the already familiar aspects of a particular actor's performance' (2003: 68). Amended lyrics to Eartha Kitt's 'Santa Baby' detailing the 'rock stars I had to kiss' rather than 'fellas' the singer 'could have kissed' and requests for labels including British designer Vivienne Westwood, who designed her costume for the Liverpool transfer, help further enforce her biography and blend Anderson with Genie.

Aside from the shared community of Pantoland, other communities exist in the form of fan bases who engage with the celebrity via a range of media platforms. The casting of someone for whom the media take an interest regardless of whether engaged in a pantomime or not means that producers and venues are aided in their marketing by way of association and exposure. The channels of operation enable such performers access to high-impact publications and broadcasts with large readerships and viewing figures with both *Aladdin* and Anderson benefitting from exposure in the *Sunday Express* as a result of her guest blog (Monetti 2009).

When the poster for *Aladdin* at the New Wimbledon Theatre was revealed, tabloid newspaper the *Daily Mail* published an article about the use of an image originally used for a 2003 PETA vegetarian campaign of Anderson wearing only lettuce leaves (*Daily Mail*, 4 December

2009). The reuse and editing of stock images is however common practice in pantomime publicity as busy production schedules preclude the organization of press launches and programmes contain advertisements for the following year's production even though the cast has not been confirmed. While this usually goes unnoticed, the commissioning of such an article reveals the impact the editors hoped Anderson would achieve due to her celebrity status. Not only does it advertise the production without appearing to do so, but it also reminds us that, 'the point of publicity and promotion is to turn advertising into news' (Turner, Bonner and Marshall 2000: 31). By reprinting the PETA poster, readers are reminded of Anderson's animal rights campaigning as well as her modelling and *Baywatch* career due to the lettuce leaves resembling a bikini. However, although appearing to focus on the use of the PETA image, the article uses the airbrushed poster to comment on an accompanying photograph of Anderson shopping with 'dishevelled hair and a tired complexion' (*Daily Mail*, 4 December 2009), humanizing the celebrity. The article also suggests that Anderson accepted the pantomime contract due to financial hardship. At a time of recession, Anderson is reported to be making sacrifices to survive, even if they include, as the article suggests, parting with gold-lined swimming pools. The article therefore highlights Anderson's extraordinary lifestyle, distancing her from the general public, while concurrently aligning her with the general public via the use of an image and reference to her financial situation. After the production opened, a number of tabloid newspapers reported on her eating crisps and chips in a local pub further shattering the notion of her extraordinary lifestyle (*Mail Online*, 16 December 2009) and enforcing her engagement with British culture. It is this blend of the everyday and exceptional that provides celebrities with what Marshall defines 'ideological power' (1997: 85), while the article contributes to the press' degradation of commercial pantomime as being full of washed-up stars.

Dyer believes that the notion of identifying or reaching the 'irreducible core' or 'true identity' of the star as a person (1986: 8) is key to understanding the celebrity's attraction, and the above article is one way cultural intermediaries satisfy the public's desire to achieve this. Marshall states, 'it is the solving by the audience of the enigma of the star's personality that helps formulate the celebrity: the audience wants to know the authentic nature of the star beyond the screen' (1997: 85) and in pantomime, the stage-door encounter provides the opportunity to achieve this.

In order to discover the celebrity's irreducible core, fans often participate in a quasi-celebrity pilgrimage to obtain a photograph or autograph, preferably, as Rojek states, 'delivered with a "personal" message to the fan' (2001: 59). Rojek identifies this as the St Thomas affect in which 'the compulsion to authenticate a desired object [results in] … travelling to it, touching it and photographing it' (2001: 62). This process of verification is a significant opportunity for individuals to interact on a personal level with the aim of humanizing a fan's so far para-social celebrity relationship. As Rojek explains, 'The physical and cultural remoteness of the object from the spectator means that audience relationships carry a high propensity of fantasy and desire' (2001: 25–26). Whereas Anderson has previously only been consumed via a screen or image, her stage-door presence in Wimbledon offers the opportunity of physical contact, and it is this prospect of turning the para-social into actual interaction, of becoming an identified fan and the possibility of a relationship that is attractive to fans. The stage-door conversation is now an integral part of the pantomime experience for autograph hunters, with celebrities obliging in order to maintain their status. Embodying the personal, autographs, often with a personal message to the fan, become proof of the individual's encounter with the celebrity and signify that a mutual exchange has occurred. The individual becomes the identified fan, and having been acknowledged personally by their idol achieves a sense of fulfilment.

Photographs capture the close proximity between fan and celebrity when such an exchange occurs. Some celebrities engage in handshakes, hugs or place their arm around the fan's shoulders to give the appearance of friendship; however, although read in this way by the fan, the action is merely a ritualized gesture. Performing the ritual of friendship strengthens the fan's imagined bond between themselves and the celebrity, and with photographs and autographs archiving the ephemeral encounter, material possessions come to act as signifiers for a fan's loyalty and personal connection to their idol, which can then be shared via social media. Such actions broadcast the personal event and depict audience member and celebrity together, not only encouraging others to 'seek a more active engagement in the lives of their idols' (Rojek 2001: 89) and thus constituting advertising for the pantomime, but also portraying an approachable celebrity who has time for his/her fans. Pictures, tweets and Facebook statuses help suggest that a fan's investment and loyalty in following the celebrity will be rewarded with personal interaction if tickets to the pantomime are booked. Other social media users' comments further validate and verify the existence of the encounter, and as a result its occurrence is firmly accepted as a shared moment occupying a place in both fan and celebrity's personal history. But while many fans' activities remain harmless, the casting of Anderson in her second pantomime reprising the role of Genie at the Liverpool Empire resulted in the arrest of her stalker (*Daily Express*, 3 January 2011). This particular encounter occurred as Anderson boarded a train after performing, whereupon an allegedly previously cautioned man followed and approached her before being arrested by police. That the episode attracted wide media coverage in national newspapers *The Metro*, *Daily Mirror*, *Daily Mail*, *Daily Express* and a number of online blogs only confirms Anderson's celebrity status while concurrently advertising the performance.

A genre that thrives on interaction, commercial pantomime has adopted celebrity casting as a way to present well-known names to audiences and capitalize from their successes in a competitive entertainment market. Regardless of talent, the celebrity pantomime cast member offers the opportunity of interaction and acknowledgement at a live event. The shared community created during performance through the recognition of aesthetic and textual referencing helps locate the pantomime in the present, while celebrity, media and theatre profit by the dissemination of news. The prospect of attending a unique event and encountering a celebrity at the theatre continues to contribute to pantomime's enduring appeal in a society obsessed by fame and for which, as Rojek states, celebrities have replaced God and the divine rights of kings as 'new symbols of recognition and belonging' (2001: 14). The consistent casting of celebrities in commercial pantomime has led to the practice becoming an expected and anticipated aspect of the genre and one that continues to evolve as pantomime embraces the popular through performance to ensure its survival.

Bibliography

Adams, W. L (2009), 'It's Panto Season in Britain, *Baywatch*-Style', *Time*, 28 December. http://content.time.com/time/arts/article/0,8599,1950006,00.html (accessed 12 October 2015).

Abhishek, S. (2013), 'How *Baywatch* Unknowingly Changed the World: The Untapped Power of TV Shows', *Huffington Post*, 25 November, http://www.huffingtonpost.com/abhishek-seth/how-baywatch-unknowingly-changed-the-world_b_3891368.html (accessed 12 October 2015).

Boorstin, D.J. (1971), *The Image: A Guide to Pseudo-Events in America*. New York: Atheneum.

Carlson, M. A (2003), *The Haunted Stage – The Theatre as a Memory Machine*. Michigan: University of Michigan Press.

Cashmore, E. (2006), *Celebrity/Culture*. Abingdon: Routledge.

Dyer, R. (1979), *Stars*. London: BFI Publishing.

Dyer, R. (1986), *Heavenly Bodies: Film Stars and Society*. London: BFI Publishing.

First Family Entertainment (2015), 'About', *First Family Entertainment*, http://www.ffe-uk.com/about/ (accessed 12 October 2015).

Frow, G. (1985), *Oh Yes It Is!: A History of Pantomime*. London: BBC Books.

Gardner, Lyn (2009), 'Pamela Anderson in *Aladdin*', *Guardian*, 16 December, http://www.theguardian.com/stage/2009/dec/16/pamela-anderson-aladdin (accessed 12 October 2015).

Giles, D. (2000), *Illusions of Immortality: A Psychology of Fame and Celebrity*. London: Arnold.

Hitchings, H. (2009), 'We Finally See Her Face … and She's Really Quite a Game Genie', *Evening Standard*, 16 December, http://www.standard.co.uk/goingout/theatre/pamela-andersons-really-quite-a-game-genie-in-aladdin-7417933.html (accessed 12 October 2015).

Koenig, R. (2011), '*Aladdin*, New Wimbledon Theatre, London', *Independent*, 11 October, http://www.independent.co.uk/arts-entertainment/theatre-dance/reviews/aladdin-new-wimbledon-theatre-london-1842866.html (accessed 12 October 2015).

Lathan, P. (2004), *It's Behind You!: The Story of Panto*. London: New Holland Publishers.

Lee, V. (2009), 'Pamela Anderson's Behind You! Oh No, She Isn't', *Guardian*, 10 December, http://www.theguardian.com/stage/theatreblog/2009/dec/10/pamela-anderson-alladin-panto (accessed 12 October 2015).

Lipton, M. (2007), 'Celebrity vs Tradition: "Branding" in Modern British Pantomime', *New Theatre Quarterly*, 23 (2): 136–51.

Lipton, M. (2008), 'Principally Boys? Gender Dynamics and Casting Practices in Modern British Pantomime', *Contemporary Theatre Review*, 18 (4): 470–86.

Marshall, D. P. (1997), *Celebrity and Power*. Minneapolis: University of Minnesota Press.

Monetti, S. (2009), 'Genie of the Lamp Pamela Anderson stars in *Aladdin* pantomime', *Daily Express*, 13 December, http://www.express.co.uk/entertainment/theatre/145815/Genie-of-the-Lamp-Pamela-Anderson-stars-in-Aladdin-pantomime (accessed 12 October 2015).

Ofcom (2015), 'Facts & Figures'. http://media.ofcom.org.uk/facts/ (accessed 12 October 2015).

'Pamela Anderson Pops to the Pub for Chips after Her Opening Night in Panto', *Mail Online*, 16 December 2009, http://www.dailymail.co.uk/tvshowbiz/article-1236125/Pamela-Anderson-Baywatch-style-costume-play-genie-lamp-Aladdin-New-Wimbledon-theatre.html (accessed 12 October 2015).

'Pamela Anderson "Stalker" Terror', *Daily Express*, 3 January 2011, http://www.express.co.uk/celebrity-news/220839/Pamela-Anderson-stalker-terror (accessed 12 October 2015).

'Pamela Anderson to Star in Panto' (2009), *BBC News*, 15 October, http://news.bbc.co.uk/1/hi/entertainment/8308554.stm (accessed 12 October 2015).

'Panto Bosses Raid the Archives for Pamela Anderson Picture (and when She Looks Like This, Who Could Blame Them?' (2009), *Daily Mail*, 4 December, //www.dailymail.co.uk/tvshowbiz/article-1232919/Panto-bosses-raid-archives-Pamela-Anderson-picture-looks-like-blame-them.html (accessed 12 October 2015).

'Panto Box Office Worth £146 Million' (2014), *Celebrate Panto*, 12 December, http://celebratepanto.co.uk/pantoboxoffice146million/ (accessed 12 October 2015).

'Panto Pamela Anderson to Star in *Aladdin*' (2009), *Metro*, 14 October, http://metro.co.uk/2009/10/14/panto-pamela-anderson-to-star-in-aladdin-at-londons-new-wimbledon-theatre-487924/ (accessed 12 October 2015).

Pavia, W. (2009), 'Interview: Christopher Biggins', *The Times*, 17 October, http://entertainment.timesonline.co.uk/tol/arts_and_entertainment/stage/article6878519.ece (accessed 12 October 2015).

Quinn, M. (1990), 'Celebrity and the Semiotics of Acting', *New Theatre Quarterly*, 6 (22): 154–61.

Rojek, C. (2001), *Celebrity*. London: Reaktion Books.

Salberg, D. (1981), *Once Upon a Pantomime*. New York: Corntey Publications.

Sladen, S. (2011), 'There is Nothing Like a Dame', *British Theatre Guide*, 27 March, http://www.britishtheatreguide.info/articles/270311.htm (accessed 24 May 2016).

Spencer, C. (2009), 'Pamela Anderson in *Aladdin* at the Wimbledon Theatre: Review', *The Telegraph*, 15 December, http://www.telegraph.co.uk/culture/theatre/theatre-reviews/6821133/Pamela-Anderson-in-Aladdin-at-the-Wimbledon-Theatre-review.html (accessed 12 October 2015).

Taylor, M. (2007), *British Pantomime Performance*. Exeter: Intellect.

Turner, A. W. (2010), *Rejoice! Rejoice! Britain in the 1980s*. London: Aurum.

Turner, G. (2004), *Understanding Celebrity*. London: Sage Publications.

Turner, G., F. Bonner and P. D. Marshall (2000), *Fame Games: The Production of Celebrity in Australia*. Melbourne: Cambridge University Press.

9

With Them, Not at Them

Bim Mason

In this chapter I aim to outline the principles that create popular appeal in two different types of street theatre. I use examples from work that I was heavily involved in: the Mummer&dada company (1985–90) and the Bigheads (2002–08). These examples are different in that Mummer&dada set out to produce shows that were static theatre on the street (although venues ranged from parks, barns, beaches, castles, fetes, festivals and circus tents) and proposed a theatrical narrative located in other places and times. In contrast, the Bigheads were mobile, almost entirely interactive, working briefly with small groups of spectators, creating a dramaturgy in the present moment. The examples are also different in that I refer to several of the seven Mummer&dada shows but there was essentially only one Bighead show, even though it was adapted for many different circumstances over six years. The difference between the examples is useful to show how common principles, such as responsiveness, are applied in different ways, emphasizing different aspects of popular appeal. Using the Bigheads, I will go into detail of the creative processes involved, from training through devising into performance and development, using the principles of open play, novelty, the attraction of risk as well as a community of conspiracy. This leads to a discussion of the interaction between playful artificiality and actual reality, in reference to the shows of Mummer&dada: the problems and opportunities, the creation of temporary communities and how this affects power relationships. Finally I indicate how empowerment operates in both examples, using the principle of an open-playing interaction. To approach these subjects I explain what infinite playing means in practice by outlining some training tactics used for walkabout performance and especially the Bigheads.

The Bigheads themselves were about one metre tall, constructed out of latex with fibre glass matting, and were therefore both waterproof and flexible. The performer's upper body was concealed when standing and the whole body was entirely concealed when crouching. Arms could protrude from slits near the ears or withdrawn to operate rotating eyeballs or a long tongue. The performers could only see through the nostrils and small holes in the eyebrows so they were connected by walkie-talkies to a 'controller' who was on the lookout for obstacles and opportunities. The optimum group size was three but on a few occasions a group of fifteen was presented. Their first outing was at the Brighton Fringe Festival in 2002 and they went on to appear around Europe and as far away as Detroit, Montreal and Singapore until 2008.

The Bigheads performances were aimed at generating an active response from spectators. This aim was partly in reaction to a current

Figure 9.1 Bighead at *Juste Pour Rire* Festival, Montreal 2005 (photo © Bim Mason)

tendency for walkabout acts to present very safe, 'cute' images that required only passive spectatorship. Their unusual appearance meant spectators engaged with the unfamiliar, providing the thrill of risk. Such novelty is popular because 'discovery and exploration imply transcendence, a going beyond the known, a stretching of one's self toward new dimensions of skills and experience' (Csikszentmihalyi 1975: 33). The Bigheads were intended to be un-ignorable; to not only make fun of a situation but to make fun *with* the spectators. The material was comprised of a few set routines that could be cued as appropriate, but was mostly improvised in response to the locations and the reaction of onlookers. This was what James Carse calls 'infinite games' (1986) without consistent rules, limits or goals, whose only aim was to maintain the playing as long as possible.

> The reaction of the female contingent is particularly interesting. A group of girls scream their heads off on seeing the arrival of the first Head ... but one very deluded adolescent places herself for a memorable photo (sandwiched between two tongues). A woman accepts a licking of her knee, but with tossed head exclaims 'You're not my type'. Another holds a Head and declares firmly: 'Damn pig!' ... That said, the insults and jeers surrounding the Bigheads are made in joy and good humour. After all that's the role of slapheads. (Guy 2005)

Why is infinite playing so important to this area of work? Within my first year as a professional performer, one of the regular jobs I was lucky enough to get was as a jester in a London tourist restaurant with a Shakespearean theme. A large part of this job was to go round the tables doing simple conjuring tricks. With my limited number of tricks, it was necessary to repeat them as I worked my way through the room. What I quickly learned was that, if I asked open questions, the encounter would always be different – 'Do you know a magic word?' might lead into play that drifted away from the premise of the conjuring. This removed the stress of 'succeeding' at the illusion and made the encounter more pleasurable as we all became involved in the moment of seeing where the game could go. The other thing that I learned was to adapt to the many different cultures within the room – from example, it was often easier to play with the southern Europeans than the more reserved East Asians who appeared to find my uninvited intrusion into their meal inappropriate because my interaction was being forced upon them. As Carse says, 'Whoever *must* play cannot *play*' (1986: 4). By pulling back and adopting a more formal manner, it was possible to meet them halfway.

Training

We begin by developing skills in leading and following, establishing ways to communicate non-verbal instructions efficiently, as well as practicing acute observation. For example, in simple mirror work there are certain positions and types of movement that are impossible to follow accurately at the same time. Once these principles have been understood, a pair can move into mirroring without a leader, with both following where they think the other wants to go, so that there is a sense of 'we' wanting to move in a certain way. In practice this involves tentative micro-proposals that, if confirmed by the partner, are advanced and developed. Although this sounds fairly basic as an exercise, developing the principle of an equal contribution to what emerges is fundamental to any one-to-one interplay and requires sophistication in being able to communicate, adapt and be aware of the qualities of another. As well as taking care to avoid either imposing an idea or of being too passive, there needs to be a highly focused engagement with the actuality of the other, in the moment: Who are they? How are they feeling right now? Where does this seem to be going? Because there is no 'goal' or endpoint, some students become anxious because they don't know what they are supposed to be doing and it takes some practice for them to realize that the unpredictability can be fun. Others may become unmotivated by the lack of a goal and it takes a while before they appreciate that the journey, not the destination, is the goal. This is practice in infinite play.

The next stage is to simulate a walkabout encounter, using both the leader-follower and the no-leader methods. One of the pair imagines that they are not a trainee performer but a 'normal' member of the public, a 'receptor'. They can be responsive to play proposals but do not initiate them. The other is the 'activator', taking the lead, for example, by setting up a game of copying actions, enlarging the version that is repeated back to them and developing any quality that they notice, such as force, elegance or hesitancy. However, if the receptor feels that the game might be developing too far or too fast for a normal member of the public they can pull back or pull out, in which case the activator must reduce their actions to mirror the 'decline'. Conversely the activator may notice signs of pleasure and can follow and develop the source of the pleasure so that there is a sense of release or 'leading out'. The outcome is that there emerges a sense of playing on an edge between aversion and pleasure, between coming together or diverging, of reassurance and challenge. So the activator must not only play within the game, they must also be aware of how the game is being played. Specifically for walkabout theatre, it is useful to experiment with different numbers of activator performers and passive spectators. If a single activator works with a group of spectators, the group may feel safe but, as a consequence of their temporary community, it may be difficult to induce them into playing but, if an activator succeeds, they may begin to feel quite powerful. By contrast, a group of performers working with a single spectator may feel oppressive, particularly if they surround the individual. These experiments can progress into different arrangements of duos and trios. They clarify the power relationships that are in play, a subject I will return to.

Of course, this raises the question of how a group of performers can improvise collectively in street situations that are unpredictable and may have many stimuli. If all the members of the performing group follow different stimuli it will disperse and be impossible to watch. To prepare for this I use training through choral work, which is similar to the no-leader mirror system but is done in small groups (e.g. five to seven). In this case the participants will not have full visual contact with the entire group all the time, unless they are arranged in an inward facing circle, which would be closed off to spectators. The group can share leadership either by changing direction so that different members are at the front or they can keep rotating individually. This is not just a fun way to improvise as a group but is a valuable training in sensitivity, accuracy of replication and developing a multidirectional awareness. It also develops an awareness of when to nudge an initiative forward (if the activity is becoming boring) and when to conform and reinforce cohesion (if the group begins to disperse).

As is suggested by Emergent Norm Theory (Turner and Killian 1972: 25), a group dynamic can encourage behaviour to be more extreme; individuals lose their fear of entering unfamiliar territory and therefore bigger risks can be taken. Each choral group will tend to have a slightly different shared 'culture' as a result of prevailing movement and performing tendencies, for example, by being more 'theatrical' (verbal, character-based) or more dance-like (non-verbal, abstract movement). These group characteristics can be heightened by facing off one group against another, almost like two individuals shifting their relationship in a pair improvisation. This provides a useful model for walkabout performance where the 'culture' of the performing group is confronted with the culture of the spectators. One of the many developments of the basic format is allowing temporary dispersal into trios, duos and even solos, while maintaining an awareness of everything else occurring around them, regrouping when the subunits become more interested in what others are doing. Another way is to encourage individuals to separate from the rest of the group in order to stimulate or provoke them, perhaps by morphing the ongoing activity into a particular sort of game. This practice in proposition-response is an excellent preparation for walkabout performance.

Devising walkabout performance

Unless there is a particular reason to remain invisible, the initial proposition of a walkabout act must have strong visual impact (which could be through exceptional behaviours), because there is likely to be a cacophony of surrounding noise in outdoor performance situations. If the image is really strong (such as the giant mechanical elephant of Royal de Luxe, 2005–6) it may be that it is sufficient for spectators to simply stand and stare, as they would watch any procession, but walkabout comes alive when there is interaction. It is a different experience to observing visual art in a gallery because it demands an active response – there is 'something going on'. The initial visual impact needs to set up open questions – What is it? What is going on? What is it for? How does it work? The greater the hook of curiosity, the better is the proposition. The unpredictability creates an element of the risk and thus, as I have suggested, has popular appeal. So, in the initial stages of devising, the big question is, what can create curiosity? However, there also needs to be some cultural connection with the public, a slight familiarity. As is well known, much contemporary visual art is not 'popular' and one reason for this is because it may be difficult to connect to without an education in the subject. Familiarity reassures and unpredictability creates excitement; one is about community and structure, the other about chaos. The third element is the shifting balance between the two; walkabout performers need to be adept at knowing when to emphasize one over the other and be able to adapt rapidly to changing situations in the moment of performance.

In the case of the Bigheads, I spent many months considering the nature of the initial visual image and researching suitable materials and construction techniques, before committing myself to the considerable investment of time required in making them. The image originally derived from a photograph of a medieval 'reredos' carving of a chimera and was thus linked to the grotesque tradition of gargoyles and the carnivalesque. I also had in mind the aesthetic of ghost train advertisements, football mascot costumes, high street promotion figures, Disneyesque dwarves and manga fantasy creatures. Although large heads are often used to caricature political figures in demonstrations, it was important to avoid easy definition in order to keep the questioning open. Similarly the gender of many of them was indeterminate and worn by both men and women. The huge, extending tongues could be seen as being simply cheeky or used more lasciviously, particularly as they emerged from the position of the performer's pelvis area suggestively. Changing the emphasis between cheekiness and lasciviousness according to the nature of the spectators was easy. Similarly, the heads could crouch down, hiding the legs, using hand gestures through the arm slits to wave and mirror reactions. This unthreatening position could draw in very small children.

Once any mask has been created it must be 'auditioned' to see what kind of movements 'fit' with it. From these we worked out some simple choreography to establish methods of travelling, arrival and departure and a cueing system (using walkie-talkies, connecting to an outside 'controller') because of the limited visibility. The training in choral work to cohere the group through minimal observation proved extremely useful. These movement routines provided default material that could give some security if the situation did not offer much to play with. However, the appropriateness of these routines could only be tested by taking them out into a real street situation. As with much walkabout performance, practical experimentation is the only way to discover the potential of the initial appearance. With such unpredictability, if too much is overdetermined, the performers may find themselves imposing a relationship on the spectators, closing down the scope of the playing. By keeping fairly neutral and observing first reactions – for example, whether the image attracts or repels – an attitude to the public and physical surroundings can begin to be established. During the first outing of the Bigheads (for a photo shoot), some spectators kept their distance, but families with small children were induced to come close and interact gently. However situations can be so different that one must be wary of making too many fixed conclusions. On the second outing teenagers screamed excitedly and playfully ran a few steps away, so the Heads began to develop this game with brief rapid advances. Over many outings some of our initial 'clever' ideas were discarded and others were discovered in moments of 'take off', when spectator reactions encourage a particular new stratagem. For example, bottles of water were carried within the Heads for the performer to drink and also to pour onto the tongues to make them look wet. One day it was discovered that this water could be flicked off the tongue and this would not only increase excitement but would also prevent spectators crowding around so tightly that others could not see. The fact that the water could create this reaction despite not being real saliva is a phenomenon that began to fascinate us, so we experimented with sneezing and spitting. This is a good example of the 'not-real' having a real effect; most theatre is already signalled 'This is play', but provocative work confuses that easy definition. It is 'a more complex form of play; the game which is constructed not upon the premise "This is play" but rather round the question "Is this play?" And this type of interaction also has its ritual forms, for example, in the hazing of initiation' (Bateson 1972: 155). A spectator can watch a theatrical play passively but a spectator watching a street fight, for example, will wonder if they need to take action or, if threatened, to recoil. A spectator watching a 'real' stunt will be engaged with the question: 'Will it be alright?' So, spectators watching the Bigheads question 'Is it safe?' and have an automatic response to the suggestion of sensuality or disgust of saliva, even though they know it is not real.

Gradually we built up a 'Users Manual' for the Bigheads that became a repository for what had been learned by different performers in a wide variety of situations and countries over several years. This covered questions of preparations, communication systems, how to travel between locations, how to create dramatic tension, how and who to excite with provocation, how to calm a situation down and how to escape. It took into account the different levels of received experience by various audiences: babies accepted the Heads as 'real' and had no fear (on one occasion a baby allowed itself to be swallowed), slightly older toddlers (and dogs) could become terrified. Older children would know they were not real but could still be strongly affected by the illusion, either by 'adopting' a head like a pet or, more commonly, hitting it without an awareness of the performer inside. Teenagers would be partially aware of the performer but would enjoy entering into the game with pubescent hilarity. Youth and some adults might feel confident to 'perform' to their friends in response to provocation. For example, at an international rugby cup final (Millennium Stadium, Cardiff, 2003), the Heads withdrew to the side of a passing tide of raucous spectators and, despite using only minimal movements, the visual impact provoked very lewd public behaviour – 'sexy' dancing and offering themselves to be licked back and front, in front of hundreds of people. This was an example of 'lift off', where the event takes on a life of its own and the performer's role becomes one of sustaining the energy, only intervening where necessary. In other situations, older adults might be more detached, empathizing with the performers, appreciating the aesthetics and what was being implied in all the various levels of play.

Real and 'not-real' in the contest for power

These different attitudes to the real/not-real conveyed different kinds of dramatic tension. Just as the water was not saliva but was treated as such, the grotesque appearance had a 'real' effect when juxtaposed with a contrasting context. For example, the surprise they created was stronger when they appeared in a mundane supermarket than when they did within a festival context. The juxtaposition with the ordinary made the location seem surreal. If the Heads mirrored normal behaviour, such as using a public phone, waiting for a bus or sitting at a restaurant table, they could include those they copied into the extraordinary picture. Similarly, if a Head placed itself right next to authority or privileged figures, it made them look absurd without having to 'do' anything. The Natural Theatre Company managed to coincide their Flowerpot Heads walkabout with a walk-past of Margaret Thatcher and the photograph of the encounter hit the front pages of several national newspapers. If there is some kind of interaction, the dramatic tension becomes even more attractive. We managed to arrange for one of the Heads to be part of the welcoming committee for a visiting royal. The simple friendly offer of a handshake from the performer made the position of privilege seem absurd.

At one festival the Heads were prevented from entering the VIP marquee by a security guard who blocked their way. Attempting to talk to the concealed performer looked ridiculous, as did calling for back-up on their radio. The tongue-tip slowly advancing towards the torso of the guard made their defiant posturing almost impossible. However, having made fun of the situation and not wanting to upset the individual, we moved on. The presence of police cars at festivals provides opportunities that have the advantage of making fun of the symbols of power rather than the individuals. Licking the car and playing with windscreen wipers created huge tension and popular interest in how much the officers inside would tolerate and how far we dared to go. During moments like these very close attention needs to be paid to the shifting balance between their reaction as humans, enjoying the attention and the cheekiness, and the role they are in costume to play, maintaining respect for the institutions they represent. Spectators will be aware that performers are similarly on a risky edge, and this has the attraction of a high-wire act. One of the key skills that are admired in street theatre by performers and spectators alike is that of being able to play on an edge between challenging an audience and reassuring them, like standing in the middle of a see-saw shifting weight to fine-tune emphasis as circumstances change. As is clear from the interest in sporting events, the spectacle of contest is immensely popular; if the contest is with those who have power over most of us, there is likely to be a complicit enjoyment in witnessing others transgressing boundaries that we might fear to cross. This complicity is a kind of community of conspiracy. In addition, because there is some ridiculing of power or its representatives, they are slightly diminished, and consequently those who feel themselves to be part of the community of conspiracy can experience a slight enlargement of their power.

It is a paradox of walkabout performance that the public act of making oneself look foolish and vulnerable can be empowering. It suggests that the imperative to conform to conventional behaviour has less power over the performer and, by implication, questions the validity or appropriateness of those conventions. Just as a circus audience may admire the daring of a performer and empathize with them, so a street audience may admire the courage and endurance of a performer, particularly if they appear to revel in the foolishness, rather than feeling embarrassed or diminished (as is often the case with those workers who are required to wear a full costume for high-street promotions). So, in the case of the sports event, referred to earlier, when the Heads provoked lewd spectator behaviour, they acted as a catalyst, giving permission for behaviour that is not 'correct', dignified or respectful but which celebrated sensual pleasure in an open joyful way, free of shame or embarrassment. This release from the constriction of norms is another form of empowerment, an upward movement.

Creating community with Mummer&dada

Having looked at the ways that the not-real impacts on real power relations, in reference to the Bigheads, I now turn to how reality impinges on theatrical illusion in relation to Mummer&dada. The first Mummer&dada group (1985) was a collaboration between students finishing two years at the Jacques Lecoq school and Lee Beagley's Theatre Exchange (also known as Kaboodle). Over the six years of its life the shows expanded in duration and scale, from a UK tour of a twenty-minute outdoor playlet on a simple carpet to international touring in theatres and with its own circus tent. It remains an unusual form of outdoor performance in its hybrid of clown theatre and serious drama. As Owen Dudley Edwards of the *Scotsman* described the first show:

> it also merits serious attention for its encapsulation of many ancient theatre conventions: the medical quacks, the lunatic duels, the ridicule of the alien mingled with fascination, the attempt at conspiracy with the audience in musical support … Clearly the result of very hard work in study and preparation: but the lively cast wears its considerable

authority lightly, and it is guaranteed to crack the most pretentious po-face. (*The Scotsman*, 12 August 1985)

Despite the expansion in scale and the difference of its shows, certain features were retained throughout its life. Shows began after a warm up in public, followed by a brass band tune and an acrobatic fanfare, which led to a direct self-introduction of the constantly multinational cast. All the shows used the death-and-resurrection structure of the Mummers plays, circus techniques, an acrobatic fight, live music and audience participation.

The obvious problem with narrative theatre in a public space, such as a street, is that the fiction is often interrupted by the actuality of the surroundings. Some brief interruptions, such as front-row children needing to find a toilet can be 'forgiven', with the audience and performers having to work harder to remain focused in the fiction. More generally, however, attempting to establish, for example, a rural idyll of Sherwood Forest (*Robin Hood Show*, 1986) in an urban environment is difficult with the urgency of ambulance sirens passing nearby. Similarly, for characters to cut themselves off from the audience by avoiding eye contact may convey either disdain or fear of them, particularly because of the close proximity and lack of physical barriers such as a raised stage. The performers may have been seen to arrive, out of character, to set up the space and equipment so the fiction may appear to be deceitful rather than magical. In order to avoid any sense of being underhand with the deception, we acknowledged it in various ways, using a deliberately artificial style and switching between relishing the fiction and undermining it through parody, for example, by using rhyming couplets and the Mummers' self-introduction ('I'm Flash Harry and I've come here to marry. From the bloody battlefield I have come, where some berk I killed and your hand I have won'). The amateur dramatic qualities, such as using wooden swords and old curtains for costumes, had the effect of disarming any illusions of pretension. The subversion of theatrical illusions such as mime or sound effects (to enhance a combat sequence) not only conveyed a playful conspiracy with the audience against the 'deceit' of the illusion, but could also provide a glimpse of conflict between the actor personas. The announcement of the nationalities of the troupe at the beginning of each show gave a snapshot of the varied individuality of its members and established a semi-authentic level of the persona of the actors. This could be employed when the 'official' performance was ruptured, either by deliberate mistakes or by real events. It allowed the performers to drop out of character and whisper offstage comments to the audience about the quality of performance of others, creating a sense of the relationships within the company. So there were several levels of performativity – the real actor, their troupe persona, the character and, at times, disguises or deceits employed by the characters. These tactics conveyed our awareness and complicity with the audience that the enterprise was just a game. We shared their community.

However, parody and deliberate amateurism is relatively easy and, for a popular audience, may convey introspective concerns – a theatre that is about theatrical forms. So, the physical skills we used were important to establish our credibility as trained performers and provide an element of real risk. Without drawing much attention to the expertise, we nevertheless were able to raise our status to balance out the status-lowering conveyed by the amateurism. Those who at first glance thought we were just 'mucking about' would visibly stop in their tracks and give us more attention. We used skills drawn from traditional popular forms – acrobatics, brass band, magic and 'fakir' stunts. However we also included more refined cultural allusions, because a street audience is not as homogenous as an indoor audience – there has not been the same level of self-selection that occurs with ticket purchase. In later shows we used references to Classical and Judeo-Christian mythologies (e.g. in *Hell Is Not So Hot*, 1988–89). Similarly, we often incorporated animal masks and simple slapstick which appealed to younger audiences. The policy was to avoid the work being pigeonholed to a 'niche' audience, so that, for example, the adults could hear and share the appreciation of younger spectators and the children would be intrigued by the adult laughter at more sophisticated jokes. Certain scenes could be appreciated at different levels simultaneously, as a display of expertise, as a play with form, as a human drama and as a literary allusion. In addition, a narrative with strong melodramatic emotions has always had universal appeal; the celebratory death-and-resurrection structure of Mummers plays contained the basis to provide these emotions. Despite the downward movement of parody, we found it was possible to shift audience perception quickly into a more elevated tragic dimension with the Flamenco singing. As a counterpoint to the linear narrative, the Dada influence provided anti-structural elements, such as seemingly random occasional entrances and mystifyingly inconsequential sequences. So this interweaving of different kinds of appeal was an opening out to make cultural connections with a wide range of audience members.

The moments of interaction with the audience could deepen this sense of creating the event with them. Spectators always identify with the experience of volunteers, imagining how they themselves might react in the given situation. As such the volunteers are representatives of the whole crowd; if they are empowered the whole crowd shares this empowerment. The moment a volunteer turns from walking onstage to facing a large crowd can be intimidating for them so we shared the experience by being physically reassuring and talking with them about how the audience appeared from onstage. Building trust helps to begin a process of inducement to play rather than using coercion. In the *Mediaeval Show* (1985) the two combatant protagonists selected a child each to joust with bamboo poles on their behalf. Having primed his champion, one of the protagonists left to make his escape into the depths of the crowd. This was a moment of open play, creating deliberate uncertainty as to what would occur, with much comic confusion. There was not a correct/incorrect outcome being demanded. In the *Robin Hood Show* (1986) a child was invited to perform the magic spell, and whatever they did or said was mirrored and exaggerated by the attendant performers. At another point the audience was asked to give a gladiatorial thumbs up/thumbs down for the demise of the villain, worked up by two opposing characters, who then switched to actor-persona level to comment on either the spectators' bloodthirstiness or their lack of resolve. In almost all the shows over the years, the resurrection moment at the end was stimulated by an appeal to the entire crowd, who were asked to raise their hands and repeat a phrase ritualistically. This could have felt painfully contrived but, because of the sense of play that had preceded it, there was always an almost universal willingness to enter into the spirit of the game. The sense of community was not only experienced in the shared sound and visual effect but also in sharing the experience of risk to overcome self-consciousness, much in the same way that group choral work eases the stress of unfamiliar behaviour.

Using these various forms of play – theatrical illusion, parody and games – the not-real could conceal serious themes and 'real' performatives. Connecting with an audience through exchange is more than just a feature of popular performing. It implies sharing their perspective and position, voicing their concerns, like the leader of a Greek chorus.

> The man who is speaking is one with the crowd; he does not present himself as its opponent, nor does he teach, accuse or intimidate it. He laughs with it. There is not the slightest tone of morose seriousness in his oration, no fear, piety, or humility. This is an absolutely gay and fearless talk, free and frank, which echoes in the festive square beyond all verbal prohibitions, limitations and conventions. (Bakhtin 1984: 167)

For this reason the empowering upward movement, combined with the downward movement of the elevated, is stimulated by the popular performer.

Mummer&dada existed during the period of political confrontation which marked Margaret Thatcher's government and this presented a challenge to producing work that had popular appeal across a wide spectrum of the public. An overtly political dimension would have set up a divisive partisanship in the audience, particularly as we were touring to rural areas and middle England as well as urban centres. However, avoiding any reference to the political situation seemed to be a self-censorship that conflicted with an aspiration for freedom and empowerment, which is fundamental to popular appeal. Direct references included the suggestion that Robin Hood's green alternative lifestyle in Sherwood Forest had some relation to the 'Peace Convoy' of New Age travellers that was being suppressed by recent legislation (the 'Battle of the Beanfield' had occurred the previous year). The following two productions made fun of the arrogance of self-righteousness with the characters of General Good (based on the figure of Lent in Mediaeval carnival iconography) and Judgement (based on a Morality Play figure). Judgement controlled the region of Purgatory and was costumed as a cross between Thatcher and moral activist Mary Whitehouse. In the climactic acrobatic fight she had to team up with the Devil in order to enforce the strict 'rules' of the underworld. In the same show, God was portrayed as a well-meaning but rather hapless and senile old man, who appeared appropriately *deus ex-machina* from a magic trunk to resolve the conflict by privileging the principle of universal love over strict adherence to the rules. So these references were light, playful and oblique, indicating an ideological standpoint that went wider than specific political positions. They made an appeal to what Turner termed 'communitas', the fellowship of humans that supersedes different norms and values.

> bluff communitas bearers are able through jest and mockery to infuse communitas throughout the whole society. For here ... there is not only reversal but levelling, since the incumbent of each status with an excess of rights is bullied by one with a deficiency of rights. What is left is a kind of social average, or something like the neutral position in a gear box, from which it is possible to proceed in different directions and at different speeds in a new bout of movement. (Turner 1969: 202)

Our ideology was also reflected in the performative elements. The highlighting of the different nationalities and languages at the beginning of the shows, as well as the very different body shapes and individual skills suggested a value in diversity. The self-deprecation by the performers of their distinct qualities mitigated against any sense of taking themselves too seriously. The emphasis on an ensemble, without stars, despite this heterogeneity, as well as the equal number of male and female performers, suggested an avoidance of hierarchical organization. The various invitations for input from spectators widened this sense of ensemble to include the whole audience in the creation of the uniqueness of each event. The avoidance of hierarchy was also reflected in the status relationships between performers and spectators. Entertainers traditionally try to please the audience by serving their tastes from a lower position. Provocateurs, on the other hand, tend to act from a superior position challenging the culture of the audience. Mummer&dada minimized status differences, asserting their skills but, by choosing to perform on the streets and these other performative elements, they avoided the self-aggrandizement characteristic of many performers. Skill denotes something to be admired, exceptional and thus outside the community of the audience. However the interlacing of the real performer who engages with the audience directly and the skillfully played role, means they are partly sharing 'as one of us' and partly 'other'. The combination of 'I am like you' and 'I can do things that you cannot' conveys an implicit suggestion of 'You could do this too'. This is an empowering theme that is attractive to those who feel their power is comparatively weak.

So, in the example of the Mummer&dada work, being *with* the audience was not just a matter of interaction but also a matter of reducing a separating distance. With the Bigheads, the mask created an unavoidable separation between the performer and the spectator; their strangeness combined with their vulnerability proposed a game that was about bridging a gap, about establishing communication with an alien being. The strangeness and intrusive behaviour provided challenge and thrill but was alternated with reassuring softer playing. This give and take created an overall equality of power relationship, with neither the audience nor the performing group imposing on or feeling threatened by the other – performing with them not at them.

Bibliography

Bakhtin, Mikhail ([1969] 1984), *Rabelais and His World*. Bloomington: Indiana University Press.

Bateson, Gregory (1972), *Steps to an Ecology of Mind*. Chicago: The University of Chicago Press.

Carse, James P. (1987), *Finite and Infinite Games*. York: Ballantine Books.

Chantal, Guy (2005), 'Têtes de Cochon', *La Presse*, Montreal, 17 July.

Csikszentmihalyi, Mihaly (1975), *Beyond Boredom and Anxiety*. San Francisco, Washington, London: Jossey-Bass Publishers.

Turner, Ralph H., and Lewis M. Killian (1972), *Collective Behaviour*. Englewood Cliffs, NJ: Prentice-Hall.

Turner, Victor (1969), *The Ritual Process*. London: Routledge Kegan Paul.

10

What's Special about Stand-Up Comedy? Josie Long's Lost Treasures of the Black Heart

Sophie Quirk

You turn off London's busy Camden High Street and down an insalubrious side road. The place you're looking for has no signage as such, just a large black heart, cast in metal, hanging from its front wall. Inside, you find a dark and comfy metal bar. Queue up a narrow, bending staircase, and across a narrow landing, until it's your turn to squeeze through a door and be greeted – warmly and smilingly – by Josie Long, cult comedian and proprietress of the monthly comedy club, Lost Treasures of the Black Heart (LTOTBH).

At around 8.30 pm, with the audience settled and performers ready, Long introduces a show packed with short sets, quizzes and games.[1] Asked how she arranges the bill, Long (2015) laughs: 'Most of the time what happens is, I forget who I've booked and then loads of people show up.' Long is the compere, and fellow comedian Nathaniel Metcalfe is the club's only regular act. The rest of the bill is unpredictable, unless you happen to have caught some hints on Twitter: there will be stand-up comedians, but there may also be writers, poets or musicians. Many acts will be performing new material in accordance with the night's theme, finding 'unsung heroes or "lost treasures" to be venerated' (losttreasurespodcast.com, 2015); others will perform established routines or work-in-progress.

The audience, in Metcalfe's (2015) words, typically number around eighty and are 'smart and comedy savvy ... consistently brilliant.' Long habitually asks newcomers to shout out, which always reveals that a large proportion of the audience are first-timers. Some of these may have prior experience of the club via its podcast, which publishes an edited version of the show, for free, online. Metcalfe (2015) identifies a 'tremendously loyal regular audience'; Long (2015) further observes that, despite this, the crowd 'varies a lot'. She arranges the club's administration such that she gets to know her audience: 'because I do the door, I do recognise people and I know that they've been coming for a while, or they've come before':

> I've known people to come every month for a year and then drift out and you see people, sort of, dipping in and dipping back out again … It's fascinating. And I think as well, like … to come to a comedy club midweek, in central London, most of the people that do it are at a certain point in their lives … and so, by definition they only come for a little bit, and then you see them a bit later. But it's lovely … I really do feel like it's a little bit of a social club.

It's 15 June 2015; tonight sees the first show following a general election that replaced a Conservative-led coalition with an outright Conservative (Tory, in UK parlance) majority. The new government promises to heighten austerity measures to which Long was already vocally opposed, both offstage and on. Long opens the show by sharing her despair, inferring that selfishness is becoming instilled in the British populace. She draws both her own passion and the volume of her audience's response to a crescendo in which she demands that anyone in the audience who voted for the Conservatives should leave, triggering enthusiastic applause. Long then supposes that it is unlikely that any Tory voters would come anyway, saying, 'I think I've got quite a strong personal brand that repels (*Long pauses before landing on her chosen word with hard emphasis*) scum [laugh]. It's scum' (*Lost Treasures of the Black Heart* 2015a).[2]

This moment captures some important characteristics of the club and of stand-up comedy generally. One is the necessity of acknowledging and responding to the performance's context. The 7 May election result is more than a month old, but failure by a politically engaged comedian to address such a monumental event here, at the club's first subsequent meeting, would be an obvious oversight and a 'disappointment' (Allen 2002: 31–32). Linked to this is the direct communication between Long and her audience. She talks not only to the crowd but also about them, interpreting their collective character: mutually opposed to Tory 'scum' and, by implication, participants in Long's concern for social justice organized on distinctively left-wing lines. Long works in dialogue with the audience, shaping the precise wording and timing of her own contribution to theirs, mirroring the procedures of everyday conversation (Double 2014: 339). This overt emphasis on dialogue with events within and beyond the gig emphasizes the immediacy and novelty of the encounter: this conversation has never happened before and can never happen again.

Most telling of all, perhaps, is Long's reference to her 'strong personal brand'. When asked what the club's unique appeal might be, Metcalfe (2015) responds: 'I think the audience like to be part of Josie's world. I think it feels a lot like you're all in a gang there.' This is echoed by one of the club's more occasional stand-up performers, Sam Schäfer (2015): 'Honestly, I think the biggest draw is Josie herself. And that is something you don't get at any other comedy club often. She is warm, personable, and enthusiastic with the crowd.' These qualities pervade the club, Long's own attitude shaping everything from the friendly welcome that punters are offered at the door to the enthusiasm with which other acts venerate obscure persons and achievements as 'lost treasures'. Her personal and ideological preferences have a perceptible effect on the way the club is managed. LTOTBH offers diverse and unpredictable gigs, but the interlacing of Long's persona through every aspect of the show is what gives these nights their coherence and clarity.

The novelty of skill; the skill of novelty

LTOTBH acts usually categorize themselves as being, or not being, comedians. It is difficult, though, to define exactly what features separate the comedians' acts from other performers'. At LTOTBH the convention is for all acts to use direct address, performing in a conversational register which acknowledges that the audience are present and that the act is a performance. Nor does the use of joking within the act form a reliable boundary. As Nathaniel Metcalfe (2015) relates:

> Even the comics tend to be doing new material to fit the brief of the club, which takes some of the pressure off the usual need for big laughs. Conversely, because it is still 'sort of a comedy night' I suspect the writers/poets probably feel a pressure to try to be funny and so they often are. The audience are aware of this too, and seem very open to anything. They're brilliant.

Writer Ian Green's (2015) practice bears this out: 'Normally at LTOTBH I try and include some sort of joke in my introduction (normally about not being a comedian) to set the audience at ease.' These complex and permeable boundaries are not specific to this club: as Double (2014: 77) has observed, it can be difficult to draw any tidy boundary around stand-up, because '[t]here are stand-up comedians who have pushed so hard at the boundaries that what they do seems to hardly fit their own category, and other performance styles have emerged that seem so close to stand-up as to differ in name only'.

Even within the nebulous category of stand-up, different practitioners and audiences may have different expectations and priorities. One important source of these differences lies at the emergence of British alternative comedy, which took place in the late 1970s and 1980s. Stewart Lee (2010: 3) relates 'contemporary British stand-up comedy's very own creation story':

> For my generation of London-circuit stand-up comedians there was a Year Zero attitude to 1979. Holy texts found in a skip out the back of the offices of the London listings magazine *Time Out* tell us how, with a few incendiary post-punk punchlines, Alexei Sayle, Arnold Brown, Dawn French and Andy de la Tour destroyed the British comedy hegemony of Upper-Class Oxbridge Satirical Songs and Working-Class Bow Tie-Sporting Racism. Then, with their own bare hands, they

> built the pioneering stand-up clubs The Comedy Store and The Comic Strip. In so doing they founded the egalitarian Polytechnic of Laughs that is today's comedy establishment. (Lee 2010: 2–3)

Lee's cynical tone recognizes the simplification inherent in this 'Genesis myth'. In truth, 'there were dozens of superb seventies acts that didn't fit this bipolar model and who were guilty of few, if any, of the ideological crimes now retrospectively ascribed to all British stand-up before 1979' (Lee 2010: 4). Lee Mack (2012: 159) reflects this criticism: 'The "alternative" comedy scene that was born in the early 1980s has a few aspects to it that I do not particularly like, namely its shunning of anything that came before it and its slightly Oxbridge mafia mentality that still prevails today.'

The creation myth does, however, reflect a genuinely game-changing moment in stand-up's evolution. Alternative comedy introduced an ethical code founded in left-wing politics, forming a site of resistance to both the acutely controversial ideological and societal upheaval foisted upon Britain by successive Thatcher governments and the racist and sexist themes prevalent in much pre-alternative 1970s comedy. It also changed expectations regarding form and content. In the 1970s, the consensus was that jokes could not be owned, and so they circulated between practitioners; Tony Allen (2000: 81), one of the key players in the launch of the alternative comedy movement, recalls pre-alternative 'acts [that] looked and sounded the same … they told jokes, old jokes, often the same old jokes'. Alternative comedians, by contrast, were expected to write their own material – befitting their own, individual voice – and in turn expected their authorship to be respected. Lee Mack (2012: 159–60) calls this 'the biggest' of alternative comedy's 'many, many positives': 'it encouraged, in fact insisted on, originality of thought'. In addition, alternative comedy was energized by the alternative cabaret scene in which it was formed. Growing up among the likes of tortoise impersonation acts and puzzling performance art, alternative comedy stand-ups prized experimentation and novelty within their own form.[3]

The term 'alternative comedy' is, again, complicated by application to the contemporary stand-up scene. It is the designated moniker for a genre of comedy – characterized by conventions established in the 1980s – which has now become dominant enough to be called main-stream (making the persistence of the term 'alternative' somewhat confusing for the uninitiated). These conventions include the under-standing that material will be written by the performer,[4] and taboos against plagiarism and overtly discriminatory material, such as racist jokes. Some practitioners, though, object that the term alternative is thereby misappropriated by a contemporary mainstream which lacks the political ethos and avant-garde artistic mission that shaped the 1980s. For those for whom the term refers primarily to this ethos of political subversion and experimentation with form, it naturally feels inaccurate to include less adventurous, commercially driven work in the alternative category. Freidman (2014: 24) observes that 'the aes-thetic principles championed by the original "alternative" circuit argu-ably still represent the gold standard' in contemporary comedy. Hence alternative comedy has arguably emerged as a genre of stand-up defined by conventions which have become dominant, wherein many consider the best work to be signified by the creative ambition and emphasis on novelty that characterized the early alternative movement.

LTOTBH has many features that reflect this 'gold standard' (Freidman 2014: 24). As Long's post-election routine illustrates, the club's politics are stridently left-wing. LTOTBH enables stand-ups to draw creative energy from a varied bill, and original authorship and novelty are prized. Acts are not only written specifically by and for the individual performer, but are often written in accordance with the club's theme for that specific event. In addition, the stand-up material is varied and frequently surprising. For example, John Luke Roberts has performed sets consisting of carefully curated, clever one-liners (*Lost Treasures of the Black Heart* 2015b); he has also performed a sexy dance, repeatedly chanting 'Ooh 'Tricia Routledge – Patricia Routledge', while displaying the image of (Long would later point out) Celia Imrie (*Lost Treasures of the Black Heart* 2012).[5] Nadia Kamil performed a feminist act 'reclaiming burlesque for alternative comedy' in which she stripped off layers of sensible clothing to reveal sequined slogans such as 'equal pay' and 'stop looking at my bum, you sexists!' (*Lost Treasures of the Black Heart* 2011). Long (2015) argues that stand-up continues to be a genre with a large degree of freedom, which can readily collapse into other forms:

> There's the freedom of the genre … It's really anything from performance art, to theatre, to spoken word, to sketch – you know, even just when stand-up is all there is, then it can be all of those things, you know. In a longer show, it doesn't always have to be funny, it doesn't always have to be anything – it just has to be what you want it to be and you have to convince people.

In adopting a porous definition of stand-up which allows for unpredictable experimentation with form, embracing 'arty and experimental' approaches, and engaging a range of acts, LTOTBH emphasizes novelty as a key component of its appeal.

LTOTBH is a departure from the ordinary model of comedy clubs for the obvious reason that it houses a wider variety of acts. For Long, though, there is another departure to be found in the club's prioritization of novelty over 'slickness'. In the introduction that accompanies the club's podcast, Long (2011) describes LTOTBH as a 'sort of kind of comedy club'. Asked why she uses these qualifiers, Long (2015) explains:

> Just to take the pressure off, really! The thing with the internet is … often people have very unreasonable expectations on what is essentially a free podcast that you're giving away … And also, like, for me, it's a work in progress night and I really want people to experiment and to take risks and just bring stuff that is unusual to it … I don't want just to book comedians, I do like booking writers and musicians and having quite a varied bill. So, on the whole it's mostly comedy and mostly amusing but I like the idea that it doesn't always have to be and it can be whatever we fancy on a monthly basis … And also just to give breathing room to the fact quite often that people are writing it solely for that night … so it's not gonna be slick.

In giving this rationale for describing LTOTBH as a 'sort of kind of comedy club', Long refers to 'unreasonable expectations', 'it's not gonna be slick'; these concepts are contrasted with the freedom to 'experiment and … take risks' and to 'bring stuff that is unusual to it'. Long's statement implicitly critiques the practice of equating a high level of skill in comedy with 'slickness', here interpreted as the habit of taking a high 'hit rate' of laughter as the sole marker of quality and funniness.

John Limon (2000: 12–13) provides an example of this attitude, saying: 'your laughter is the single end of stand-up … there need not be anything *but* jokes. Constant, unanimous laughter is the limit case'. Some comedy fans and theorists may understandably see this as common sense. Yet many practitioners point to the damage that such purist, laughter-centric interpretations of quality can do in practice. Tony Allen (2002: 35), for example, places the processes of producing a 'tight twenty' in direct opposition to the processes of innovation:

> The pressure to conform and succeed is obvious and the impetus to cut the clever stuff and stitch together a 'tight twenty' as good as the next guy's is almost overwhelming; but it's also soul-destroying … given the competitive service-industry environment, it's not difficult to understand why so many contemporary comedians have such a limited range of attitude and mostly conform to a narrow range of generic types.

For Allen, the pressure to produce a safe and consumable tight twenty leads only to blandness and conformity. Conversely, Long (2015) notes that replacing the tight, well-rehearsed routines with more novel and experimental work can be risky:

> Quite often I really am winging it. Like, I'm trying to sort of, you know, make stuff up and create a little bit of improvised stuff and muck around and see if I can do some experiments … so quite often, as a result, I find it quite a challenge and quite a frightening experience, 'cause I'm sort of trying really hard to … make something happen out of nothing and I'm always worried that I'm gonna die on my arse …

> But that's the thing I think is what makes it thrilling ... is that I always know there's gonna be some sort of improvisational challenge for me.

This implies that being reliably funny is something that must be gambled if the more vital material that comes from experimentation and improvisation is to be won. Long (2015) prioritizes the thrill of this process, accepting – and asking her audience to accept – that this carries a higher risk of failure, at least in terms of laughter.

Long exerts a conscious effort to create an atmosphere where experimentation, and its attendant risk, may be indulged and appreciated. For example, she welcomes punters personally, chatting to them as she casually gathers their five-pound entrance fees into a pint glass; she distributes cakes and fruit; gives out prizes and invents new games and competitions for the audience to play each month:

> I think it shapes ... the attitude of the [audience] ... If you come into a room and there is a quite a marked atmosphere ... it will affect you ... I like the idea of making it a little bit more shambolic and homely and sweet-natured, and the idea of immediately trying to be a bit generous with it, and make it quite clear that it's not really running at a profit and stuff like that ... It does influence people ... I like the idea of giving people more than they expect ... the idea of surprising people with gifts and games and trying my hardest to think of ... ways to make it a fun night, you know? (Long 2015)

Generosity is central to the club's ethos and atmosphere. The crowd are encouraged to be supportive, enabling artists to take risks and innovate: in return, Long finds ways of giving the audience 'more than they expect'. For the acts, this permissive atmosphere can entail a welcome release from the pressure to prioritize laughter and the opportunity for other facets of the act to be valued. As stand-up Sam Schäfer (2015) relates:

> I love performing at LTOTBH. It gives me a chance to put the idea of something being interesting over the idea of it being funny, or more importantly, it creates an environment that supports that approach ... If you can demonstrate or teach something new to the audience, and

> be enthusiastic about it, in my experience at least, the idea of it being especially funny is secondary.

While laughter remains an important feature of the night, LTOTBH asserts that it need not be the sole aim, nor the only measure of quality. Work is valued and judged by a range of artistic standards, including innovation and originality. Most stand-up emphasizes its trappings of spontaneity and hence of novelty. As Long and Allen each identify, however, slick and well-rehearsed stand-up can corrupt the authenticity of this process. In deprioritizing – or at least risking – a high hit rate of laughter, LTOTBH aims for a more genuinely novel experience. The skill that is emphasized is not the production of slickness but the management of experimentation: the skill of preserving novelty.

Battling the widening gulf: The importance of intimacy and direct connection

Mark Thomas (2015) recalls how the initial alternative scene – where comedians had shared a stage with an inventive array of left-wing theatre companies, street performers, musicians and performance artists – was whittled down into a single, dominant form: stand-up comedy. It was the alternative comedy revolution of the 1980s that established stand-up as an industry in its own right. At the time Thomas was establishing himself as a comedian, 'mid-ranking comics, who are competent, could earn three times the national average wage in a year' just by gigging. From the outset, commercialization sat uncomfortably with alternative comedy's political allegiances. Speaking specifically of the disintegration of theatre companies following cuts in subsidy, Thomas (2015) observes:

> What's interesting about that … is you have the withdrawal of subsidy, the withdrawal of collective endeavour…and you get the emergence of a singular, solitary performer. A performer who is motivated, who … writes their own material … who will travel where the work is, who is

> on three times the national average wage … they have vested interest in getting on and doing well because they know they'll pick up work on the back of it. What we have is the creation of a Thatcherite art form … We are the bastard children of Margaret Thatcher … I am a small-to-medium sized business!

By the mid-2010s, the lucrative stand-up circuit has evolved into an even bigger industry with complex structures that, some claim, function to the detriment of the form. Friedman (2014: 159) identifies a set of 'tastemakers' who exert decisive influence over which emerging comedians come to prominence. For example, comedy scouts have a critical role in channelling specific practitioners towards the particular (and, he suggests, largely imagined) markets that differentiate the comedy audience. In addition, big comedy agencies such as Off the Kerb and Avalon are frequently identified as wielding uncomfortable levels of power. In 2012, comedy website Such Small Portions created a list of the 100 most influential people in comedy. This included practitioners, commissioners and journalists, but was topped by an agent: Off the Kerb's Addison Cresswell. One of the list's creators, Tim Clark (2012), explained, 'despite the creative talents of all the people on the list, we felt that the ultimate influence on who is watched, who is given the limelight, and how our comedy is shaped is decided by a handful of powerful comedy agents'.

Of course, many comedians can thank influential facets of the industry such as critics, agents and TV companies for connecting them with substantial audiences who would otherwise have been beyond their reach. However, the uncomfortable implication is that the relationship between comedians and their audiences is mediated through a top-down system in which Freidman's (2014: 159) 'tastemakers' manipulate the means by which performers connect with their public. Such industry influence arguably corrupts the very ideals of popular performance as articulated, for example, by Schechter:

> Today the term 'popular theatre' is still associated with democratic, proletarian, and politically progressive theatre … without having to

> conform to externally-imposed standards or depend on institutional approval, artists can say what they please, and may please the public in ways that more controlled, formulaic art cannot. (Schechter 2003: 6)

For Schechter, popular performance is characterized by immediate and unmediated relationships between performer and audience. By contrast, the presence of powerful businesses and individuals who act as mediating forces in the comedy industry implies the insertion of 'externally imposed standards' and dependency upon 'institutional approval'. Industry structures interfere with the direct exchange that Schechter describes, creating an artificial gulf in what should be an authentic connection between performers and audiences. Performers' material and audiences' expectations are driven to conform to industry ideals that possibly shape public demand as much as they respond to it (Friedman 2014: 160–61).

Another gulf is created by the sheer scale on which the industry operates: money, commercialism, fame and prestige all play their part in disrupting the direct connection that Schechter describes. Following the success of his own 2009 BBC TV series, *Stewart Lee's Comedy Vehicle*, Lee (2012: 5) felt he had to make a concerted effort to allow audiences to 'feel part of a living process, rather than simply being onlookers at a minor celebrity spectacle'. This concern is intensified in regards to the emerging form of 'arena' comedy: massive gigs that enable stand-up comedians to perform to audiences of over 10,000 people in one hit (Lockyer 2015: 587). Long has called such shows 'a rip off,' asking, 'what's the point?' (Herring 2014). She elaborates, 'I don't wanna go to watch comedy in arenas ... I like, to be honest, to be in a very small room. I like – like – 100 people or less ... you know, for me, bigger than about 500 people and it just loses what's special about it' (Long 2015). Asked what this 'specialness' consists of, Long identifies two key features: the authentic connection that may be made between performer and audience, and the spontaneity that this engenders:

> There's something really real, and in and of the moment, about [stand-up] ... There's a really interesting interplay between the fact that you

> know someone's lying and you know someone's tricking you, but they also have to seem authentic. And the best stand-up has real, genuine authenticity, sharing, vulnerability to it, and I think that's really important. And on top of that there's the realness of the fact that things can change and go wrong, there's no fourth wall. You can talk to people, you have unexpected events, you fuck up and muck around and people improvise and people, you know, talk to the crowd. And I think – all of that – it just has a certain something to it that makes it really feel special and exciting and like each time is, you know, an individual event. (Long 2015)

This account of stand-up's specialness is reflected in results of a survey by Lockyer and Myers, which captured the audience experience. Two of the factors that audience members cited as important to their enjoyment of stand-up comedy clubs were the 'unexpected and unpredictable potential' (Lockyer and Myers 2011: 175) – the novelty of the encounter, as reflected in Long's celebration of the propensity for 'unexpected events' and the opportunity to 'fuck up and mess around' – and 'proximity and intimacy' between audience and performer (Lockyer and Myers 2011: 177–78), as celebrated in Long's comments on authenticity, vulnerability, sharing and being 'tricked'. Sam Schäfer (2015) echoes the intimacy theme:

> I think there are people who like stand-up for the sense of connection. That they are hearing a real person express themselves honestly and without barriers to the audience. And that there is potential to see your own life reflected back, and to maybe feel better about situations or feelings you've had, that you're not alone, that other people think the same, and it's ok, it's funny.

Nathaniel Metcalfe's (2015) analysis again emphasizes the intimacy of the connection that may be struck between stand-up comedian and audience member:

> I think it's communal experience, and I think people enjoy laughing with other people. I also think [stand-up] has a confessional quality and I think people enjoy the gossipy nature of hearing other people

> talking about their own lives in great detail. Sometimes you relate to what a stand up is saying, sometimes you're appalled by it, sometimes you want to be their friend and everything in between.

Lockyer's (2015: 599) later survey capturing the audience experience at arena gigs highlights that 'the lack of interaction and intimacy between the comedian and the audience is a main limitation of arena stand-up comedy'. While smaller clubs allow the possibility of heckling, and permit the comedian to read diversity and nuance in audience response, the vast spaces involved in arena comedy create a gulf across which such detailed dialogue cannot take place. Arena comedy still involves direct address, eschewing the fourth wall between audience and stage, but it disrupts the direct connection that many see as one of stand-up's defining and crucial characteristics.

In addition to affecting the relationship between performer and audience, the physical gulf affects the nature of the comedian's material. Lockyer (2015: 591–92) finds that, in order to succeed with such large crowds across a massive space, arena comedy demands material with 'universal appeal', which in turn means 'discouraging comic material that is ambivalent and confusing'. Take, for example, a routine in Michael McIntyre's *Showtime* (2012), which was performed at the O2 Arena and subsequently released to an even greater and more distant public via DVD. McIntyre recalls watching beach volleyball on television during the recent 2012 Olympics hosted in London. The routine is based upon cultural norms and assumptions that are easily recognizable; that, as a heterosexual man, his main interest in beach volleyball will lie in ogling scantily clad female players, and that this compromises its legitimacy as a sport. For example, he suggests that the placement of such titillating programmes on respectable BBC channels was incongruous, especially as daytime viewing. He claims that he usually enjoys such material alone and online, hinting that it may be equated with pornography. He also reinterprets the players' communication via hand signals placed at the small of their own backs, observing that the players seem to be pointing to their own buttocks in case the viewer 'were under any doubt as to what you were supposed to be looking at' (McIntyre 2012). As Lockyer's findings predict, this is a routine that eschews challenge and ambivalence. The premise is that beach volleyball is for ogling. This being understood, the jokes are uncomplicated: McIntyre says what he means in straightforward terms.

The relative intimacy of LTOTBH allows for a less direct and more nuanced approach. In the following routine, Sam Schäfer mocks the formulaic nature of old-fashioned mother-in-law gags – an archetypal staple of pre-alternative comedy – while also critiquing the archaic attitudes towards women that they display. Reading from a book of 'pub jokes' his Nan gave him for Christmas, he begins:

> 'What do you call a blonde mother-in-law? An airbag!' And – and I wouldn't. [Big laugh] I, I'm, I'm not married for one [small laugh] Um, and if I was, I'd probably be more polite and, sort of, go by her name, because I wouldn't want to upset my wife and [laugh] um, I mean, I, I imagine I love her [laugh] I'm not quite sure what her hair colour has to do with it, either [laugh] Um, I mean, I, I'd probably just call her by her name. Um. Something like Carol [small laugh]. (*Lost Treasures of the Black Heart* 2012)

Schäfer relies upon an intimate connection with the audience to communicate his material through the complicating lens of dramatic irony. He plays the credulous fool who mistakes the book for literal advice. Central to this performance is a shy, slightly hesitant delivery that forms a striking contrast to the booming, break-neck energy with which McIntyre fills his enormous stage. Schäfer asks his audience to understand, implicitly, that the literal content of the routine is being used to flag up the unpleasant real-life implications of attitudes towards women embodied in the joke-book gag. It also demands that the audience interrogate their own ideological stance not only as regards attitudes to women – as the routine relies upon a shared, though unstated, understanding that the pub jokes are inappropriate because of their content – but also as regards attitudes to political correctness in comedy, as the gag's type is being attacked along with its theme. McIntyre's routine makes no such demands; it takes an easy point of reference (that beach volleyball is for ogling) and allows the audience to use it unquestioningly.

It is worth noting that arena comedy itself has novel and innovative features. Rather than dismissing it as a watered-down or debased version of the real thing, Lockyer (2015: 590–93) identifies arena comedy as an emerging form characterized by, for example, an emphasis on increased physical movement and observational material. The sheer scale of the venue, and the distance from performer to audience, may entail less opportunity for an 'unexpected and unpredictable' interplay between the performer and audience, but it does offer a kind of rarity that lends the experience its own specialness. It's a big night out – a rare treat on a grand scale – and can be looked forward to with a confidence and excitement informed by 'audiences' prior knowledge and experience of the stand-up comedian's performance' (Lockyer 2015: 594). The arena gig embraces commercialism, offering heightened prestige and celebrity for a ticket price that may be ten times higher than LTOTBH's. Audiences feel that this implicitly guarantees them a high-quality theatrical spectacle and high quantity of laughter production, and the form is evolving to meet those expectations (Lockyer 2015: 593–96). Given the centrality of direct communication to stand-up as a form, we may arguably see arena comedy – which subverts this key feature – as daringly experimental.

LTOTBH offers a more unpredictable and intimate experience. For Long, this division between commercial and artistic priorities also draws a significant barrier at the more modest end of the contemporary circuit:

> I try and make it an atmosphere where people who maybe don't gig a lot … or maybe don't feel like the circuit is really a fun place for them, [can] come and do my club … I like it when it feels like it's a curated thing, you know? … For me, it kind of does have to feel welcoming and warm … I think maybe in some ways it's a little bit snobby on my part but, like, I don't like these big barn clubs that are really blokey

> and aggressive and, kind of, full of hen dos and stuff. It's just not what I enjoy. I like people who are trying to be a bit arty and experimental, or just obstinate and weird, you know. (Long 2015)

Long describes LTOTBH as a kind of haven on the margins of the mainstream circuit. While the mention of 'hen dos' suggests that 'barn' clubs cater to a profitable market in audiences for whom the night out comes first, and the choice of entertainment second, all types of act at LTOTBH are presented as carefully curated artworks. As such, it attracts, in Ian Green's (2015) words, a 'very relaxed' audience who welcome the club's potentials for spontaneity, novelty and experimentation: '[T]he night acknowledges and revels in its nature as something slightly more organic and less rehearsed than many comedy nights, and people are happy to pay £5 because they know the organisers will make sure they have a fun few hours, even if they don't know what to expect.'

Long's policy on booking acts combats the gulf between performer and public imposed by the complex structures of the comedy industry. The club's performers cover a striking diversity of experience and fame. LTOTBH has seen acts from such TV-bolstered personalities as Robin Ince, Stewart Lee and Sara Pascoe, and less famous but established acts like John Luke Roberts and Chris Coltrane; Long also welcomes much less experienced comedians, occasionally even hosting performers' first gigs (losttreasurespodcast.com 2015). The club's marketing and ethos signal that all acts should be awarded equal respect, minimizing the attention given to celebrity and industry hierarchies. In this way, LTOTBH actively fights the manipulation and mediation of the industry machine, inviting direct and authentic connections between audience and performer.

The club does, of course, impose its own restrictions. As noted earlier, the DIY ethos is itself something that Long creates consciously and intentionally. Long also has control of the bill. Asked whether she ever refuses requests from would-be performers, Long (2015) responds:

> No, but I do tend to say to people, if I really don't know them, I do say … I like to have at least met someone or seen them once. And

Figure 10.1 Illustration by Josie Long, part of her series Another Planet for the *Guardian* newspaper (© Josie Long, courtesy of the British Stand-Up Comedy Archive, University of Kent)

> I have people ask who've never performed and I do tend to say to them, 'look, do five or six gigs and come back' … But then sometimes – I'm just quite whimsical about it – because sometimes I'll be like, 'ah, fuck it, come on then!' So it sort of depends what mood you catch me in, whether or not I'm up for it.

To an extent, Long is merely describing a succinct – and rather liberal – set of measures which accomplish necessary quality control. Long (2015), though, highlights that her selection policy can be interpreted as skewed and restrictive: 'mine is a little bit more of a weird set of barriers, 'cause mine's like, *do I like you? Do I know you?* Which I think can still feel a little bit unnecessarily exclusive for people. But … yeah it's a different kind of value system' (original emphasis). In this sense, Long directs and manipulates the tastes of her audience in a manner equivalent to the mechanisms of the commercialized industry. The important difference is that Long's construction of the bill represents another way in which her persona and preferences are interlaced with the whole of the club's management and presentation; an organizing principle that is transparent, rather than hidden or ignored. This offers, in Metcalfe's (2015) words, a way to be 'part of Josie's world': a direct connection, rather than a widening of the gulf.

The interlacing of performer and interpretation

LTOTBH is shaped by Long's preference for artistic diversity and novelty and by the wish to preserve the special connection between performer and audience that is available to popular performance forms. Long's left-wing politics are the source of the low door fee and DIY ethos; the personal qualities projected in her persona, such as warmth, playfulness and generosity, shape the attitude of both acts and audience. As Schäfer (2015) puts it, 'the whole night is just her wanting to have a good time, and hoping other people agree with her idea of what a good time is'.

Long's comments on her own creative decisions suggest that she sees the skill of preserving novelty and the intimacy of direct connection between performer and audience as profound and important features of stand-up as a form. Furthermore, they are features that she feels are under threat on the more commercial circuit. Stewart Lee has identified a binary split in the contemporary stand-up industry, organized along these very fault lines, which became perceivable by 2004:

> There was now an obvious split in the circuit. You could make a living doing your regular twenty minutes at Jongleurs and The Store [large, commercial venues], with some lucrative Christmas corporate gigs thrown in … and never bother to go north to the [Edinburgh Festival] Fringe. Or you could shuffle about in what seemed to be this new underground scene, and take your show to Edinburgh at a massive loss, and get written about in a broadsheet, and try and get some arts centre gigs, and let nerds all over the land know about your work via these new-fangled social networking sites … If the phrase hadn't lost its meaning once already, you could almost say we were witnessing the birth of a new Alternative Comedy, in opposition to

> the crowd-pleasing composite that the Alternative Comedy of old had become. (Lee 2010: 36)

Lee (2010: 35) notes Long as a significant figure, citing her 'evenings with an almost arts-and-crafts flavor during which young weirdos read half-formed ideas off crumpled bits of paper' as a key example of the 'new Alternative comedy' style. By 2008, the movement had gained enough recognition to be written about as a distinct, emergent form by academic and LTOTBH performer Broderick Chow (2008). By this point, the title 'DIY comedy' was in common parlance, signifying the performer-driven and anti-commercialist ethos of the new circuit. Chow again named Long as an important participant.

Long (2015) concurs with Lee's assessment of the mid-2000s as a significant period, saying:

> I definitely felt … especially nine [or] ten years ago, I really did feel part of a really vibrant group of peers who loved running weird nights and making sure there was loads of stuff on … a whole new circuit like Robin Ince and Pappy's and loads of people like that were really going for it and doing mad stuff. Yeah, I felt part of that, and proud, as well, to be a part of it.[6]

Long is, though, cautious about identifying clearly demarcated movements or timescales, saying, 'I feel like the comedy scene has always been, and will always be, really vibrant and exciting … There's always people doing really cool stuff in comedy. So, I feel more confidently glad to be part of an industry where there's this wellspring of, like, new, strange, wonderful people bringing their ideas.'

Wherever a particular stand-up's work is situated in terms of tribal affiliation or market placement, artistic decisions will be influenced not only by technical demands – such as the size of the space, the finance available or the expectations of the audience – but also by the ideological stance and business model that the performer adopts. All comedians make decisions about how to situate their work (Ritchie 2012: 188): the decision to ignore conceptual, artistic or political preferences itself reflects an ideological position. This means that the individual performer's work cannot be understood without reference to their personal priorities and preferences.

Stand-up comedy is becoming a big, rich and increasingly international business. It has established centres across the world – primarily in North America, Australia and parts of Europe – and is spreading into new countries and new continents (Lockyer 2015: 586). This chapter has argued that LTOTBH bears distinctive marks of the particular context to which it so intimately responds: it is a London club, a post-British-alternative club, a reaction to the scale and mechanisms of stand-up's commercialization in the twenty-first century and an expression of Long's persona. All stand-up may be expected to reflect its environment in this way. Yet the principle that stand-up performance as a whole be identified with, and understood through, its contexts is not specific to LTOTBH or to its milieu. The interlacing of the performer and their role is always an important organizing principle by which stand-up comedy can be understood. Hence, the individual performer's personal priorities and preferences must be central to our understanding of their work, and to our understanding of a growing artistic form, massive international industry and significant, wide-spread mechanism of social communication.

Notes

1 Since the time of writing, the show's start time has changed to 8.00 pm.

2 In this and all transcripts, square brackets denote audience response; italics in rounded brackets denote comedians' actions.

3 For example, Mark Thomas (2015) fondly remembers sharing the bill at his first gig with tortoise-impersonation act Cyril the Tortoise, and later booking the Ice Man, a performance artist who would attempt (unsuccessfully) to melt a large block of ice.

4 In fact, there have always been solo performers who worked with writers off-stage (Double 2014: 416); latterly, the practice of employing directors for longer shows is becoming increasingly common (Double 2014: 432–33). Nonetheless, the emphasis is still very much on individual

authorship. A comedian's material is expected to cohere with his or her persona and hence is strongly identified with the person who performs it. The involvement of other creators is usually treated as something of a badly-kept secret.

5 Patricia Routledge and Celia Imrie are respected British actresses, both more than 30 years Roberts' senior. Routledge is best known for her role as snobbish battleaxe Hyacinth Bucket in BBC TV sitcom *Keeping Up Appearances*; Imre for a range of hit TV and film comedy.

6 Robin Ince is a fellow stand-up comedian. Pappy's are a sketch group: they form the basis of another chapter in this volume.

Bibliography

Allen, T. (2000), *Attitude: Wanna Make Something of It? The Secret of Stand-Up Comedy*. Glastonbury: Gothic Image.

Chow, B. D. V. (2008), 'Situations, Happenings, Gatherings, Laughter: Emergent British Stand-up Comedy in Sociopolitical Context', in J. Malarcher (ed.), *Comedy Tonight!* Tuscaloosa: University of Alabama Press, 121–33.

Clark, T. (2012), 'Who Are the Most Influential People In Comedy?' *Huffington Post*, 24 August, http://www.huffingtonpost.co.uk/tim-clark/who-are-the-most-influential-comedians_b_1616914.html (accessed 4 September 2015).

Double, O. (2014), *Getting the Joke*, 2nd edn. London: Bloomsbury.

Friedman, S. (2014), *Comedy and Distinction: The Cultural Currency of a 'Good' Sense of Humour'*. London: Routledge.

Green, I. (2015), personal interview, by email, 29 July.

Herring, R. (2014), *Richard Herring's Leicester Square Theatre Podcast*. 'Episode 41: Josie Long', 18 April, http://www.comedy.co.uk/podcasts/richard_herring_lst_podcast/episode_41_josie_long/ (accessed 30 September 2015).

Lee, S. (2010), *How I Escaped My Certain Fate: The Life and Deaths of a Stand-up Comedian*. London: Faber and Faber.

Lee, S. (2012), *The 'If You Prefer a Milder Comedian Please Ask for One' EP*. London: Faber and Faber.

Limon, J. (2000), *Stand-up Comedy in Theory, or, Abjection in America*. Durham, NC: Duke University Press.

Lockyer, S. (2015), 'Performance, Expectation, Interaction and Intimacy: On the Opportunities and Limitations of Arena Stand-up Comedy for Comedians and Audiences', *The Journal of Popular Culture*, 48 (3): 586–603.

Lockyer, S., and L. Myers (2011), '"It's About Expecting the Unexpected": Live Stand-Up Comedy from the Audiences' Perspective', *Participations: Journal of Audience and Reception Studies* 8 (2): 165–88, http://www.participations.org/Volume%208/Issue%202/2c%20Lockyer%20 Myers.pdf (accessed 2 April 2015).

Long, J. (2011), 'Intro', *Lost Treasures of the Black Heart* [podcast], http://www.losttreasurespodcast.com/mp3/intro.mp3 (accessed 13 April 2015).

Long, J. (2015), personal interview, by telephone, 22 July.

Lost Treasures of the Black Heart. (2011) [Podcast], episode 8, 7 December 2011, http://www.losttreasurespodcast.com/mp3/08-lost_treasures_of_the_black_heart-2011-12-07.mp3 (accessed 30 September 2015).

Lost Treasures of the Black Heart. (2012) [Podcast], episode 9, 8 February, http://www.losttreasurespodcast.com/mp3/09-lost_treasures_of_the_black_heart-2012-02-08.mp3 (accessed 30 September 2015).

losttreasurespodcast.com (2015), http://www.losttreasurespodcast.com (accessed 1 September).

Lost Treasures of the Black Heart. (2015a) [Live performance]. The Black Heart, Camden, 15 June.

Lost Treasures of the Black Heart. (2015b) [Live performance]. The Black Heart, Camden, 7 July.

Mack, L. (2012), *Mack the Life*. London: Bantam Press.

McIntyre, M. (2012), *Showtime* [DVD]. London: Open Mike Productions.

Metcalfe, N. (2015), personal interview, by email, 16 July.

Ritchie, C. (2012), *Performing Live Comedy*. London: Methuen.

Schäfer, S. (2015), personal interview, by email, 1 August.

Schechter, J. (2003), *Popular Theatre: A Sourcebook*. London: Routledge.

Thomas, M. (2015), Linda Smith Lecture, University of Kent, 12 May.

11

'It Feels Like a Group of Friends Messing Around Onstage': Pappy's and Live Sketch Comedy

Oliver Double

It's Saturday, 28 February 2015, and the comedy trio Pappy's are performing to an audience of 250 people at the Gulbenkian Theatre, Canterbury, as part of a night of sketch comedy. Sharing the bill with them are retro slapstick trio the Three Half Pints and five-man improvised comedy troupe the Noise Next Door. The only solo stand-up on the bill is the compère, Alex Smith.

About halfway through the thirty-minute act, Pappy's sing a song in which Tom Parry wears a series of different gloves, and Matthew Crosby and Ben Clark sing a series of questions to him, trying to guess what kind of ridiculous character he is representing with each one. The song's last big punchline – which involves a boxing glove – unleashes seven seconds of laughter and applause, and the performers pause to make room for this, before launching into a final triumphant chorus. The audience clap along with the rhythm, and Tom shouts, 'Come on, everyone! It's Saturday night!' before kicking the boxing glove out into the audience like a football. During the applause and cheering which greets the end of the song, Tom jumps down off the stage to retrieve the boxing glove. The punter who caught it chucks it right at him, and he gets a laugh by commenting, 'That was a really good shot!'

Matthew tries to restore order and starts introducing the next sketch based on the *Choose Your Own Adventure* series of children's books. Tom interrupts him to comment on the fact that the audience don't seem familiar with this type of book, causing Matthew to lose his temper: '*No no no, we're doing a sketch at the moment, we're on stage! Y'remember??*'

Tom responds with a mocking, high-pitched 'Oooo!' then continues to horse about with the boxing glove, throwing it at a man walking back in from the toilets. As the laughter continues to bubble, the man throws it back and Tom kicks it like a football, getting a cheer. He gets another laugh by gleefully announcing, 'This is so much better than doing sketches!'

Now Matthew admonishes him and confiscates the glove, provoking Tom to taunt him.

'Come on, *Dad!* [laughter]', Tom says, before adopting the voice of an old-fashioned bratty American teenager, reminiscent of the type found in 1960s beach party movies: 'We're just having a good time! [laughter] Stop being so square!' He uses his fingers to form glasses around his eyes to mock the bespectacled Matthew and gets six seconds of laughter as he struts around the stage like that.

'Have you ever seen a teenager before?' says Matthew. 'That is not what they do!' He gets extended laughter for doing a mocking impression of Tom's mocking impression.

Now Tom turns to a young lady in the front row, who – as Alex Smith established in his introduction to the show – is only twenty years old and sitting next to her mother. Tom has been eyeing her mock-lasciviously since Pappy's took the stage. 'Seen one?' he says. 'I've been looking at one all night!' This gets twenty-three seconds of laughter and applause.

Such impromptu moments encapsulate Pappy's' distinctive style of sketch comedy. Critics talk about 'their ultra-exuberant, gloriously ramshackle brand of humour' (Kettle 2013) and say that, 'They create a gang-show mentality, but make sure that the audience feels like the fourth member of the gang. So their sense of fun becomes infectious.' (Maxwell 2012) The comedian Richard Herring has described their shows as feeling 'like a group of friends messing around onstage' (in Cook 2008). Tom Parry recalls that after their first Edinburgh show, he was approached by a woman who told him: 'I saw your show yesterday … we've got sons. And all it reminded me of was when they were, you know, ten, eleven, and they used to put on plays in our front room and we used to have to sit down and watch them put on a play' (Pappy's 2015a).

Such comments suggest that Pappy's comedy is naïve, chaotic and fuelled by simple, unaffected matiness rather than craft and technique. However, the sheer volume of audience response at the Gulbenkian suggests otherwise. The twenty-three seconds of laughter and applause at the end of the above routine is a conspicuously fulsome response in professional comedy, and it is indicative of their reception on this occasion, the audience laughing and applauding frequently throughout their time onstage. It is unlikely that an act that was genuinely naïve and chaotic could win such regular, consistent approval, and closer inspection reveals the careful craft behind the ramshackle sense of fun, based on key aspects of their performance which have been important components of live sketch comedy throughout its history and increasingly dominate the form today.

An uneasy fusion of theatrical and music hall elements

In Britain, sketches originated in music hall – appearing as early as 1855, when Charles Morton presented *The Enchanted Hash* (Macqueen-Pope 1950: 92). This was illegal, because sketches constituted stage plays, and the 1843 Theatres Act dictated that only licensed theatres were allowed to present these. Nonetheless, music halls continued to present sketches in defiance of the law, and the Lord Chamberlain finally addressed the legal situation in 1912, allowing central London music halls to stage sketches as long as they sat alongside a minimum of six variety acts (Russell 1996: 69).

The sketch went on to thrive in the twentieth century in revue, seaside entertainment and variety theatre, where comedians like Harry

Tate, Robb Wilton, Sandy Powell, Frank Randle, Sid Field and Jimmy James built their careers in ensemble sketches (as opposed to solo front cloth routines). Later, the student revue became important in the development of the comic sketch, with shows performed by the Cambridge Footlights and the Oxford Revue spawning professional theatre shows like *Beyond the Fringe* (1960) and *Cambridge Circus* (1963), both of which were commercially successful on both sides of the Atlantic.

However, the immediate roots of today's sketch scene lie in the British comedy circuit of the 1990s, with a number of key acts emerging. The Cheese Shop formed in around 1990 and included such performers as Ben Ward, Gerard Foster, Dave Lamb and Gordon Southern in their line-up. They ran a comedy club at the George Canning pub in Brixton, compèring the night and performing sketches alongside the stand-up acts they booked, and here developed material for a series of Edinburgh Fringe shows (Southern 2015). They were followed by more prominent groups like the League of Gentlemen and the Mighty Boosh.

The most important influences on Pappy's were Big and Daft (1997–2002) and We Are Klang (2003–10). The anarchic Big and Daft grew out of a comedy club in Finchley run and compèred by Ray Peacock, who started performing sketches with actor Jon Williams and stand-up Rob Rouse between the other acts. By the time of their first Edinburgh Fringe show, they had stopped playing multiple characters and had instead adopted consistent personas based on 'exaggerated versions of ourselves' (Peacock 2015). Meanwhile, We Are Klang was made up of three solo stand-ups – Greg Davies, Marek Larwood and Steve Hall. Hall recalls that they were most influenced by 'those groups who deliberately smudged the boundaries between sketch [and] stand-up', and they enjoyed playing stand-up nights at venues like Up the Creek and Maxwell's Full Mooners, as opposed to nights specifically dedicated to sketches, where they found an 'unhelpfully rarefied atmosphere' (Hall 2015).

The original line-up of Pappy's was made up of a group of friends who had met at the University of Kent – Matthew Crosby, Tom Parry, Brendan Dodds, Sam Pay, Steve Purcell and Dave Puckridge – plus Ben Clark, a friend of Parry's from his native Wolverhampton. In 2004, they began staging a series of thrown-together monthly shows under the name Pappy's Fun Club, each time writing and rehearsing entirely new material over the course of a weekend – and performing it for an audience of friends and family at the Old Coffee House on Beak Street in London.

After more than a year of this, the team had slimmed down to a quartet made up of Crosby, Parry, Clark and Dodds and started appearing as a guest act in other people's shows as well as staging their own nights. They felt slightly out of step with the other sketch comedy that was around at the time, like the ex-Footlights dominated Sketch Etc. at the Betsey Trotwood on Farringdon Road or Doug Sketchy with Doug Faulkner at the Albany in Great Portland Street, but got good advice from a group called Dalton Trumbo's Reluctant Cabaret, who offered them a regular slot at the monthly shows they ran at the Ram Jam Club in Kingston upon Thames. Like Klang, Pappy's Fun Club generally preferred playing alongside stand-ups in ordinary comedy clubs to specialized sketch nights, and this undoubtedly shaped their approach to performance (Pappy's 2015b).

They did their first Edinburgh Fringe show in 2006, being nominated for the Edinburgh Comedy Award for their 2007 show the following year. After two more Fringe shows, Brendan Dodds left the group, and to mark the change, they adopted their current, shortened name of Pappy's. Having continued to work as a busy live act since 2004, they are currently one of the longest-established troupes in the current sketch comedy scene.

Pappy's' place in the history of live sketch comedy can be best understood in the light of one key point – that the sketch is, as Lois Rutherford has noted, 'an intermediate dramatic form, an uneasy fusion of theatrical and music-hall elements' (1986: 150). Legitimate theatre saw sketches as a threat, because they contained elements present in plays, notably characters, dialogue and plot. However, they also involved key aspects of popular performance styles like music hall and stand-up comedy – improvisation, audience interaction and a blurring of the boundaries between performer and role.

As live as comedy gets

The first key aspect of Pappy's comedy is that it is *present-tense performance*, playing on the immediate circumstances of the particular show and emphasizing the fact that it is firmly rooted in the here and now. This quality has been noted by critics like Brian Logan, who describes their shows as 'just about as live as comedy gets' (2011a). It is something the group consciously strives for. Tom Parry believes that creating the feeling that 'We're all here and this is happening now' is what 'elevates [comedy] above anything else' (Pappy's 2015c).

This present-tense quality is most conspicuous when the performers leave the established text to improvise in response to something happening in the venue – a long-established technique which certainly existing in music hall sketches. For example, the Lord Chamberlain's office noted disapprovingly that Arthur Roberts was an 'improvisatore who never sticks rigorously to his text' (Rutherford 1986: 144).

Since their earliest days Pappy's have made improvisation central to their work, and Parry believes that this has its origins in their anarchic, semi-planned early shows: 'A lot of people always assume we're from an impro background and we're not at all. It was like it was kind of forced upon us really that we had to try and think on our feet a lot, because no-one knew their lines, no-one knew the sketches well enough' (Pappy's 2012).

Having adopted improvisation out of necessity, they began to develop it as a conscious, deliberate strategy, with three of the Edinburgh shows finishing with Parry coming on and engaging in long, improvised rants in the character of a Quaker or a deranged tax man, being comically undercut by Crosby or Clark when his powers of spontaneous comic invention began to wane. More recently, they have dropped the device of structuring such improvised sections into the show. As Clark explains, they have found other ways of keeping the work improvisational: 'You're able to do that as *you* in between scenes or during a scene breaking down rather than like, "Oh, this is Tom's improvising character"' (Pappy's 2015a).

Parry's throwaway comment that his horseplay with the boxing glove is 'so much better than doing sketches' raises an important point about how Pappy's' shows are structured. The sketches – and other set-piece routines like songs – are contained within a loose, improvisational frame in which the performers talk directly to the audience and mess around together without adopting any clear characters. Unconsciously echoing Rutherford's point about the mix of 'theatrical and music-hall elements' in sketches, Brian Logan suggests that Pappy's have no 'pretence that they're anywhere but right here, right now. But their act resembles theatre, too' (2011a). While there are elements of conventional narrative theatre in the sketches (characters, settings, plot), these sit alongside the spontaneity and emphasis on the immediate performance situation that can be found in the stand-up comedy clubs in which Pappy's cut their teeth.

These more present-tense aspects are particularly conspicuous in the improvisational frame, but even the fictional settings of the sketches are lightly worn. The performers might pretend to be the Three Musketeers reading out the football results, athletes at a medal ceremony or act out a fantasy sequence about Ben's future marriage to a member of the audience, but all of these settings are conjured up in the most rough and ready way possible. This makes it easy to temporarily push the sketch to one side to make way for spontaneous comments about how the show is going.

However, the improvisational frame is where the immediate performance situation becomes absolutely central, and anything that happens can become an opportunity for spontaneous, anarchic fun. Almost everything in the excerpt described in the introduction is improvised and responds to the here and now of the show – reacting to the boxing glove being thrown, arguing over the interruption and joking about a particular front-row punter.

Improvised shenanigans like these emphasize the here and now of the show, but also create an 'infectious' sense of fun and the feeling that this is just 'a group of friends messing around onstage'. When Tom shouts, 'Come on, everyone! It's Saturday night!' he is explicitly exhorting the audience to let their hair down and play.

The fourth member of the gang

Present-tense performance is closely related to the second key aspect of Pappy's' performance technique: an *intense relationship with the audience* which makes them feel like 'the fourth member of the gang'. There is something of a divide among sketch groups between those which acknowledge the audience and address them directly and those which adopt a fourth-wall approach.

Gordon Southern recalls that with the Cheese Shop, 'The "4th wall" was pretty much a constant especially in the early days', acknowledging that this was an uneasy fit in a London comedy club: 'It was a bold move doing our sketches that often erected a 4th wall and then transitioning into stand up. The results varied to say the least' (2015). Similarly, Ray Peacock admits that Big and Daft – an acknowledged influence on Pappy's – were not immune to the temptations of the fourth wall:

> Both myself and Jon were from a drama background so had a slightly better understanding of the fourth wall and how to utilise it than Rob, I know that by the third show we were keeping it 90% self-contained for the audience to just watch – which with hindsight was the wrong call and I'd have to throw my hands up to that. (2015)

Pappy's, on the other hand, started out in stand-up clubs and Crosby, Parry and Clark have all performed as solo stand-ups. This has shaped their performance style, because like stand-up comedians, they address the audience directly for much of the time they are onstage. However, whereas a solo stand-up can give the audience his or her undivided attention, Pappy's have to divide their attention between the audience and each other, and they have become expert at this kind of *bidirectional focus*. This is present in Matthew and Tom's boxing glove argument, as each of them alternates between shouting straight at the other and looking out to the audience.

This kind of sharing of focus is a conscious strategy, and they have developed a gesture to refer to it when working on new material. Pointing the index fingers towards each other means interaction between members of the group, and pointing them straight forward means playing straight out to the audience. As Ben Clark explains, 'quite often we'll start with a sketch and we're like, "Yes, but this feels quite fourth wall", and … we wanna turn it out, we wanna make it present and in the room rather than turning in on ourselves and shutting the audience out' (Pappy's 2015a).

One way they 'make it present in the room' is by letting the show spill off the stage into the auditorium, and allowing individual punters to directly participate in it. This is a long-established technique in sketch comedy and was certainly happening as early as the 1930s. John Fisher describes one of the first Crazy Gang revues at the London Palladium, 1933's *Crazy Month*: 'To conjure up the atmosphere of that production one need only mention that at different times during the show Bud [Flanagan] could be seen chasing a screaming chorus-girl all over the auditorium with an axe at the ready, while during the interval he was to be found serving hot-dogs to the audience from the stage' (Fisher 1973: 56).

We Are Klang – a direct influence on Pappy's – provide a more recent example. Steve Hall recalls that, '[A]lmost straight away there was space to fuck about with members of the audience … the audience interaction seemed a natural part of what we were trying to do – whether it was getting them to sing along, or throw bread at us, or contribute insults' (Hall 2015).

Pappy's have made this kind of technique their own. For example, within two minutes of taking the stage at the Gulbenkian, they temporarily set aside the initial quick-fire sketches to respond to the minor exodus of male punters making their way out of the auditorium to the toilets. Matthew climbs aboard an exiting punter to ride piggyback, before falling off and commenting on his own physical incompetence in comparison to the slick slapstick skills of the previous act: 'The Three Half Pints make it seem very easy'. The other two clown around in a similar fashion, and all of this tomfoolery yields over a minute of continuous, unbroken laughter.

A key technique in maintaining bidirectional focus is mugging, which the seminal alternative comedian Tony Allen has defined as

Figure 11.1 Pappy's perform Last Show Ever at the 2012 Edinburgh Fringe. Matthew Crosby takes Tom Parry by the arm, as Ben Clark stands and grins from among the audience (photo © Idil Sukan)

'sharing exaggerated little cameos of [the performer's] own feelings with the audience via looks, double takes and visual asides' (Allen 2002: 29). Ben mugs expertly while Matthew and Tom argue, looking out to the auditorium and opening his mouth to register gleeful mock amazement, then continuing to smile sheepishly at the audience as the fracas plays out. The awkwardness he communicates with his mugging entirely fits his role as the quietest and most downtrodden member of the group, and the amusement we see on his face mirrors the audience's own enjoyment of the argument and thus creates a kind of collusion.

Crosby explains how the members of Pappy's use mugging to comically undercut each other: 'At least one of us is looking at the audience going, "You're right." ' Clark describes this as a 'lovely trick' because 'you can be on the same side as the audience' (Pappy's 2015a). Each member of the trio appeals to the audience, trying to win them round to his individual point of view. When Tom responds to Matthew's anger with a falsetto 'Oooo!' he is looking straight out to the auditorium, asking the audience to share his mocking view of his comic sparring partner.

Matthew goes beyond mugging when Tom kicks the hurled boxing glove, snatching it up off the stage and announcing, 'I am confiscating this!' before passing it to somebody in the front row – who happens to be my son, sitting right next to me – and telling him, 'You – look after that, don't throw it!' Both of them are trying to enlist the audience, individually or collectively, as allies. My position sitting right next to the newly appointed boxing glove guardian allows me to experience at first hand just how effective this technique is in making the audience feel involved in the show.

It is a time-honoured technique. Sketch comics in variety theatre would often appeal directly to the audience, trying to get them to sympathize with their plight or convince them of the idiocy of the other characters. For example, in Sid Fields' classic golfing sketch, based on a series of comic misunderstandings, Fields and his golfing partner Jerry Desmonde express their growing frustration with each other by glancing at the audience with exasperated expressions on their faces. Fields' catchphrase – 'What a performance!' – is another tool for expressing his frustration with the situation, and he says it to the audience several times in this sketch (*London Town* 1946).

In the Harry Tate sketch 'How Are You?' Tate is held up outside a country pub by a man who forcefully engages him in an absurd, long-winded conversation. By the time the man leaves, the pub is closed, and Tate turns to the audience wobbling his false moustache with indignation and lets out his frustration: 'And I might have had a drink!' ('Harry Tate (1934)'). Similarly, in his fireman sketch, Robb Wilton is exasperated by his fellow fireman at the other end of a speaking tube who asks him about the football sweepstake instead of dealing with the emergency at hand. He turns to the audience and says, 'Would you believe, football sweeps and people's lives at stake. I don't know!' Then he goes back to the speaking tube and asks, 'What have *I* drawn?' ('Robb Wilton (1934)').

Pappy's have extended this long-established technique. In variety, the frustration the comic shares with the audience is contained within the narrative of the sketch and is essentially the frustration of the character. With Pappy's, the competition for audience approval happens outside of the sketches in the improvisational frame, and it is the performers themselves who look to us as allies.

The audience meet us first as people

This immediately raises the third key aspect of Pappy's' performance: their use of *clearly defined stage personas*. Like Big and Daft and We Are Klang before them, Clark, Crosby and Parry play versions of themselves for much of their time onstage. This is established as soon as they come on, as Crosby explains: 'At the start of our sets now … we go out at the start to say hello to the audience … there'll often be five or six minutes of us just messing around together onstage with the audience. And it's the closest we've ever got to three-man stand-up' (Pappy's 2012). This establishes their stage personas straight away, and according to Parry it allows them to break out of a sketch to address the moment, as well as creating a layering of different identities:

> [T]he audience meet us first as people, before we go into any kind of roles. So that when we're on stage in character, if something happens, and we become Matthew or Ben or Tom to recognise it, then that isn't odd, and we haven't lost. So it's almost like you're playing two roles … when I'm, say, being Julius Caesar onstage, I'm being *Tom in Pappy's* being Julius Caesar. (Pappy's 2015a)

As in stand-up comedy, although it might seem that the members of the group are simply 'playing themselves' onstage, in fact they adopt heightened personas, selecting elements of their personalities to amplify and exaggerate. *Tom in Pappy's* is different from the offstage Parry. In the act, he is more boisterous, effusive, childish and occasionally lecherous – as in his comments to the 'teenager' in the front row. While Tom is the most anarchic presence, he is counterbalanced by Matthew, who takes the traditional straight-man role even though he gets many of the laughs. He is nerdy, uptight and teacherly, constantly trying to keep the show on track in the face of Tom's daft disruptions. It is absolutely true to form when he responds to Tom's foolery with the boxing glove by saying, 'I am confiscating this!'

If Matthew ostensibly has the highest status, Ben has the lowest. Cheerful and innocent, he is the quietest of the three and is often found grinning from the sidelines while the other two fight it out. Peter Davison has noted that in variety sketch acts, 'One of the devices for gaining audience sympathy is by the presentation of one of a duo or trio as witless' (1982: 29). This is the role Ben plays in Pappy's, as Parry explains: 'Whenever we want to reach out to an audience … getting pathos, and getting the audience [to] *feel* … that's gonna come through Ben … It's also why most of our cruelty onstage is directed at Ben … in terms of like slapstick and stuff like that' (Pappy's 2015a).

Although the personas they adopt in Pappy's are heightened and fictionalized – each fulfilling a different function within the trio – there is still no clear dividing line between the private performers and the roles they play onstage. Crosby recalls meeting a BBC producer who was surprised at how different he was from the Matthew she had seen in Pappy's, saying, 'Oh! I sort of thought you were quite an angry, grumpy person, but you're actually very laid back.' Similarly, Parry talks about the misunderstandings which the gulf between Clark's onstage and offstage selves can bring about: 'Ben takes quite a hit actually, because he's very stupid in Pappy's. And obviously [he] isn't stupid at all [offstage]' (Pappy's 2015a).

What this highlights is that, as in stand-up, the boundaries of fiction and reality are fuzzily drawn in this kind of sketch comedy. The silly settings of the sketches themselves are blatantly, transparently fictional, but in the improvisational frame it is much more ambiguous what is true and what is not – and sometimes they get laughs precisely by playing on this ambiguity. The introduction to the gloves song starts with Matthew asking Ben, 'Anyway, Clarky, have you got any plans for your time here in Canterbury?'

> **Ben reacts as if this is a genuinely impromptu question which has stumped him:** 'Errr – n, no? No. [laughter]'
> **Matthew persists:** 'OK. Nothing at all?'

> **Ben still seems to be floundering, but manages to come back with something:** 'Oh, er – I might buy some gloves.'
> **In contrast with Ben's convincingly natural-sounding speech, Matthew's delivery now starts becoming heightened, as it might during a sketch:** 'You're gonna buy some-? This is great *news!* What kind of gloves you gonna buy?'
> **Ben is still flummoxed:** 'I – I don't know! They're just gloves!'
> **Matthew's delivery becomes even more heightened:** 'But no, Ben, they're never just *gloves.* The kind of gloves a person wears says a lot about who that person really is.'
> **Now Ben's delivery starts to match Matthew's heightened tone:** 'Are you sure?'
> **He picks up his guitar, prompting six seconds of laughter.**

The audience laugh because they suddenly recognize that they have been fooled. The beginning of the exchange sounds genuinely ham-fisted, and the audience buy into the idea that they are hearing an absolutely real, bona fide attempt at casual conversation, awkwardly thrown into the middle of the act. Ben's reactions are performed exquisitely, his confusion so believable that he makes it look as if Matthew really is leading him into a comedy cul-de-sac. However, when he picks up his guitar, it becomes clear that this is not a moment of genuine spontaneity but a cleverly disguised introduction to a well-honed song.

Such gags work by playing on the fuzziness of the boundaries that separate the planned from the spontaneous, the fictional from the real. In Pappy's work, genuine improvisation sits alongside moments of planned spontaneity, so that even seasoned reviewers find it hard to tell which is which. For example, in 2009, the *Daily Telegraph*'s Mark Monahan confessed: 'I still can't decide if the quartet's frequent, barely-suppressed giggles are entirely un-scripted, but it doesn't matter either way.' The following year, he had become more cynical, complaining about 'their over-reliance on fauxcorpsing' becoming 'rather tired and selfcongratulatory' (Monahan 2010).

Art which conceals art

If Pappy's create the feeling that they are just a group of friends messing around onstage, this belies the *skill* behind their performance. Indeed, they laugh when I mention that one of the key elements of their style might be skill, and Crosby comments self-deprecatingly, 'That's where it slightly falls apart' (Pappy's 2015a).

Nonetheless, carefully concealed skill has long been part of comic performance and was certainly present in the music hall tradition. Brian O'Gorman has written of 'that art which conceals art', referring to the fact that while variety performers might have looked like they were simply having a 'lark', in fact it took 'many years of refinement' to learn their skills and polish the act (1998: 3). Similarly, Pappy's exhibit a high degree of performance skill to create the impression that their work is simply thrown together in the spirit of fun. On reflection, Parry acknowledges the structure and technique that lie behind the apparent anarchy:

> I think for all us, our favourite comedians are the ones who try and hide how clever they are … people like Harry Hill and Tim Vine and Andy Zaltzman are so smart but they act so stupidly. And they never want the audience to see how smart they are. And I think they're a big inspiration to us because it's like if you come out and it looks like it's thrown together and it's shambolic and then behind it all there's a plan, then you always know that that's coming, you know. You think, 'Oh you guys don't think we know what we're doing,' and actually when it goes badly that's how it looks, like we don't know what we're doing. But actually we do know. (Pappy's 2015a)

A vital aspect of their skill is the ability to perform in such a loose, relaxed style that the whole act seems to be spontaneous. This requires considerable acting ability, which only becomes apparent when they directly draw attention to it. The gag which introduces the gloves song is a good example, requiring Clark to act his confusion realistically enough to fool the audience in order for the punchline to work.

Frustrated by Monahan's cynicism, Parry argues that, '[F]auxcorpsing isn't fun to do. Like, pretending something is real when it isn't is actually hard work, it's proper acting' (Pappy's 2015a). The moments in which amusement or awkwardness are faked realistically enough to fool both audiences and critics are actually carefully constructed and performed. Crosby talks about how they require the group to 'try and *not perform*', moving from their usual 'upbeat' and 'open' style and instead 'deflat[ing]' the performance.

Another great skill is their ability to genuinely improvise. It is relatively simple for a solo stand-up comedian to move between prepared material and improvisation, but in a trio this demands skilful collaboration. There is a high level of *complicity* between the members of the group, as well as with the audience. This seems to suggest a connection with the kind of clown theory espoused by Lecoq and Gaulier, although neither is a conscious influence on Pappy's.

Gaulier uses the concept of working in 'major' or 'minor', which John Wright helpfully defines: 'The person "in major" is the person whom we, in the audience, should be looking at. That is the person who's driving the scene and making the action at that moment. The person "in minor" works in support of the major role ensuring that we keep focus on the person who we should be looking at' (2006: 65). He goes on to explain that this idea allows performers to collaborate onstage because 'the roles are exchanged and not stolen', with partners taking turns to work in major or minor, thus 'mak[ing] us into secret associates rather than outright competitors' (66).

This has some relevance to Pappy's. They use the analogy of jazz to elucidate how they improvise together, explaining that when one of them solos (by going into a long improvisation) the other two will provide a subdued rhythm section (by toning down their performance and not interrupting). The idea of soloing seems to suggest working in major, while the rhythm section suggests working in minor.

However, on other occasions their improvisation seems to be more competitive than cooperative. A good example is the argument about the boxing glove, in which two members of the group compete for the status of being in major. When Tom says, 'We're just having a good time,' he is looking straight at Matthew, but pointing out to the audience to indicate he believes they are on his side. When they do mocking impressions of each other, not only are they trying to convince the audience of the ridiculousness of the other, but also competing for which one of them can do the funniest impersonation. On the face of it, they are not willingly exchanging the major role, so much as trying to steal it from the other in an outright contest to win the audience's approval. In reality, they may be secretly collaborating in the shared project of making the audience laugh, but they are going beyond the restrictions of Gaulier's major-minor technique to do so.

Their ability to improvise together in this way has developed organically, through depth of experience. As Parry puts it, 'It's like a muscle that you exercise, being live and … responding. It is just like going to a gym and becoming more muscular' (Pappy's 2015a). Because it is organic and lacks conspicuous structuring devices, it can come across as sheer natural exuberance, but there are moments where the skill becomes visible enough to be acknowledged and rewarded by the audience.

The argument is a good example. It is clearly a spontaneous moment, initiated partly by the individual punter throwing the glove at Tom, and yet it has the same kind of comic satisfaction as the actual sketches. It plays on the established personas – Tom loudly showing off, Matthew trying to keep him under control, Ben watching sheepishly from the sidelines – and finishes with a clear, strong punchline. This is a callback to an earlier incident, highlighting Tom's skill in being able to spontaneously invent gags that directly respond to this particular show. The applause which greets the line is an acknowledgement of this skill.

Sketch comedy has changed

According to a *Guardian* article from 2011, '[S]ketch comedy has changed. In the early 2000s, it tended to be tightly scripted and performed behind a strictly observed fourth wall. Today, a standup's skills – direct audience address, spontaneity – would be more to the fore' (Logan 2011b). Crosby recalls how different the live sketch scene was in 2004 when Pappy's started:

> The sketch circuit has changed a tremendous amount … since we started … Sketch nights you'd see a lot of people who had spent a lot of time on the costume and learning their lines, which for us were the two least important things … So we'd always have an awful time at sketch nights and a fun time at stand-up nights, because we could have a bit of back and forth with the [audience]. (Pappy's 2012)

The shift in the 'intermediate dramatic form' of the sketch has been to decrease the importance of the theatrical elements of characters, dialogue and plot, in favour of the elements drawn from forms like music hall and stand-up – present-tense performance, an intense relationship with the audience and clearly defined stage personas based on the performers' own personalities.

Undoubtedly, this shift has been partly inspired by the success of Pappy's, and a small sample of sketch shows at the Edinburgh Fringe in 2015 reveals the extent of their influence. The basic styles of The Pin (clever metacomedy, deconstructing the conventional sketch in a variety of ways), Max and Ivan (two-man team playing multiple roles in sketches forming a narrative about a fictional town), Kitten Killers (female trio presenting a series of sketches often ending with blackouts) and BEASTS (anarchic male sketch trio) vary widely, but all of them contain key performance elements seen in Pappy's' work.

Each of these very different shows makes heavy use of direct address, and most involve audience interaction, with individual punters or the audience as a whole joining in – a far cry from the fourth-wall based approach of 1990s sketch acts like the Cheese Shop. Each show is structured to include discrete sketches contained within an overall frame in which the performers appear as versions of themselves. Each show also contains moments of real – or beautifully faked – spontaneity, in which the performers improvise (or appear to) in response to the particular circumstances of the particular show. Although their comedy is very different from Pappy's', The Pin's Ben Ashenden acknowledges the older group's influence on his own sketch duo's developing style:

> The fourth wall has been crumbling for us as the years go by. Now we tend to do as much as possible directly to the audience, occasionally dipping into a 'scene' before returning to the audience and telling them that we find that sketch utterly bizarre. I don't think we're as open to 'breaking' the scene, once we're in one, as groups like Pappy's are. It's a looseness that we admire, and are increasingly trying out – but it requires such confidence and flexibility that it's not something we've mastered. (2015)

The influence is strongest in BEASTS, who share with Pappy's the device of structuring their show around the idea that their performance is in jeopardy and could fail at any minute. As with Pappy's, the improvisational frame is as important, if not more important, than the sketches themselves and there are similarities in the group dynamics of both trios. Ciarán Dowd shares Tom Parry's joyfully out-of-control exuberance. The other two try to persuade him not to go ahead with his 'Naked Baker' sketch, and it is his unstoppable, misplaced enthusiasm which fuels the laughter when he finally comes onto the stage in a baker's hat, flour on cheeks, completely naked except for the loaf of bread he holds in front of his genitals. Owen Roberts adopts the same kind of straight-man role as Matthew Crosby, vainly trying to keep Ciarán under control and get on with the show. It is Owen who sends Ciarán off when he comes on as the Naked Baker and chides the audience for responding to this with a disappointed, pantomime-style 'Ahhh!'

The Pappy's-like touches are not surprising given that the show was directed by Tom Parry, and this kind of directing work is one very tangible means by which their influence has spread. As well as directing two shows by BEASTS, Parry has also directed two shows each with Max and Ivan and female sketch trio Birthday Girls. The Kitten Killers' Kat Cade acknowledges:

> In the 3 years I have been performing Sketch Comedy the biggest influence I have witnessed is Tom Parry's direction of sketch and character

> acts at the Edinburgh Fringe. He is one of the most sought after directors. Max and Ivan and Birthday Girls … are both arguably two of [the] top sketch groups from the past few years and have been a big influence on Kitten Killers and what we understand as the 'standard' for sketch comedy. (2015b)

The extent of Pappy's' influence on the live sketch scene can also be attributed to their longevity as a live act. Historically, sketch comedy has been associated with television and radio, and successful sketch acts often leave most of their live work behind once they enjoy success in broadcast media. This was particularly true of the Oxbridge student review tradition, with cast members of *Cambridge Circus*, for example, going on to star in *Monty Python's Flying Circus* and *The Goodies*. More recent examples include the League of Gentlemen and the Mighty Boosh, both of which developed their live shows into eponymously titled radio shows and subsequent TV shows. Pappy's have appeared on TV – notably in two series of their BBC sitcom *Badults* – but this has not brought them the same level of success and critical recognition as their live shows.

However, broadcast comedy's loss has been the live sketch scene's gain. Because they have not transferred wholesale to television, they have remained a powerful presence on the circuit, inspiring newer acts to adopt and adapt the key elements of their comedy. Their longevity has also allowed them to develop to the point where their skill in moving between improvisation and prepared material, working with the audience and playing with their established personas is extremely sophisticated. Perhaps what really allows them to get such big responses from audiences is that the skills that underpin their act largely remain invisible, because they have managed to retain the feeling of 'ramshackle exuberance'. The Pin's Ben Ashenden argues that Pappy's biggest influence is that their performance has 'an unbreakable sense of pleasure and giddiness':

> It's like a sort of magic spell you can set on a room: if you're genuinely grinning away, you can perform the piece 'for the first time' and the audience can feel that, I believe. We've been astounded at what

> a difference it can make: and it was … watching Pappy's a few years ago that we realised they were doing something we hadn't yet – truly enjoying themselves on stage, rather than worrying about the craft too closely. (2015)

It is this genuine pleasure in performance that masks the careful, precise craft behind their comedy and creates the highly believable illusion that they are nothing more than a group of friends messing about onstage.

Bibliography

Allen, Tony (2002), *Attitude: Wanna Make Something of It?* Glastonbury: Gothic Image.

BEASTS (2015), [live show] *Live DVD*, Pleasance Courtyard (Upstairs), Edinburgh, 17 August.

Ashenden, Ben (2015), email, 28 August.

Cade, Kat (2015), email, 16 December.

Cook, William (2008), 'Pappy's Fun Club: London', *The Guardian* (*The Guide* section). 23 February, 41.

Fisher, John (1973), *Funny Way to be a Hero*. London: Frederick Muller.

Hall, Steve (2015), email, 21 July.

'Harry Tate' (1934), https://www.youtube.com/watch?v=OnmOAUBGwrA (accessed 20 July 2015).

Kettle, James (2013), 'The Boys Who Never Grew Up', *The Guardian* (*The Guide* section). 20 June, 20.

Kitten Killers (2015), [live show] *Woof*, Underbelly George Square (The Wee Coo), Edinburgh, 18 August.

Logan, Brian (2011a), 'The Three Stooges: These Men Are Aiming to Resurrect the Sketch Show – with a Time-Travelling Dinosaur and a Wise Old Owl', *The Guardian* (*G2* Section). 5 May, 22.

Logan, Brian (2011b), 'From Sketches to Standup: The Great Escape', *The Guardian* (*G2* Section). 9 August, 19.

London Town (1946), [Film] Dir. Wesley Ruggles. UK: Rank.

Macqueen-Pope, W. (1950), *The Melodies Linger On*. London: WH Allen.

Max and Ivan (2015), [live show] *The End*, Pleasance Dome (Queen Dome), Edinburgh, 20 August.

Maxwell, Dominic (2012), 'Pappy's; Edinburgh Comedy', *The Times* (*T2* section). 15 August, 9.

Monahan, Mark (2009), 'Pappy's Fun Club's World Record Attempt', *Daily Telegraph*. 12 August, 24.

Monahan, Mark (2010), 'Not a Bunch of Idiots, After All', *Daily Telegraph*. 19 August, 25.

O'Gorman, Brian (1998), *Laughter in the Roar*. Westbury, Wiltshire: Badger Press.

Pappy's (2012), interview with Oliver Double, Patisserie Valerie, Canterbury, 29 February.

Pappy's (2015a), interview with Oliver Double, Gulbenkian Theatre, Canterbury, 28 February.

Pappy's (2015b), interview with Oliver Double, Prince of Wales, Brixton, 14 June.

Pappy's (2015c), interview with Oliver Double, King Charles I, Kings Cross, 27 July.

Peacock, Ray (2015), email, 15 July.

'Robb Wilton' (1934), https://www.youtube.com/watch?v=AVazfGnMGyg (accessed 21 July 2015).

Russell, Dave (1996), 'Varieties of Life: The Making of the Edwardian Music Hall', in Michael R. Booth and Joel H. Kaplan (eds), *The Edwardian Theatre*. Cambridge: Cambridge University Press.

Rutherford, Lois (1986), '"Harmless Nonsense": The Comic Sketch and the Development of Music-Hall Entertainment', in J. S. Bratton (ed.) *Music Hall: Performance and Style*. Milton Keynes and Philadelphia: Open University Press.

Southern, Gordon (2015), email, 10 July.

The Pin (2015), [live show] *Ten Seconds with the Pin*, Pleasance Dome (Queen Dome), Edinburgh, 18 August.

Wright, John (2006), *Why is That so Funny?* London: Nick Hern Books.

Conclusion

Louise Peacock

In the introduction, Oliver Double put forward the four key features of popular performance as defined in this volume. So, in retrospect we can not only confirm the importance of those key features but can also demonstrate how connections can be seen across the modes of performance considered here. The same key features appear in each of the chapters and sometimes they are used in very similar ways by performers from different periods of history or with different areas of expertise. This edition opened with an investigation of the binary positions which exist between what we have defined as popular performance (low, illegitimate, informal, improvised, commercial, entertaining and frivolous) and what may be regarded as legitimate theatre (high, legitimate, formal, literary, subsidized, aesthetic and improving). At the heart of each chapter of this collection lies the belief that each of the forms of performance explored here is as worthy of consideration as any example of what might be termed legitimate theatre and each writer analyses a form of popular performance which has previously been under-represented in academic literature. It is clear that popular performance not only offers, and has offered for decades, entertainment and enjoyment to its audiences but that it bears rigorous examination – indeed that it rewards critical and academic engagement because by considering the key features of popular performance through the forms represented here we can come to a fuller understanding of the skills, techniques and structures which drive it.

Demands on audience

It is also clear that the forms of popular performance considered here make particular demands upon their audiences, rarely allowing them to sit passively to receive the performance as was common in conventional theatre (in the way Double outlined in the introduction). Consequently, as Matthew Reason recognizes 'performances that engage audiences actively through participation also emancipate and empower and are consequently radically liberating' (2015: 272). Indeed the forms considered here make demands on their audiences which can be empowering when they lead individual audience members to become engaged in an act of co-creation as a result of an increased level of participation on the part of the audience. Prentki and Selman (2003) recognize this increased engagement 'in popular theatre the audience, even in those instances where it is not called upon to intervene actively in the performance, is engaged on a different level' (132). One of the primary ways in which the audience is engaged in the performance is through interpreting the performers who may appear to present their actual personalities on stage, who may exaggerate features of their everyday selves or who may construct a fabricated persona to engage the audience.

Audience interaction: The layering of participation

Popular performers make choices about whether to present themselves or a fictional version of themselves to their audience. Citing Brown (2014), in Chapter 6 Michael Mangan suggests that 'one of the most important elements of a magician's show is the persona he creates, and "with the *persona* you create, there's a sort of narrative that comes with it" And usually, of course, that persona is a complete fabrication'. In Chapter 4 Adam Ainsworth suggests that similar personas were created by variety performers and then those personas were subsequently adopted by other performers in much the same way that a role in a play might be played by different actors. In this case Ainsworth states that Dixie Haygood's persona Annie Abbott would be appropriated by numerous performers on both sides of the Atlantic for the next thirty years, with each adopting and adapting Haygood's stage names, her claim to possess an enigmatic power and the tricks she employed to 'demonstrate' it. There is in these examples a blurring of fact and fiction so that the audience believes they are seeing and interacting with an authentic individual whereas the performer's real identity is concealed behind their adopted persona. Other popular performers adopt a deliberately less secure persona which allows the audience to see glimpses of what might be the real self as the performer shifts from one layer of presentation to another. For one performer discussed in this collection, that layering is overtly represented by layers of masking and costume which are removed as part of the act. As Lynn Sally explains in Chapter 7, MsTickle's costume for her burlesque act consists of three layers; the first of these involves a face mask which makes the performer look like a Hollywood starlet but when this is peeled off another mask lies beneath. This time it is a full body mask making the performer look like a blow-up sex doll. Only when this is removed does the audience see the performer's own body. This is an unusually clear depiction of the layering of person, persona and role which is common in popular performance.

In Chapter 1 Caroline Radcliffe highlights the difficulty critics and commentators can have when analysing live performances which occurred before the advent of film, 'It is unclear whether he [Leno] performed these recitations in costume or not, but given his widespread fame and established status as a "national treasure", it is likely that he was able to abandon all characterization and finally perform as "himself"'. Leno's established performance style involved the presentation of detailed characters but his fame also reached such a pinnacle that it was possible for him to give recitations as himself without the costumes and characterizations which had contributed to his fame. The distinction would have been immediately evident to his contemporary audience but remains uncertain for us.

The concept of less physically evident layering, in which the performer's individual identity is overlaid with a performance persona which may, in turn, be overlaid with a role is best explained by Michael Wilson in Chapter 3 when he asserts that 'this is not Karl Valentin the actor playing the role of the Father, but Karl Valentin in his role of Valentin the cabaret persona, playing the role of the Father, in a way that the both the Father and the comic persona are simultaneously visible'. This layering of performer and role requires an act of interpretation and deciphering on the part of the audience who have to make rapid subconscious decisions as to whether they are responding to the performer or to a projection of persona or character by the performer. The same technique is identified by Leigh Woods as being part of Olga Petrova's act: 'she offered a classic instance of personality reconfigured as performance'. The performer makes a dual or even triple presentation to the audience which then engages in an act of interpretation in order to understand who they are watching. Simon Sladen identifies a similar layering at work in pantomime with the inclusion of celebrity performers: 'the presence of the performer's body provides the illusion that the audience is, in this case, witnessing the celebrity uncovered, un-airbrushed, unedited and free to perform as "self"; but "self" in Anderson's case is mediated via the Role and rarely manifests'. Here the audience may be encouraged to believe that the performance gives them access to the celebrity performer's uncovered self but, as Sladen recognizes, the performer is rarely presented without the protective layer of a role. In the case of Pappy's Double suggests that the performers consciously introduce both their everyday selves and their performance selves to the audience to aid the audience in understanding who they are responding to: 'This establishes their stage personas straight away, and according to Parry it allows them to break out of a sketch to address the moment, as well as creating a layering of different identities'. That this layering occurs in so many of the popular performance forms considered in this book points towards its important connection with two of the key features of popular performance suggested in this volume. By layering performance identities, popular performers are able to draw attention to the performative nature of their act and, by shifting from one layer of performance to another, they are able to exist in both a performative frame and in the here and now. They are able to address the audience directly both from within the role and by stepping out of the role to comment either on their own performance or on their fellow performers. In fact, Bim Mason addresses this directly in Chapter 9 where he suggests that 'there were several levels of performativity – the real actor, their troupe persona, the character and, at times, disguises or deceit employed by the characters'. He goes on to claim that this layering 'allowed the performers to drop out of character and whisper off-stage comments to the audience about the quality of the performance of others, creating a sense of the relationships within the company'. Direct address to the audience of this nature encourages the audience to feel that they are witnessing a unique show in which a particular mistake or event has occurred which has prompted the performer to drop out of character and comment on it. It also highlights the popular performer's awareness of the audience in the here and now. There is no need to pretend that the show is going well if it is not because the structures and conventions of popular performance allow any unusual moments, good or bad, to be directly acknowledged.

Even in a show which is running entirely as planned, popular performers use direct address to the audience to encourage the creation of a particular performer/spectator relationship, one in which the spectator is expected to engage in an act of co-creation with the performers. In its simplest form direct address allows the performer(s) to acknowledge the audience's presence. This can be seen in my chapter on Grock where a number of examples are given of the performer engaging directly with the audience either through looks or through use of the spoken word (often, in Grock's case, a simple catchphrase). In such instances no direct response is demanded of the audience beyond an invitation to laugh. Direct address can also be used to help build a relationship between performer and audience as Caroline Radcliffe notes in relation to Dan Leno's use of patter which 'provided Leno with a particularly direct form of audience address, creating an intimacy between the performer and the spectator'. While intimacy is encouraged no direct response is demanded of the audience. However, in pantomime, as identified by Sladen in Chapter 8, the audience often engages in what can be defined as a to-and-fro exchange between the stage and the audience and these 'Call and Response conventions between Audience, Comic and Dame represent allegiance, reliance and a sense of trust between the tripartite of "characters" and are fundamental in establishing the pantomime's shared community for performance'. Using direct address in order to create a shared sense of community is also noted by Sophie Quirk in her discussion of how Josie Long comperes the Lost Treasures of the Black Heart comedy club in Chapter 10. In this instance, Long uses direct address to encourage a sense of group identification in her audience by targeting another 'outside' group: 'She draws both her own passion and the volume of her audience's response to a crescendo in which she demands that anyone in the audience who voted for the Conservatives should leave, triggering enthusiastic applause'. Long draws her audience together by identifying a group who would be unwelcome in the club ensuring that those present feel that they truly belong. In Chapter 11 Double also addresses this idea of creating the feeling that the audience belongs but in the case of Pappy's they ensure that the audience belongs by creating 'an *intense relationship with the audience* which makes them feel like "the fourth member of the gang"'. Central to popular performance forms is the desire to remove barriers between the performers and the audience. Two of the acts considered in this collection actively involve the audience on stage during the performance. This is, of course, the most overt kind of audience participation in which spectators become a kind of performer on stage alongside the actual performer. Dixie Haygood, as Annie Abbott, requires several audience members to participate on stage during her act to facilitate the demonstration of her skills. As Ainsworth states in Chapter 4, 'At times the illusionist will require participants to perform solos, at others they will need to contribute to an orchestral section and at key moments all those involved will be brought together simultaneously'. The audience members on stage occupy a liminoid space, caught between being audience and being performers. They are in the hands of the performer and are required to do what is asked of them or risk jeopardizing the show. In the Annie Abbott act, participants form part of the illusion and contribute to the notion that the illusions are in fact reality because real audience members are engaged in trying to move her while she uses her 'powers' to resist. Derren Brown's audience members also contribute to the show and Mangan offers a detailed account of how Brown misdirects them to get the responses he needs for the show to work. Mangan draws attention to this requirement that the audience respond in a particular way: 'And of course we know that she *will* choose wrongly. If she gets it right, the show is as good as over – so the laws of theatre demand that she get it wrong. The question the audience is invited to ask itself is, *why* does she get it wrong?' suggesting that for the remainder of the audience the enjoyment lies not in whether or not she gets it right but in working out why she got it wrong. For Derren Brown and the Annie Abbott act, audience participation is central to the act and, while for other acts considered in this collection the audience's responses are a necessary part of the act, for these two performers the participation of audience members enables the *material* of the act, potentially shifting the way in which the act proceeds.

A number of the performers considered here engage in a process of sizing up the audience in order to judge how best to perform to them. Woods recounts how Petrova would 'walk past the box office and go down the side aisle through the auditorium to the door leading to the stage ... to feel out the temper of the gathering and ... size up the house'. Also Quirk recognizes that Josie Long, who comperes at the LTOTBH, helps to inflect the audience mood by working on the door and welcoming the audience: 'These qualities pervade the club, Long's own attitude shaping everything from the friendly welcome that punters are offered at the door' so that Long can both judge the nature of the audience she will perform to and help to shape their expectations from the moment they enter the club.

One of our key features highlights the importance of a direct performer/audience connection 'eschewing any notion of a fourth wall' and in the introduction to this volume Double reinforces the importance of this connection: 'Rather than focusing on an imaginary fourth wall, popular performers look directly at the audience and share their gaze around the auditorium so that every section feels included'. Nowhere is the lack of a fourth wall more apparent than in street theatre where, as Mason suggests in Chapter 9, 'attempting to establish, for example, a rural idyll of Sherwood Forest in an urban environment is difficult with the urgency of ambulance sirens passing nearby'. There is a potential unruliness in popular performance. In some settings, as in street theatre, the audience is unrestrained by the usual seating conventions of a theatre. In others such as the venues for burlesque shows, comedy clubs and sketch comedy performances the audiences may be drinking during the performance and a number of these performances are sites where heckling is not uncommon. Any performance which encourages audience participation faces the risk that such audience participation may not go entirely to plan. When discussing The Bigheads, Mason suggests that 'their unusual appearance meant spectators engaged with the unfamiliar, providing the thrill of risk'. Just as direct address has proved to be central to popular performance so risk or the perception of risk is at play in many of the performances considered in this book.

In street theatre performances the audience members are engaged in a more active process in deciding what is required of them in response to the action unfolding in front of them. Mason suggests that 'A spectator can watch a theatrical play passively but … [a] spectator watching a 'real' stunt will be engaged with the question: "will it be alright?" So, spectators watching the Bigheads question, is it safe?' The usual boundaries of theatre in which the performers occupy one space and the audience another have been breached and, for the audience, this calls into question all their assumptions about the safety or reality of what they are watching. When the Bighead characters come towards them, audience members recoil as if the 'saliva' dripping from their mouths is real even though they know that it is all part of the performance. While there is no actual threat to the audience, here the audience members are engaged in a constant process of assessing the potential risk.

Quirk's chapter on LTOTBH addresses risk in a different way when she identifies that the performers may fail to deliver their act in the way the audience expects. The consequent risk here is that the audience will not have the good night out for which they have paid. However, in the world of popular performance it appears that risk-taking is in fact a significant part of the enjoyment of and engagement with the performance. Following ideas established by Lockyer and Myers, Quirk points out that 'two of the factors that audience members cited as important to their enjoyment of stand-up comedy clubs were the "unexpected and unpredictable potential" … and "proximity and intimacy" between audience and performer'. Popular performance audiences enjoy seeing the moments in which performers make, or appear to make, mistakes. Audiences laughed at Grock when he fell backwards into a drum (see Chapter 5). The audience for Pappy's enjoyed being tricked into thinking a performed exchange was real. Spontaneity and its consequent mistakes remind the audience of the liveness of the event and create a unique (or seemingly unique) performance which the audience member can treasure as an experience which few others have had. Ainsworth's chapter on Variety highlights the role the perception of risk might play in an audience's response to performance. His account of Annie Abbott creating the illusion of collapsing under the physical stress of the performance she is giving is used as a way of drawing the audience together in a moment of unity in response to her collapse. Quite often in popular performance what creates the illusion of risk or what makes the audience feel surprised by what they see is that the act involves some skill or novelty which inspires wonder or amazement in the audience.

Skill and novelty

These unusual demonstrations of skill and novelty require a greater level of engagement because novelty may make the nature of the act or performance unfamiliar. The audience member cannot, therefore, rely on previous theatrical experiences or the conventions of naturalistic theatre to guide them in understanding what response might be expected of them. In a form like pantomime, for example, the audience understands from the outset what is expected of them and may contribute to the performance without being prompted

The importance of skill and novelty can be traced across all the chapters in this volume, and reflecting on the varying content of the chapters, is it possible to see that notions of skill and novelty can mean different things to different performers. For example, the chapters on magic, the Kingston Empire and Grock reveal the ways in which popular performers rely on specialist skills to attract an audience. Mangan identifies a list of skills needed by the contemporary magician which includes 'sleight of hand, physical misdirection and control of the audience's perception through well-judged patter'. This list provides a remarkable overlap with the one provided by Ainsworth in his assessment of the Annie Abbott act where he cites Harrington and Harrington as saying that the act relied on 'a combination of misdirection, legerdemain and a working knowledge of fulcrums'. In the chapter on Grock, I recount how while still young, Grock 'learnt to play several instruments, taught himself to walk the tightrope on a line set up in his back garden, practised acrobatics and contortion and learnt some magic tricks'. It is evident that part of the attraction of each of these performance styles lies in the performers' ability to awe their audiences, to leave them wondering how the trick or stunt has been managed and to force them to acknowledge that they do not have the necessary skill to do the same. Indeed, as can be seen in Ainsworth's analysis of Betty Knox's contribution to the variety act she shared with Wilson and Keppel, sometimes the performance is presented as a challenge to the audience to force them to recognize the performer's superior skill: 'In this mode the performer seems to say to the audience: "See what I can do" and although Betty remains silent throughout the dance she commands the audience's attention and indicates when they should express their appreciation of her acrobatic ability by orienting her virtuoso performance to them directly.'

This provocation of awe sets the performer apart; other techniques which are used to make the performers seem out of the ordinary can also be seen in the way the performers exercise skill vocally as well as or in place of physical skill in such a way as to create a sense of novelty. In this way Woods explores how Olga Petrova could command the sound of a baritone and a high falsetto toward the voices she applied and how she introduced bird calls, including parrots, into her turns, and her impressions of cats made another crowd-pleaser. Here the pleasure for the audience lies in admiring the skill but also in being surprised that such a skill might exist.

In a similar vein Wilson pinpoints the importance of Valentin's vocal delivery and I highlight Grock's delight in mishandling and deliberately misunderstanding what his partner is saying. Playing with language is another distinct skill which is regularly presented as part of popular performance. Being unable to manage language efficiently is only one of several forms of incompetence which can be seen in popular performance. My chapter on Grock discusses the presentation of the competent as incompetent where the focus is on tricking the audience into believing one thing of the performer (that he is so stupid he would try to move the piano to the stool rather than the other way around) before the performer is revealed to be highly competent (in this case as a pianist). Another such example is found in Chapter 11 when Double cites an example from Pappy's act where two of the performers have a conversation in which one of them appears to be entirely groping for words before seguing into what is clearly a carefully rehearsed song. At this point the audience realize they have been had – and the performers' skill has been used to surprise the audience with skill drawn from the illusion of incompetence. This paradox of the highly competent presentation of incompetence is also explored in my chapter on Grock.

There are other paradoxes at play in the way in which skill is presented in popular performance. Sladen highlights a moment in Pamela Anderson's performance in Aladdin when she enters playing a saxophone: 'While sexually suggestive, the entrance displayed her musical talent and increased the nature of the unique event as the audience bore witness to a rare Anderson saxophone recital'. In this case the audience's expectation of the performer's skill was low and they were entertained to discover that she had some hitherto unknown ability. Much of Sladen's chapter focuses on the fact that the audience are there to observe Anderson's celebrity rather than really expecting a performance from her. In Ainsworth's chapter Dixie Haygood as Annie Abbott displays considerable skill but the skills in which she excels (legerdemain and misdirection) are not the skills she claims to have which are instead 'electric, spiritualistic, electro-biological [and] odic power'.

On the borders between fiction and reality

According to Mangan, for Derren Brown 'the presence of a live audience offers a sense of immediacy and an implied guarantee (on one level at least) of the "authenticity" of the performance'. This question of authenticity has arisen again and again throughout the chapters in this book. Double discusses Pappy's audience being taken in by the performance of an apparently spontaneous clumsy conversation which is revealed to be performed: 'The audience laugh because they suddenly recognize that they have been fooled. The beginning of the exchange sounds genuinely ham-fisted, and the audience buy into the idea that they are hearing an absolutely real, bona fide attempt at casual conversation'. For the audience of a piece of popular performance the boundary between fact and fiction is often fuzzy. Audiences of magic understand cognitively that there is no such thing as magic, that what they are watching is illusion, but there is still a desire to be convinced by the reality of what is happening in front of them. In a sketch comedy setting, the audience realize that not all the sequences or sketches depict the performers as their everyday selves but still, through skilled performance, they can be lured into believing that they are seeing the performers' real selves revealed. As has been demonstrated throughout the book and earlier in this conclusion the audience is often uncertain as to the degree of authentic self being revealed by the performer. When attending a live performance they may wish to believe that they are seeing the real unmediated authentic self and the desire simply to see the performer in the flesh may motivate some popular performance audiences. Sladen provides evidence as to the impact of casting Pamela Anderson on ticket sales but even when the performer is on stage in front of them, the audience may find it hard to discern the degree to which she is concealed behind a persona.

There is every indication that there is a large audience which seeks out performance forms which demand active participation and which offer the audience the chance to see things go wonderfully right or entertainingly wrong. The world of popular entertainment is rich and varied, as this volume has demonstrated. Its insistent concern with meeting the audience in the moment, with encouraging a human response of laugher, of surprise or of amazement makes it ever more relevant in a world in which so many of us encounter the world through the mediation of a screen however large or small. To be in a performance space knowing that the performer may, at any moment, address you directly may require you to speak or even to enter the performance space demands a level of engagement from the audience which is met by the commitment of the performer(s) to be present in that moment, connecting with the audience in a demonstration of skill that recognizes the importance of a live and potentially unruly relationship.

Bibliography

Prentki, Tim, and Jan Selman (2003), *Popular Theatre in Political Culture: Britain and Canada in Focus*. Bristol: Intellect.

Reason, Matthew (2015), 'Introduction to Part 2: *Participations* on Participation: Researching the "Active" Theatre Audience', *Participations: Journal of Audience and Reception Studies*, 12 (1) (May): 271–80.

Index

Abbey, Richard 99
Abbott, Annie 99–100, 115, 271, 274–5, 277–8, 280
acrobat 64, 99, 106–7, 120
aerialist 99, 107
Ainsworth, Adam 25, 270–1, 274, 277–8, 280
Aladdin 183, 187–191, 193, 195
alcohol 2, 15, 98, 162
Aldershot Hippodrome 104, 106
Alhambra 46, 69
Allen, Robert C. 166–7
Allen, Tony 9, 18, 20, 22, 24, 227, 230, 255
Ambassador Theatre Group 181–2
Anderson, Pamela 25, 182–3, 184–7, 187, 195–6, 198, 279, 281
animal acts 64, 99
Antoine, André 10, 12, 24
Antonet 121–2, 125–8, 130–1
applause 17, 19, 47, 66, 83, 103, 109, 145, 162, 164, 224, 247–9, 263, 274
Artaud, Antonin 12
Ashenden, Ben 265–6
Aston, Olly 106, 113. *See also* Empire Melody Masters
audience. *See also* direct address; direct connection
  active audience 15, 19, 24, 270, 276
  behaviour 2, 7, 11–12, 15, 88, 162, 274, 276
  expectations 11, 88, 124, 126, 132, 163, 234, 242, 277, 280
  family 98, 183, 216
  impact of venue 11, 15, 79, 88, 126–7, 138, 161, 172, 235–6
  manipulation of 146, 275
  middle-class 32, 38, 41–2, 51, 92
  street 216
  theatre 4, 9, 10, 11, 13, 15
  working-class 5–6, 32, 38, 41, 79
audience participation
  co-creation 83, 146, 152, 164, 270
  ritualized 11, 163, 188–9, 274
  volunteers 17, 83, 101–3, 115, 217
audience/performer relationship 20, 24–5, 108, 115, 239, 254, 257–9, 264
audience response 77, 82, 128, 132, 224, 247, 249, 260, 272, 276–7
auguste 121–2, 124, 131–2
authenticity 61, 139, 232, 235, 280

Bailey, Peter 47, 98
Baker, Richard Anthony 113
Baldwin, Michelle 165
Barfe, Louis 112–13
Barker, Clive 22
'bar turn' 106–7
Baywatch 182, 184–6, 191–3, 195–6
Beagley, Lee 214
BEASTS 264–5
Berman, Shelley 14
Beverley Sisters 22
Big and Daft 250, 254, 258
Biggins, Christopher 186
Bigheads 25, 203–5, 209–11, 214, 220, 276
Billington, Michael 4, 140, 149
Bombshell Girls 168
Boorstin, Daniel J. 185
Booth, J. B. 37
Brand, Jo 22

Brecht, Bertolt 6, 9, 12, 25, 76–85, 89, 90, 92, 167
Brighton Fringe Festival 204
Broadcasting Act 1980 180
Brook, Peter 2, 5–7
Brown, Derren 21, 25, 137–9, 141–2, 144–56
  Infamous 139, 147, 150–1, 154
  Miracle 139–41, 149, 153–5
  Svengali 139–41, 144, 149, 152
burlesque 10, 48, 161–175, 229, 271, 276
Bus Boys 107
Buszek, Maria Elena 166–7
Butsch, Richard 12, 15, 16

cabaret 59, 76–80, 82–4, 86–90, 92, 94
Cade, Kat 265
Calvert, Louis 17
call and response 188–9
Cambridge Footlights 250
camp 165–6, 182
Campbell, Herbert 37, 179
Carlson, M. 109, 186
carnivalesque 38, 209
Carse, James 205–6
Cashmore, Ellis 184
catchphrase 119, 125–6, 133, 189, 257, 273
celebrity 108, 148–9, 169, 171, 179–99
Champion, Harry 37
Charter Theatre (Preston) 181
chaser act 65–6, 107
Cheese Shop 250, 254, 264
Chevalier, Albert 36
choreography 109, 111, 115, 163–4, 210
Chow, Broderick 242
Chudley, Allan 106–7
circus 107, 120–4, 126–8, 134, 203, 214–15
Clark, Ben 247, 250, 255–6
Clark, Johnson 1, 5, 16
Clark, Tim 233
Cleopatra's Nightmare 107–8, 110
clowns 7, 9, 11, 20, 23, 25, 85, 92, 119–135, 214, 262
Coborn, Charles 40
Cocteau, Jean 9–10
collaboration 8, 76, 92, 115, 214, 262
Colleano and Sole Brothers' Huge Circus and Menagerie 107, 116
comedy 3–5, 9, 13–14, 85, 115, 166
  character 36
  clubs 11, 15, 223–43, 276–7
  physical 83, 89–90, 107, 111
  sketch 19, 247–67, 280
  spoken 35, 87, 92
  stand-up 9, 18–20, 223–44, 247–67, 251, 253, 258, 277
  280
compère 105, 223, 247
communitas 219
complicité 123, 125. *See also* complicity
complicity 213, 216, 262. *See also* *complicité*
costume 21, 38, 111, 122–6, 131, 147, 186, 190–2, 195, 271
Crazy Gang 255
Crosby, Matthew 247, 250–2, 254, 256, 258–9, 261–2, 264–5
Csikszentmihalyi, Mihaly 205
culture
  celebrity 169, 171, 181
  mainstream 171
  patriarchal 165, 167, 171, 174
  raunch 167
  striptease 167
curtain speech 62, 64–5

Dalton Trumbo's Reluctant Cabaret 251
Dames 186, 188–9
dance
  ballroom 44–5
  clog 31, 33, 49, 51, 107

polka 37, 44–5
sand dance 64, 108–10, 115
dancer 33, 46, 64–5, 99, 106–7, 110, 115
Darnley, Herbert 35–6, 42, 46
Das Aquarium 75, 87
Das Christbaumbrettl 75, 84–8, 90
Davis, Tracy C. 104
Davison, Jon 124, 126, 129
Davison, Peter 19, 259
Dawkins, Richard 154
De Freece, Walter 40
devising 203, 208–9
Diderot, Denis 10, 15
Die Dreigroschenoper (*The Threepenny Opera*) 82, 92
Die rote Zibebe 25, 75–82, 84
direct address 8, 11–14, 34, 100, 109, 163, 216, 220, 225–6, 273–4
direct connection
authenticity 22
empowerment 218
facial expressions 111, 127–8, 133, 256–7
direct interaction 92, 131, 144–5, 231, 251, 255, 264
Dodds, Sherill 163–4, 166, 172
double act 18, 119, 121–3, 132, 135
Double, Oliver 98, 104, 106, 113, 225–6, 243, 270, 272, 274, 276, 279–80
Drury Lane 32, 35, 41, 179–80
Dyer, Richard 184, 186, 196

eccentric 34, 39, 106, 111, 115, 120–3
Empire Melody Masters 106. *See also* Aston, Olly
empowerment 188, 203, 214, 217–18
entrée 119, 122–8, 130–4
Eplett, Fred 44
Era, The 3, 7

fairytale 180
fame 31, 48
feminism 167, 173
First Family Entertainment Ltd 181–3, 187
Fo, Dario 9
Forgacs, David 50
fourth wall 8–15, 24, 83–4, 153, 163, 190, 235–6, 254–5, 263–5, 275–6
Friedman, Sam 233–4
Frow, Gerald 180

Gaulier, Philippe 262–3
Gay, Maisie 21, 23
General Election (2015) 224, 228
Genie of the Lamp 183, 189, 191–3, 195
Getinthebackofthevan 4, 15
Giles, David 181
glamour 140, 171, 186–7
Glover, Jimmy 35
Granville Barker, Harley 1, 19–20, 22, 24
Great Raymond, The 97
Green, Ian 226, 239
Grock 21, 25, 119–34, 273, 277–9. *See also* Wettach, Adrien
Grotowski, Jerzy 13, 15–16
Gulbenkian Theatre, Canterbury 247, 249, 255

Halberstam, Jack 173, 175
Hall, Steve 250, 255
Hancock, Tony 32
Harris, Augustus 179
Harum Scarum Girls 107
Hasselhoff, David 182, 193
Haygood, Dixie 99, 271, 274, 280
headliner 58, 59–61, 64–6, 68–9
heckling 10, 19, 190–1, 236
Herring, Richard 248
Hill, Anette 101–2, 115
Hodges, W. L. 112
Hollywood 169, 171, 182
Houdini, Harry 140, 147–8, 153
Howerd, Frankie 18–19
hypnotism 142–3

illusion 97, 100–3, 124, 140–2, 155, 205, 214–16, 218, 272, 275, 277, 279–80
impressionist 99, 106
incompetence 84–5, 129–30, 132–3, 255, 279
interval act 106–7
Irving, Henry 2–3, 15, 37

Kamil, Nadia 228
Kammerspiele, Munich 75–7, 79, 81, 83, 92–4
Karlstadt, Liesl 25, 75–6, 78–81, 87–95
Keith-Albee Exchange 69
Keppel, Joe 107–111, 115–16, 278
Kershaw, Baz 31, 46
Kilgariff, M. 111
King, Harry 37
Kingshot Theatres 104, 112
Kingston Empire 25, 97–116, 278
Kitten Killers 264–6
Knowles, R. G. 37
Knox, Betty 107, 109
Knox, Jean Patricia 'Patsy' 109

Lady Ace 168
Lady Gaga 173
Langtry, Lily 58
Lathan, Peter 180
Lauder, Harry 17
La Vie Parisienne 112
Lecoq, Jacques 125, 214, 262
Lee, Stewart 3, 226, 234, 239, 241
legitimate theatre 2–3, 5–8, 12–15, 19, 24–6, 37, 46–7, 56, 81, 98, 251, 269
Leno, Dan 25, 31–51, 179, 271, 273
Levy, Ariel 167
Liepe-Levinson, Katherine 167
Little Georgia Magnet *see* Abbott, Annie
Limon, John 230
Lipton, Martina 182, 187
Little Tich 1, 5, 16, 19, 20–2, 24–5
liveness 91, 115, 138, 163–4, 172, 277
Liverpool Empire 193, 198
Lockyer, Sharon 234–8, 243, 277
Logan, Brian 4, 15, 252–3, 264
London Palladium 104, 107, 255
London Pavilion 101, 103
Long, Josie 223–5, 228–32, 234–5, 238–43, 275
Lord Chamberlain 1, 249, 252
Lost Treasures of the Black Heart (LTOTBH) 223, 225–6, 228–32, 237–9, 241–3, 275, 277
Lynn, Sally 25, 161–77, 271

Mack, Lee 227
magic 7, 11–12, 21, 25, 66, 100–3, 137–57, 216–17, 270, 278. *See also* Brown, Derren
Mangan, Michael 25, 270, 275, 278, 280
Marshall, P. David 183–4, 197
mask 169–171, 194, 210, 213–16, 220, 267, 271
Mason, Bim 7, 11, 15–16, 25, 273, 276
Maurin's Marvelous Fountains 99
Maxstadt, Karl 80
McGrath, John 6–7
McIntyre, Michael 236–7
McNair, Brian 167
Mediaeval Show 217
Meissler, Josef 44–5
Melodrama 33, 47, 78, 113, 217
Mentalism 25, 141–2, 144, 148
Mesmer, Franz Anton 143
Metcalfe, Nathaniel 223–6, 235, 241
Midas Productions 181
Middlesex Music Hall 38
Midwinter, Eric 112

Millican, Sarah 22
Milligan, Spike 32
mind control 142, 144–5
Mirza, Shazia 4
Molière 9
Monahan, Mark 260, 262
Morton, Charles 46, 249
Mother Goose 179
MsTickle 165, 168–75
Mummer&dada 203, 214–20
Münsterer, Hans Ot 77–8, 81–3
music hall 32–49, 51, 59, 70, 97–8
Myers, Lynn 235, 277

Nally, Claire 166–7
narrative
 burlesque 165, 167–8, 171–2, 174–5
 drama 4, 203, 215, 217, 253
 fairy-tale 11, 180
 frame 19, 31–2, 188
 magic 140, 143, 147, 155, 270
 sketch 257, 264
naturalism 12, 24, 36–7, 153
Natural Theatre Company 212
Nelms, Henning 100–1
New Penny Magazine, The 46–7
New Wimbledon Theatre 25, 183
Noise Next Door 247
novelty
 frivolity 108, 165
 impact 16–17, 205, 225
 skill 106, 279
 spontaneity 229, 232, 235, 239
 style 62, 87, 92, 106, 203, 227–9
Nowell-Smith, Geoffrey 50

Old Mo *see* Middlesex Music Hall
O'Gorman, Brian 261
O'Grady, Paul 151, 183
Off the Kerb 233

palimpsest 161, 165, 168, 174–5
pantomime 112, 140, 179–99, 265, 272, 274, 278
Pappy's 4, 26, 242, 244, 247–67, 272, 274, 277, 279–80
parody 35, 79, 124, 129, 151, 165–7, 215–18
Parry, Tom 4, 15, 247–8, 250–4, 256, 258–9, 261–3, 265, 272
Pastor, Tony 70
patriarchy 173, 175
patter 1, 19, 26, 33–5, 40, 42, 49, 145–6, 152, 190, 273, 278
Pavilion 47, 104
Peacock, Louise 11, 17, 20, 23, 25, 129, 279
Peacock, Ray 250, 254
performer
 character 21, 110, 191, 216
 comic 25
 identity 25
 layering 23, 86, 92, 99–100, 155, 165, 186, 220, 243, 270–3
 persona 21–3, 123–4, 251, 264
 personality 21, 23, 123–4, 137, 264
 role 8, 100, 190–1, 243, 251
Petrova, Olga 23, 25, 55–72, 272, 275, 279
Prentki, Tim 5–6, 270
present
 moment 8, 18, 21, 85, 89, 100, 138, 155, 203
 tense 155, 252–4, 264
props 115, 123, 130, 133, 163, 168
proscenium 11, 161, 163
provocation 174, 211–12, 279
Punchdrunk 13

Qdos Entertainment Ltd 181–2
Quinn, Michael 183
Quirk, Sophie 26, 274–5, 277

Radcliffe, Caroline 25, 31, 271, 273
Randi, James 153–4
Reason, Matthew 270
revue 14, 21, 60, 104, 107, 112, 114, 249–50, 255

risk 101, 103, 203, 208–9, 213, 216, 218, 229, 230–2, 275–7
Roach, Catherine L. 166–7
Robert-Houdin 140, 145, 147–8
Roberts, Arthur 252
Roberts, John Luke 228, 239
Roberts, Owen 265
Robin Hood Show 215–17
Rojek, Chris 181, 189, 197–8
Ross, Becki 167
Russell, Dave 98
Rutherford, Lois 251–3

Sackett, Robert Eben 80, 85–6, 91
Salonhumoristen 79–80
Salberg, Derek 180
Schäfer, Sam 225, 231, 235, 237, 241
Schechter, Joel 6, 233–4
Schneeman, Carolee 175
Schulte, Michael 76, 78, 90, 93, 95
Scott, Harold 48
Sellers, Peter 32
Selman, Jan 5–6, 270
Seyler, Athene 13, 110–11
Sharratt, Bernard 5, 23
Shteir, Rachel 165
Simplicisssimus 80–94
skill
  appreciation of 11–12, 16, 100, 133, 153, 220, 278–9
  comedy 230, 232, 241
  dance 18, 110–11, 115
  improvisation 262–3, 266
  invisible 17–18, 261, 266
  juggling 125
  language games 87–8, 279
  magic 125, 147, 155, 278
  mimicry 68
  musical 18, 120, 132–4, 194
  physical 17, 90, 120, 124, 129, 132–3, 216, 255
  playing the crowd 14, 18, 213, 241
  theatrical 18
  vocal 17, 68, 279
Sladen, Simon 25, 272, 274, 279–81
slapstick 17, 31, 33, 180, 188, 216, 247, 255, 259
Slave of the Ring 192
Slipper Room 161–2, 172
Sontag, Susan 166
Sounes, Clarence 98, 104
Southern, Gordon 250, 254
spesh act 106–7
spontaneity 17–18, 20, 164, 232, 234, 239, 253, 260, 277
Stafford, Alan 107–8
stage name 99, 135, 271
Stanislavski, Konstantin 10–11, 13
starlet 169, 171, 271
States, Bert O. 109–10
Stedman Jones, Gareth 47
Steinmeyer, Jim 100, 103
street theatre 7, 11, 25, 203–20, 276
striptease 166–7
subversion 129, 215, 228
Surrey Comet 97–8, 100–3, 112–14
syndicate 56, 104

Tate, Harry 257
Taylor, Millie 188–9
Theatre Royal (Drury Lane) 32, 35, 41, 179–80
Théâtre Libre 10, 12
Thomas, Mark 18
Three Half Pints 247, 255
Tigger 166
Tivoli 1, 19, 20, 46
Towsen, John 123–4
Traies, Jane 41
training 32, 122, 203–4, 206–8, 210
transgression 165–8, 175, 213
Trick of the Mind 151
Tricks of the Mind 142
Trommeln in der Nacht (*Drums in the Night*) 77–8, 93–4
tug-of-war 17, 102–3
Turner, Alwyn W. 180

Turner, Graeme 185, 193
turns 47, 55, 59, 68, 97–9, 104, 279
'twice nightly' 97

underground scene 165, 168, 172, 241

Valentin, Karl 21, 25, 75–95, 272, 279
variety theatre 3, 7, 16, 18, 25, 46–7, 98, 104, 249, 257
Vatermord 77
vaudeville 7, 25, 55–72, 107
villain 23, 186, 189, 217
Völker, Klaus 78, 82, 84, 93
Volksänger 79–80, 94
Von Embden, Max 128–9, 132–3

walkabout encounters 204–5, 207–10, 212–13
Warrington Hippodrome 103
Watson, Stanley 104, 114
We Are Klang 250–1, 255, 258
Wedekind, Frank 80, 94
West End (London) 37, 48, 183
Wettach, Adrien 120–3, 127, 130, 134. *See also* Grock
whiteface 121–3, 131–2
Widow Twankey 189, 193
Wilde Bühne cabaret 77
Willson, Jacki 167, 174
Wilmut, Roger 106, 112–13, 115
Wilson, Jack 107, 115–16
Wilson, Michael 25, 272, 279
Winter, William 79
Wishee Washee 189, 193
Wood, J. Hickory 33, 49, 179
Woods, Leigh 25, 272, 275, 279
Wright, John 125, 262

Lightning Source UK Ltd.
Milton Keynes UK
UKHW020737161118
332438UK00005B/219/P

9 781350 089686